GLOBALIZING TRANSITIONAL JUSTICE

# OXFORD
## UNIVERSITY PRESS

*Oxford University Press is a department of the University of Oxford. It furthers the University's objective of excellence in research, scholarship, and education by publishing worldwide.*

Oxford    New York
Auckland    Cape Town    Dar es Salaam    Hong Kong    Karachi    Kuala Lumpur    Madrid
Melbourne    Mexico City    Nairobi    New Delhi    Shanghai    Taipei    Toronto

With offices in
Argentina    Austria    Brazil    Chile    Czech Republic    France    Greece    Guatemala    Hungary
Italy    Japan    Poland    Portugal    Singapore    South Korea    Switzerland    Thailand
Turkey    Ukraine    Vietnam

Oxford is a registered trademark of Oxford University Press in the UK and certain other countries.

Published in the United States of America by
Oxford University Press
198 Madison Avenue, New York, NY 10016

First printing in paperback, 2016.
ISBN 978–0–19–022137–9 (paperback : alk. paper)
The Library of Congress has cataloged the hardback edition as follows:

---

Library of Congress Cataloging-in-Publication Data

Globalizing transitional justice : contemporary essays/Ruti G. Teitel.
     pages cm
    Includes bibliographical references and index.
    ISBN 978-0-19-539494-8 ((hardback) : alk. paper)
    1. Transitional justice. 2. Human rights. 3. Criminal justice, Administration of.
I. Teitel, Ruti G., editor of compilation.
    K5250.G56 2014
    340.115—dc23

                                                    2013042323

---

### Note to Readers

This publication is designed to provide accurate and authoritative information in regard to the subject matter covered. It is based upon sources believed to be accurate and reliable and is intended to be current as of the time it was written. It is sold with the understanding that the publisher is not engaged in rendering legal, accounting, or other professional services. If legal advice or other expert assistance is required, the services of a competent professional person should be sought. Also, to confirm that the information has not been affected or changed by recent developments, traditional legal research techniques should be used, including checking primary sources where appropriate.

*(Based on the Declaration of Principles jointly adopted by a Committee of the American Bar Association and a Committee of Publishers and Associations.)*

---

**You may order this or any other Oxford University Press publication by visiting the Oxford University Press website at www.oup.com.**

*To Nataša Kandić and Baltasar Garzón, heroes of global transitional justice*

# Contents

# Acknowledgments

THE PAPERS COLLECTED here have been previously published. I am grateful to the editors of the journals and volumes concerned for permissions wherever necessary to include them here. There has been some modification of text and footnotes, to update the arguments and citations. Thanks are due as follows:

Chapter 1. Transitional Justice Globalized, *International Journal of Transitional Justice* 2008; doi: 10.1093/ijtj/ijm041.

Chapter 2. The Universal and the Particular in International Criminal Justice, 30 *Columbia Human Rights Law Review* 285–303 (1999).

Chapter 3. Transitional Justice: Post-War Legacies (Symposium: The Nuremberg Trials: A Reappraisal and Their Legacy), 27 *Cardozo Law Review* 1615–31 (2006).

Chapter 4. Human Rights in Transition: Transitional Justice Genealogy (Symposium: Human Rights in Transition), 16 *Harvard Human Rights Journal* 69–94 (2003).

Chapter 5. Bringing the Messiah Through the Law, chapter in *Human Rights in Political Transitions: Gettysburg to Bosnia*, 177–193, edited by C. Hesse & R. Post. Zone Books (1999).

Chapter 6. Transitional Justice as Liberal Narrative, chapter in *Experiments with Truth: Documenta 11—Platform 2*, 177–193, Okwui Enwezor et al., eds., Hatje Cantz Publishers (2002).

Chapter 7. The Law and Politics of Contemporary Transitional Justice, 38 *Cornell International Law Journal* 837–62 (2005).

Chapter 8. Rethinking *Jus Post Bellum* in an Age of Global Transitional Justice: Engaging with Michael Walzer and Larry May, Symposium Issue on Just and Unjust Wars, *European Journal of International Law* 24 (1), *European Journal of International Law* 335 (2013).

Chapter 9. Transitional Rule of Law, chapter in *Rethinking the Rule of Law after Communism* (Adam Czarnota, Martin Krygier, and Wojciech Sadurski, eds.) (CEU Press, 2005).

Chapter 10. The Alien Tort and the Global Rule of Law (Symposium: Moralizing Capitalism), 185 *International Social Science Journal* 331 (2005).

Chapter 11. Transitional Justice and the Transformation of Constitutionalism, chapter in *Comparative Constitutional Law* (eds. Rosalind Dixon and Tom Ginsburg, Edward Elgar 2011).

Many of the chapters, in various versions, have been presented at workshops and as public lectures in various places around the world, where I have benefited from the exchanges. In particular, I would like to express my gratitude to the following institutions and colleagues, whose comments and support have been especially helpful: First and foremost to my home institution New York Law School, for research support via the Ernst C. Stiefel fund faculty workshop, as well as summer research grants. Next, my gratitude to NYU Straus Institute for the Advanced Study of Law and Justice, where I was able via my 2012–2013 residence fellowship to conclude this book in a truly supportive interdisciplinary setting. I am also grateful for my ongoing nexus to the London School of Economics where I am a Visiting Fellow, and where I have been able to work in a global and interdisciplinary way on some of the issues raised in this book. I am grateful as well to Hebrew University Law School's Transitional Justice Program and the Fried Gal Foundation for the opportunity to chair an ongoing colloquium where I have been able to be part of an international exchange with faculty and students on these issues in a dynamic regional context. I have benefitted from exchanges at the University of Ulster Transitional Justice Institute as well.

I have been the beneficiary of the comments of many colleagues and friends. My gratitude to Oxford University Press and to John Louth and Blake Ratcliff who saw an idea in this book and helped make it happen, and to Alden Domizio for his help in the editorial process. My gratitude to Camille Broussard, to Carolyn Hasselmann and the NYLS Library, and to my RA's, Claudio Guler, Mitchell Markowitz and Lauren Marinelli for research assistance, as well as to the students of the Transitional Justice Network Project. My gratitude to Stan Schwartz for word processing and other assistance. My great thanks to colleagues in a number of institutions where I have been able to benefit from conversations on these topics over the years, including Kora Andrieu, Finnuola Ni Aolain, Christian De Vos, Pierre Hazan, Bronwyn Leebaw, Mary Kaldor, Frank Munger, Edward Purcell, Iavor Rangelov, Gerry Simpson, Jack Snyder, and Leslie Vinjamuri. Last, my thanks to Rob Howse for his endless solidarity.

# Introduction: Transitional Justice Lived

THE ESSAYS COLLECTED in this volume address more than a decade of practice and study of transitional justice around the world, since my book of that name was published in 2000. Whether one thinks of contemporary conflicts in the Middle East, or earlier ones in South Africa, the Balkans, Latin America or Cambodia, a remarkable amount of experience and experimentation has by now occurred with transitional justice.

In the recent political awakenings in the Middle East, the call for accountability has been front and center: from the demonstrations in Tahrir Square, to the demands of the international community and its court in the midst of the Libyan conflict. Indeed, in the latest political changes, what has become clear is that transitional justice is no longer a byproduct or afterthought, but rather, appears itself to be the driver of political change. Where transitions are fraught and democratization a distant goal, transitional justice is both a goal of political transformation as well as a means to it. We can see changing expectations of law and other demands at this time, especially in light of tensions between its demands and politics.

One can see the demand for justice and accountability underway on many levels: beyond war, beyond the transitional state, ranging across the public and private sectors to civil society, with implications for the rethinking of the meaning of transitional justice at this time; where it is accountability—conceived in rule of law terms—that appears to offer a distinctive source of legitimacy. Yet, it is a relative legitimacy, which as we will see is always informed by a transformative politics of often limited and unstable transitions.

To appreciate the road traveled since the time when the notion of "transitional justice" crystallized, at the end of the twentieth century, we must see how transitional justice emerged from, and came to be identified with, a vital debate over how to reckon with the abuses of predecessor regimes, particularly in light of the aims of democratization and state-building associated with the political transitions of that era. At that time, I was commissioned to write an advisory memorandum for the New York–based Council on Foreign Relations (CFR) aimed at clarifying a debate and making recommendations about justice that had surfaced at the time of the Latin American transitions. In the policy memorandum, I advocated a broader view of transitional rule of law than that originally posed at the CFR debate. Indeed, given the nature of the transitional context, I argued that, wherever the criminal justice response was politically unwise or simply impractical, other ways should be considered to respond to the predecessor regime's wrongdoing and repressive rule, and, moreover, that such alternatives could advance the rule of law. "The extraordinary transitional form of punishment characterized as the 'limited' criminal sanction is directed less at penalizing perpetrators and more at advancing the political transformation's normative shift."[1]

Early on, my interest was the particular character of the challenges of transition in relation to justice: in work leading to my book, *Transitional Justice*, published in 2000 by Oxford University Press, during the late eighties, at the time of the Soviet collapse, I introduced the term "transitional justice"[2] in light of the Latin American transitions away from military rule. In proposing this term, my aim was to account for the self-conscious contingent construction of a distinctive conception of justice associated with periods of radical political change after past oppressive rule. As would become clear, the path chosen fell short of ideal conceptions of justice. Rather, transitional justice was an exercise in law and politics where line drawing was endemic, informed by felt necessities, as well as by a country's long-standing traditions relating to the rule of law; "The conception of justice in periods of political change is extraordinary and constructivist: It is alternately constituted by, and constitutive of, the transition. The conception of justice that emerges is contextualized and partial: what is deemed just is contingent and informed by prior injustice."[3]

With the collapse of communism, and the East European transitions, it became evident that this provisional feature constituted the preeminent characteristic of transitional justice: the structure of the legal response was shaped by the circumstances and parameters of the associated political conditions. Further, one could also see that the direction of the transition was itself conditional upon the degree of commitment to normative political change. Several conclusions followed: Transitional justice might not then reflect the ideals of rule of law set out in established political systems. Moreover, in such hyper-politicized moments, one can see that the law operates differently, though of course this is a question of degree; it is near impossible to meet all of the traditional values associated with the rule of law, such as general applicability and procedural due process, as well as more substantive values of fairness or analogous sources of legitimacy.[4]

After this post–Cold War phase reflecting the proliferation of transitional justice, there has been over two decades of experimentation and change in the nature of conflict as well. I argue here, as this volume's title reflects, that we have now turned to a new global phase, where further to the leading essay in the book, "Transitional Justice Globalized," the volume elaborates a contemporary paradigm of transitional justice associated with the distinctive context of global politics. In analyzing the development of this field against this context of global politics, this book sets out these developments both through a genealogical lens along a proposed three-part framework and substantive analysis of the transitional justice in the context of these periods.

## Early Debates

The established controversy over transitional justice at the beginning of the third-wave transitions toward the end of the twentieth century (a periodization the overview essay following this Introduction sets out)[5] involved a somewhat artificial zero sum and dichotomous framework that centered on a set of apparent foundational dilemmas and related binaries: "punishment versus impunity," "truth versus justice," "justice versus peace."[6]

In these debates, the role of the state loomed large, with the problem of justice revolving almost exclusively around state actors and related institutions and purposes. In transitional justice's early days, the central concern was framed in terms of how a successor regime ought to respond to abuses perpetrated by the state and against its own citizens. This primary concern with state behavior often emphasized retribution against official perpetrators. Drawing a line was seen as necessary for the transformation of dictatorial or other repressive regimes, as Aryeh Neier, among others, framed at the time: "What is to be done about the Guilty?"[7]

I reframed the question in a backgrounder to a Council on Foreign Relations debate on "impunity" in the Southern Cone: How should a society come to terms with a collective violent repressive past?[8] At the time, one can see that often the path of transitional justice followed a constitutional approach, in its emphasis on the problem of strong state transitions, conceptualized in terms of constraining bad state action and actors, as well as recognizing individual rights and responsibilities. Indeed, throughout Latin America, Eastern Europe, and South Africa, commitments to a new constitutionalism were associated with varying forms of transitional justice, punitive or administrative.[9]

## Globalizing Transitional Justice

More than two decades on since the early post–Cold War period, how have the central questions changed? At present, I argue the changes amount to a "global" paradigm of transitional justice. The very problem of justice is being reconceptualized through a global politics of accountability, often in the context of *weak* rather than *strong* states, and beyond the primary focus on abuses of state power with evident implications for the transformative challenge. Accountability for past wrongs is being demanded in situations where there is no clear or consolidated political transition. Indeed, there is evidence of its normalization to intra-conflict context. Consider some of the claims to transitional justice during the Balkans conflict and now in the Arab awakening, for example, Egypt, Libya or in the Syrian war.

If, before, the centrality of the transitional problem was the predecessor regime and its excesses, and the related aim—constitution-style delimitation of state power—now, the challenge of contemporary transformation is that it engages directly nonstate actors at all levels and their behavior and entails changing social norms building civil society,[10] and a demand for adequate institutions and capacity building.[11] In an increasing number of weak and failed states, from Eastern Europe to the Middle East and Africa, the overriding goal is the assuring of a modicum of security and the rule of law that, even without other political consensus, one might say, has become a route to contemporary legitimacy.

As the introductory essay of this book, "Transitional Justice Globalized," sets out, the global phase or paradigm of transitional justice today is characterized by at least three key dimensions: First, one can see the expansion of the aegis or normalization of transitional justice, that is, the sense of the departure from the original 1980s' transitions associated with justice-seeking for exceptional times. Now, instead, transitional justice is more often than not conceived as disassociated from the *politics* of transition; its globality is comprehended by two models discussed below, which arise as a result of its new normalization: the international law model and the bureaucratic model.

The globality of transitional justice today is also evidenced along a matrix of the passage of time, in that we can see the relevant period for transitional justice extending beyond the immediate times of regime transition. What was initially conceived as *transitional* justice has become normalized as accountability for certain kinds of very serious systemic wrongs, such as crimes against humanity, applied increasingly even while a conflict is underway, and certainly before any definitive political transition, as was seen in the context of the Kenyan elections.[12] One also saw this in the Balkans, with the UN Security Council creation of an intra-conflict adjudicatory tribunal[13] and, more recently, with Libya and the Security Council referral of the situation and Qaddafi regime to the International Criminal Court.[14] Hence, here we can observe the increase of issues and actors around the transition across war/ peace lines in this moment with the recent acceleration in attempts to use the law to impose ex ante settlements via transitional justice mechanisms.

Significant controversy remains about the ongoing viability of local responses and processes and the relationship to international interventions[15] as well as regarding the potential role of the law in peacemaking and reconciliation.[16] Indeed, these two recurring debates—justice versus peace and international versus local—continue and overlap in interesting ways, as is discussed here in some of the essays, for example, Chapter 5, "Bringing the Messiah through the Law." Last, in terms of the manifest expansion of the ambit of the discourse and practice of transitional justice, one also can see efforts to address past wrongdoing by state and even nonstate actors long after regime change has occurred, in some cases as in Latin America's Southern Cone, decades later, reflecting various political failures and social pathologies in the states concerned, despite regime change.

With the normalization of the field, some of the essays in this book address not only the practice of transitional justice over the past decade or so, but also its development as a field of scholarship that "crosses" disciplines. The struggle over the nature, parameters, and control of the field is sometimes intense: with much at stake within academia and in the broader society.[17] Christine Bell has argued against the current conception of transitional justice as a "praxis-based interdisciplinary field,"[18] characterizing it as a departure from "the original focus of transitional justice discourse [which] was that human rights requires accountability in transitions rooted in the discipline of law." Although we might differ upon the "original focus," there is no question that, over time, the focus has been expanded to include a much broader range of mechanisms, goals, and inquiries across a range of discipline/approaches which are discussed in this book.

But what to make of these interdisciplinary developments? Insofar as its basis is in praxis, there is a dimension that has developed that is bureaucratic in nature. Yet, the inquiry into the character of the field may well be the tail wagging the dog. There is a larger debate stemming from transitional justice becoming a demand of the international community in cases of political transition, and the engagement of a range of actors, from the UN to various consultancies and NGOs in supplying this demand from the outside, as it were, through training, advice, and related functions. What is its relationship to other sectors such as of peace, security, and development?[19] For example, what is its relation to the UN and its Security Council? Of late, the UN has endorsed justice practices as part of its approach to new states.[20] Might controversies about international versus local responses be best understood as part of this broader policy question of what discourses, what institutions, and what actors will be engaged in the transitional project? Some practitioners in the field advocate a holistic or eco-logical approach,[21] while others invoke "best practices." But what does this mean? "Best" according to what measure? To what extent can such practice-based approaches aiming at a general rule, that is, of best practices, be sensitive to politics, to context?

Of course, on the ground, the issues do not neatly fall into just one discipline or another, perhaps not surprisingly, given that we are talking about massive instances of systemic abuses, in multiple and very diverse social, political, and cultural contexts.[22] Even more crucially, to what extent do such practices match those of one discipline, such as law or politics? This goes to the question of how to conceptualize the field. From the vantage point of the normalizing models, for example the praxis-bureaucracy model, "justice" becomes just one piece in the "tool box" of practices. Yet from the formal-legalist side, seen as a priori obligatory, this hardly makes sense considering that, from its very beginnings, transitional justice was conceptualized as a distinctive conception of justice, which was tightly connected to a state's political transforma-tion, and to substantive commitments—of a political and constitutional character.

## Emergent Models: Bureaucracy and Law

As the first essay in this volume elaborates, the landscape today reflects a global politics of transitional justice, often engaging stakeholders who are not direct participants in the transition itself, such as international actors and institutions, as well as global civil society.[23] In a world that is increasingly interdependent but lacks political integration there is a strong tendency to superimpose international law as the governing normativ-ity in resolving these issues. This is closely connected to the ascendance of international criminal law and tribunals, and even more so to the discourse of legal punishment that this generates.[24]

What might the direction in the proliferation of transitional justice tell us about the changing circumstances of political transition? One can see the turn to this dis-course even ex ante and intra-conflict, where societies face a threat of the use of violence, particularly where ethnic and civil strife exists, with a shifting adaptation in our sense of the relationship law bears to violence.[25]

In this light, given changing borders of international conflict and accordingly of political transition, the contemporary management of transitional justice resonates as an issue of global governance. The parameters of jurisdiction are changing, and there is greater transnational engagement on these issues (as taken up in the first essay here), and where conflict is often cross-border, then how to manage is a matter of global governance where the central question is: When and where should there be supranational intervention?[26] What principle might guide the choice between international and the local responses to issues of wrongdoing? Here some of the hardest dilemmas are faced in places such as Cambodia, Sierra Leone, Iraq, and Libya. One kind of solution is to adopt hybrid local/international mechanisms, for example, as in East Timor and Sierra Leone.[27]

Overall, the global paradigm has given rise to two preeminent models or approaches operating in contestation with one another, with varying weight given as to what justification exists for such global engagement on these issues, for example, between practice-oriented efficiency and legal obligation.

## What Is to Be Done? The Rise of the Bureaucratic Model

Here, one can see a significant interest in framing transitional justice as a global question and likewise in delivering a global answer, such as "best practices." The "bureaucratic" approach tends to theorize across regions and transitions, aiming at a general rule. It appears to be guided by a scientific analogy, and the notion of delivering a formula or prescription to states. This approach is epitomized by the leading nongovernmental organization (NGO) in this field—the International Center for Transitional Justice,[28] which conceives of transitional justice as a set of responses to a problem that demands a solution, where lessons can be learned worldwide. Hence, it consults with states and proposes an array of transitional justice practices.[29] Other institutions involved in the bureaucratization of transitional justice such as the UN and other NGO institutions, both domestic and international, have helped develop a series of transitional justice practices that are framed in international human rights law terms.[30]

But, there are issues with the model, insofar as it departs from the pragmatic politics of the 1980s, as bureaucratic decisionmaking regarding transitional justice is being formulated by technocratic elites and not sufficiently informed by local politics. Some of the issues involved in interventions by international bureaucracy have been articulated in the work of David Kennedy, in his critical writing about humanitarian aid[31] and international intervention. Although other scholars, such as Harvey Weinstein and Laurel Fletcher, surmise that there may well be times for international intervention,[32] that determination depends on a number of factors, which often involve granular, careful assessment of relative institutional legitimacy indeed, as taken up toward the end of the book, and, therefore, interventions that may well be at their most justified when local institutions of justice are at their weakest.

## International Law Model

In *Transitional Justice*, I identified a turn to the alternative normativity of international law, an early trend in the late 1980s' wave of transitions, as a way to mediate the core dilemma of transition between the adherence to established positive law and the demand for potential transformation and discontinuity. This is seen, for example, in the statute of limitations debates, occurring over punishment in post-communist Eastern Europe,[33] where international law appeared to offer an alternative normativity that addressed and appeared to solve the problem of retroactivity. Beyond offering an alternative process, international law also seemed to solve the problem of normative change associated with transition, of the value switch between regimes, for example, by proposing a highly circumscribed set of offenses: as in the words of the Rome Statute, proscribing those "most serious crimes."[34]

A major change in transitional justice today is its increasing application via legal processes and institutions, particularly through human rights law and international criminal law. Today, the global paradigm and the demand for its enforcement has been associated with two other features primarily associated with international criminal justice—weak state, therefore, limited sovereignty and likewise, limited immunities for political leadership. In the characterization of the offense against "humanity," all are potentially aggrieved. Enforcement is disaggregated, a development that goes hand in hand with weak state justice.

The so-called exceptional or "ad hoc" tribunals were established to deal with specific transitional situations, such as the International Criminal Tribunal for the former Yugoslavia (ICTY) and the International Criminal Tribunal for Rwanda (ICTR), and then evolving into a permanent regime with a standing tribunal, the International Criminal Court (ICC). Together with the jurisprudence of the regional human rights courts, there are now a host of enforcing institutions that appear to a greater or lesser degree to generate new legal obligations in this area.

The surge in developments in transitional criminal law and related jurisprudence is explored in various essays in this volume, as well as in other responses that inform transitional justice. Essays such as "The Alien Tort and Global Rule of Law" take up other forms of legalization, such as civil litigation and the demand for reparatory rule of law, as well as others devoted to transitional constitutionalism, as set out below.

What these essays all share is a preoccupation with the global paradigm, the ascendance of international law and related institutions and the tensions raised, which is how to reconcile these normative commitments and obligations with other transitional values and context on the ground. In the international criminal context, the

Rome Statute of the International Criminal Court gives us a norm, in the commitment to the jurisdictional principle of "complementarity"[35]: where there is willingness and capacity, the domestic jurisdiction should prevail. Conversely, it is in instances of political failure that international intervention is at its most justified.

Similar issues are being confronted in Latin America in the context of challenges with its regional human rights tribunal. Kathryn Sikkink emphasizes human rights trials as essential to contributing to the rule of law.[36] A variant of this thesis can be seen for example in the work of political scientist Leigh Payne, whose approach is characterized by ecumenicism, and a "holistic" view of transitional justice. She advocates an overall "justice balance" approach, that is, arguing against too much punishment, but also against amnesties where there is no investigatory process.[37] Others taking a pragmatist position are Jack Snyder and Leslie Vinjamuri, who argue for "sequencing", i.e., putting peace before justice, particularly in situations where prosecutions could endanger fragile peace negotiations, such as in the UN referral of Bashir/Sudan.[38]

Yet, even in instances of political failure, international law does not constitute one universal norm nor an absolute; instead, international law contemplates interpretation. Indeed, the rise of judicialization allows for case-by-case consideration, where ultimately these responses ought to be measured by the aim of change in a more liberalizing direction together with relevant goals such as a measure of human security.

Perhaps, the best way to understand these competing conceptions is in terms of a contestation over what space transitional justice ought to occupy, but, as will be seen, both models are inadequate because they are conceptualized as disconnected from the transitions' substantive political commitments and values.

## Road Map

What follows is a mapping of the book. I begin with a short overarching chapter grounded in an editorial written at the beginning of the century, entitled "Transitional Justice Globalized," which also doubles as the title of the volume because it offers both a way of identifying and understanding the global paradigm of transitional justice and a good summary of many of the themes explored in the individual essays. It also serves as a basis for an introduction for this volume, providing a road map through various pieces, situating them in context, and providing a narrative of how the theory and the practice of transitional justice have evolved in response to political events, but also, to broader social, political, and legal tendencies associated with the post–Cold War period, ranging from globalization to the judicialization of international conflict to the new humanitarian intervention.

The remaining essays in the book fall into three Parts, which pick up on these strands characterizing the global paradigm: *Roots,* relating to the origins of contemporary developments, *Narratives* addressing transitional justice as a site for contestation about the past and future, and *Conflict, Transition, and Rule of Law* analyzing the situatedness of transitional justice today along a continuum of violence and international law. A word about each of these.

*Roots* returns to the early twentieth-century instances of transitional justice that continue to have great salience today, in particular post–World War II cases, with chapters on what distinguished those moments and their response, characterized by high-profile international trials. "Transitional Justice: Post-War Legacies" analyzes the legacies of the post-war transitional justice, identifying ways these trials have shaped current understandings. "The Universal and the Particular in International Criminal Justice" explores the move to individual accountability in transitional justice, and raises the question of what is sought via this form of judgment in the courts.

The next Part, *Narratives,* addresses the appeal of the transitional justice discourse to offer an account of the complexity of interactions of goals, actors, processes, and institutions in such periods. It begins with an essay entitled "Transitional Justice Genealogy," which offers an account of the evolution of the field. "Transitional Justice Genealogy" traces an intellectual history of the central ideas in a tripartite framework starting with the development of international criminal justice processes and institutions from the exceptional (as experienced in the Balkans and post-genocide Rwanda) as they have developed a permanent feature of contemporary international affairs, and ending with the globalization of transitional justice and its "normalization," a central theme in this volume.

Building on "Transitional Justice Genealogy," *Narratives* continues with the next essay, "Bringing in the Messiah through the Law," which takes up the heady expectations for international criminal justice and explores their relationship to peacemaking. The essay follows a story being told in the Balkan trials of how the end or aims of justice is peace. It takes up the first international tribunal convened during a conflict, the International Criminal Tribunal for the former Yugoslavia, which was established by the U.N. Security Council under Chapter VII of the U.N. Charter, explicitly to deter and to reconcile warring factions in the Balkans. The broader account here informs the next chapter, "Transitional Justice as Liberal Narrative," which aims to reframe our understanding of the present uses of criminal justice in terms of the liberal aims shared across transitional justice modalities.

The next Part, *Conflict, Transition, and the Rule of Law,* turns its attention to post–Cold War issues in transitional justice, and in particular, to the evident connection between transitional justice and changing conceptions of security. In the "Law and Politics of Contemporary Transitional Justice," I discuss various trials associated with transitions in the Balkans and in the Middle East, which specifically reckon with the problem of reconciling multiple and competing purposes of transitional justice as well as the aims of human security.

The next chapter, "Rethinking *Jus Post Bellum* in an Era of Transitional Justice," explores the parameters of transitional justice and its relationship to war. Comprehending seemingly pervasive conflict, from ethnic to civil wars,[39] even intra-conflict, justice-seeking plays a greater role at a time where there is more persistent intra-state conflict, and post-conflict settlements, and plausibly returns to the "law of war tradition." In "Rethinking *Jus Post Bellum* in an Era of Transitional Justice," the just war tradition is evaluated in a comparative perspective. I argue that the discourse of transitional justice is playing an ever-greater role in conflict and conflict studies, and particularly that transitional justice in its global paradigm reflects a move away purely from a *state* security model to *human* security model, with an impact on conflict and its resolution. Against this background, I explore the relationship between transitional justice and the "just war tradition," proposing that transitional justice is playing a new and ever bigger role, not just post-conflict in enforcing the law of war, as well as in punishment for the violations of human rights, but also in setting out the terms by which to adjudicate the justice of the initiation of war. The complexity and multiplicity of potential purposes is a distinctive characteristic of contemporary transitional justice.

Globalization and the rule of law are the subjects of the last part of the book. "The Alien Tort and Global Rule of Law" takes up corporate accountability in the context of violations of the law of nations, even as the jurisdictional setting continues to be contested in the domestic constitutional setting in the United States, as seen in the 2012 U.S. Supreme Court decision in *Kiobel*.[40] Although as of this contemporary precedent, some traditional "nexus" must be present to bring grave violations to U.S. courts, other sites for reparatory justice-seeking remain and the normativity has only become further entrenched.

In this vein, the book ends with an essay on the dynamic relationship of transitional justice and constitutionalism in the twenty-first century. It explores the extent to which many of the values and commitments associated with transitional justice have, by now, become entrenched in constitutions and international human rights instruments, and raises the question of what impact these new duties may have on the normative questions raised here. On the one hand, constitutions are indubitably shaped by transitional commitments; conversely, the question is just how do these substantive commitments and interactions shape and steer the ongoing direction of transitional justice? Indeed, the proliferation of constitutional commitments, as well as of international human rights norms set out in both domestic and regional rights norms, may well mean that one can no longer conceive as before of a fully self-contained understanding of transitional justice particular to moments of radical political change, and may need to recognize the fact of the relationship of international law obligations to transitional justice. Ultimately, this goes to the question of the current relationship transitional justice bears to rule of law. Often these questions are deliberated over in terms of absolutes, but this book concludes that the normative question is less formalist, and more a matter for careful interpretation in light of relevant normative materials.

The *Epilogue* revisits some of the difficult questions posited by the global paradigm. Drawing from essays in the volume, the book concludes by reckoning with the tension between the normativity evoked by justice-seeking with the political considerations and context associated with transition. Current debates reflect the absence of guiding principles to manage the relationship of global transitional justice and a need to reset the terms of engagement. The questions that lie at the heart of the global paradigm, such as of the normative relationship of the local to the international, cannot be answered in a categorical or absolute way. These are critical issues to be, at least in part, defined by the relevant political community, and which are in turn defining for them.

## Notes

1. *See* RUTI G. TEITEL, TRANSITIONAL JUSTICE 217 (2000).

2. *See* Ruti G. Teitel, *Transitional Justice: A Bridge between Regimes* (United States Institute of Peace, Grant Application, 1991) (on file with author).

3. TEITEL, *supra* note 1, at 6.

4. For discussion of whether it makes sense to think about this in terms of an exception in the law, see Ruti G. Teitel, *Transitional Rule of Law, in* RETHINKING THE RULE OF LAW AFTER COMMUNISM (A. Czarnota, M. Krygier & W. Sadurski eds., 2005).

5. *See* Ruti Teitel, *Transitional Justice Genealogy*, 16 HARV. HUM. RTS. J. 69 (2003).

6. *See* PIERRE HAZAN, JUDGING WAR, JUDGING HISTORY: BEHIND TRUTH AND RECONCILIATION (2010).

7. *See* Aryeh Neier, *What Should Be Done about the Guilty?*, N.Y. REV. BOOKS, Feb. 1, 1990.

8. *See* TEITEL, *supra* note 1, Preface, at 231 (citing Ruti Teitel, *How Are the New Democracies of the Southern Cone Dealing with the Legacy of Past Human Rights Abuses?, in* TRANSITIONAL JUSTICE: HOW EMERGING DEMOCRACIES RECKON WITH FORMER REGIMES (Neil J. Kritz ed. 1997)).

9. *See* S. AFR. CONST., 1996; *see* A MAGYAR KÖZTÁRSASÁG ALKOMÁNYA [CONSTITUTION OF THE REPUBLIC OF HUNGARY].

10. *See* I. Rangelov & R. Teitel, *Global Civil Society and Transitional Justice, in* GLOBAL CIVIL SOCIETY 2011: GLOBALITY AND THE ABSENCE OF JUSTICE 162–77 (M. Albrow & H. Seckinelgin eds., London: Palgrave Macmillan) (2011).

11. *See* David Kaye, *Justice Beyond The Hague: Supporting the Prosecution of International Crimes in* COUNCIL ON FOREIGN RELATIONS SPECIAL REPORT (June 2011), *available at* http://i.cfr.org/courts-and-tribunals/justice-beyond-hague/p25119.

12. *See* Situation in the Republic of Kenya, Case No. ICC-01/09-19, Decision Pursuant to Article 15 of the Rome Statute on the Authorization of an Investigation into the Situation in the Republic of Kenya (Mar. 31, 2010), http://www.icc-cpi.int/iccdocs/doc/doc854562.pdf.

13. *See* Statute of the International Criminal Tribunal for the Former Yugoslavia, S.C. Res. 808, U.N. SCOR, 48th Sess., 3217th mtg., U.N. Doc. S/RES/808 (1993), *annexed to Report of the Secretary General pursuant to Paragraph 2 of Security Council Resolution 808 (1993)*, U.N. Doc. S/25704 & Add. 1 (1993) [hereinafter ICTY Statute].

14. *See* S.C. Res. 1970, ¶ 4, U.N. Doc. S/RES/1970 (Feb. 26, 2011).

15. *Id.*

16. *See* L. Fletcher & H. Weinstein, *Violence and Social Repair: Rethinking the Contribution of Justice to Reconciliation*, 24 HUM. RTS. Q. 573 (2002).

17. *See* C. Bell, *Transitional Justice, Interdisciplinarity and the State of the 'Field' or 'Non-Field'*, 3 INT'L J. TRANSITIONAL JUSTICE 27 (2009).

18. *Id.*

19. *See, e.g.*, MARK FREEMAN, NECESSARY EVILS: AMNESTIES AND THE SEARCH FOR JUSTICE 374 (2009).

20. *See* U.N. Secretary-General, *The Rule of Law and Transitional Justice in Conflict and Post-Conflict Societies: Rep. of the Secretary-General*, U.N. Doc. S/2004/616 (Aug. 23, 2004).

21. *See* HAZAN, *supra* note 6; *see also* ICTY Statute, *supra* note 13.

22. *See e.g.*, REMAKING A WORLD: VIOLENCE, SOCIAL SUFFERING, AND RECOVERY (V. Das et al. eds., 2001).

23. *See* I. Rangelov & R. Teitel *supra* note 10.

24. *See* RUTI G. TEITEL, HUMANITY'S LAW (2011).

25. *See* I. Rangelov & M. Theros, *Abuse of Power and Conflict Persistence in Afghanistan*, 12 CONFLICT, SECURITY & DEV. 227 (2012). *See* MARY KALDOR, NEW AND OLD WARS: ORGANIZED VIOLENCE IN A GLOBAL ERA (1999).

26. There is a growing literature on evaluation, see ASSESSING THE IMPACT OF TRANSITIONAL JUSTICE: CHALLENGES FOR EMPIRICAL RESEARCH (H. van der Merwe, V. Baxter & A. Chapman eds., 2009); *see also* Colleen Duggan, Editorial Note, Special Issue: *Transitional Justice on Trial—Evaluating Its Impact*, 4 INT'L J. TRANSITIONAL JUST. 315, 320 (2010); *see also* Oskar N.T. Thoms et al., *State-Level Effects of Transitional Justice: What Do We Know?*, 4 INT'L J. TRANSITIONAL JUST. 329, 332 (2010).

27. *See* J. Snyder & L. Vinjamuri, *Trials and Errors: Principles and Pragmatism in Strategies of International Justice*, 28 INT'L SEC. 5 (2003).

28. *See* INTERNATIONAL CENTER FOR TRANSITIONAL JUSTICE, www.ictj.org (last visited Feb. 12, 2014).

29. For an explanation of transitional justice as conceived by the International Center for Transitional Justice, see http://ictj.org/sites/default/files/ICTJ-Global-Transitional-Justice-2

009-English.pdf (last visited Feb. 12, 2014).

30. *See* Report of the Special Rapporteur on the Promotion of Truth, Justice, Reparation and Guarantee of Non-recurrence, Pablo de Greiff, Aug. 9, 2012, A/HRC/21/46, p. 5, *available at* http://www.ohchr.org/Documents/HRBodies/HRCouncil/RegularSession/Session21/AHRC-21-46_en.pdf

31. *See* DAVID KENNEDY, THE DARK SIDE OF VIRTUE: REASSESSING INTERNATIONAL HUMANITARIANISM (2005).

32. *See* Fletcher & Weinstein, *supra* note 16.

33. *See* TEITEL, *supra* note 1, at 20–121.

34. *See* Rome Statute of the International Criminal Court art. 8(2)(c), July 17, 1998, 2187 U.N.T.S. 3 [hereinafter Rome Statute] (("Affirming that the *most serious crimes* of concern to the international community as a whole must not go unpunished and that their effective prosecution must be ensured by taking measures at the national level and by enhancing international cooperation") (emphasis added); *see also* Rome Statute art. 5 which enumerates crimes that fall under its jurisdiction).

35. *See* Rome Statute Preamble, para. 4. ("Emphasizing that the International Criminal Court established under this Statute shall be complementary to national criminal jurisdictions").

36. KATHRYN SIKKINK, THE JUSTICE CASCADE: HOW HUMAN RIGHTS PROSECUTIONS ARE CHANGING WORLD POLITICS (2012).

37. T. OLSEN, L. PAYNE & A. REITER, TRANSITIONAL JUSTICE IN BALANCE: COMPARING PROCESSES, WEIGHING EFFICACY (2010) (arguing for a rule of "balanced justice," constituted by formula of practices of amnesties and truth commissions).

38. *See* Snyder & Vinjamuri, *supra* note 27.

39. This can be seen in the U.N.'s expanded focus of study beyond periods of transition, see Report of U.N. Secretary General, *supra* note 20.

40. *Kiobel v. Royal Dutch Petroleum Co.*, 133 S. Ct. 1659 (2013).

# 1 Overview

*This brief essay was solicited by the* International Journal of Transitional Justice *in 2008 as their first editorial by a board member. The essay sets out what is, as the title indicates, the central theme of this book, the increasing detachment of transitional justice from local politics and its corresponding transformation into a form of global law and politics, especially through international criminal law, as well as the application of transitional justice-like accountability for the past outside the context of political transition, even during ongoing conflict.*

# 1    Transitional Justice Globalized

INTEREST IN TRANSITIONAL justice has surged in legal scholarship, in the human rights field generally, and most notably in the domain of politics. "Transitional justice" is an expression that I coined in 1991 at the time of the Soviet collapse and on the heels of the late 1980s' Latin American transitions to democracy. In proposing this terminology, my aim was to account for the self-conscious construction of a distinctive conception of justice associated with periods of radical political change following past oppressive rule. Today, we see that an entire field of inquiry, analysis, and practice has ensued that reflects scholarly interest in this topic: the launching of this journal, the publication of books in a wide variety of related areas such as rule-of-law and post-conflict studies, international centers and research institutes dedicated to work in this area, interest groups, conferences, domains, websites, etc. One cannot help but be struck by the humanist breadth of the field, ranging from concerns in the fields of law and jurisprudence, to those in ethics and economics, psychology, criminology, and theology.

Moreover, these scholarly and practice agendas reflect ongoing developments in the phenomena of transitional justice: justice-seeking efforts; ongoing debates regarding issues of accountability versus impunity; and the dedication of institutions to prosecution, truth-seeking, and the restoration of the rule of law.

To appreciate the road that has been traveled, one might return to the late 1980s and early 1990s, when the modern-day notion of 'transitional justice' crystallized. At that time, transitional justice emerged from, and came to be identified with, a vital debate over whether to punish predecessor regimes, particularly in light of the aims of democracy and state-building that were associated with the political transitions of that era. In an advisory memorandum for the New York-based Council on Foreign Relations, I advocated a more expansive view of the question of punishment. I suggested that wherever the criminal justice response was compromised or otherwise limited, there were other ways to respond to the predecessor regime's repressive rule. And I noted that such alternatives could develop capacities for advancing the rule of law. Indeed, with the collapse of Communism, and in the context of the Eastern European transitions, it became evident that this feature constituted the pre-eminent characteristic of transitional justice: the structure of the legal response was inevitably shaped by the circumstances and parameters of the associated political conditions. Justice might not, then, reflect the ideal. And, moreover, in such hyper-politicized moments, we learned that the law operates differently, and often is incapable of meeting all of the traditional values that are associated with the rule of law, such as general applicability, procedural due process, and more substantive values of fairness or analogous sources of legitimacy.

This broader historical intellectual context enables us to reflect upon the evolution of transitional justice over the last 15 years. This contextual approach can usefully illuminate the paradigmatic framing of the contemporary global scheme associated with the beginnings of the 21st century.

At present, we find ourselves in a global phase of transitional justice. The global phase is defined by three significant dimensions: first, the move from exceptional transitional responses to a "steady-state" justice, associated with post-conflict related phenomena that emerge from a fairly pervasive state of conflict, including ethnic and civil wars; second, a shift from a focus on state-centric obligations to a focus upon the far broader array of interest in non-state actors associated with globalization; and, third and last, we see an expansion of the law's role in advancing democratization and state-building toward the more complex role of transitional justice in the broader purposes of promoting and maintaining peace and human security. As will be seen, these changes do not necessarily work in a linear or harmonious direction, but instead may well result in chaotic developments and clashes in the multiple rule-of-law values involved in the protection of the interests of states, persons and peoples.

The now historical "punishment-impunity" debate has given way to a marked demand by diplomats and legal scholars for more judicialization and tribunalization at the global level. There is a call for complex forms of accountability associated with the rise of private actors who are implicated in violent conflict, both as perpetrators—e.g., paramilitaries, warlords, and military contractors—and as victims, as we see the ever greater toll borne by civilians in contemporary conflict. In addition to a myriad of local responses, still in operation are the United Nations special tribunals—the so-called "ad hocs" that were set up pursuant to the UN Security Council's "Chapter 7" peacemaking power in the midst of ethnic cleansing in Bosnia, and in response to the genocide in Rwanda. These experiments have had mixed results: for example, the "untimely" death of Slobodan Milošević just days before his trial's close leaves a sense of unfinished business, as the aborted proceeding cheated international society of the satisfaction of a final judgment. Moreover, anxiety regarding the limits of the ICTY also derives from the sober recognition that so far, in these waning days of the tribunal, the two persons most responsible—General Radko Mladić and Radovan Karadžić—still remain at large.

Yet, there is also a broader lens through which to appreciate the impact of the global justice trend, which goes to the broader aims of the tribunal, beyond any strict retributive or deterrent effect. While ostensibly committed to positivism—that is, to the notion of mere application of pre-existing law according to established criminal justice principles and concepts, as set out in its landmark *Tadić* decision—in their jurisprudence the tribunals have also reflected teleological goals including broader, non-criminal justice goals such as the achievement of peace in the region. As the ICTY appellate chamber has declared, the law applied "must serve broader normative purposes in light of its social, political and economic role."

The broader normative impact can be seen in the substantial developments in local justice and the evolution of the work of the domestic judiciary in the Balkan region, where, since the launching of the ICTY, remarkably, there are now scores of war crimes cases in the region including hundreds arising out of indictments issued by the special court in Serbia, as well as national courts in Croatia, and Kosovo's internationalized courts. Furthermore, the normativity more broadly affects the political discourse and civil society in the region, both regarding domestic politics, and in regional issues such as accession to Europe, where compliance with the UN tribunal has, in and of itself, become a benchmark of greater European cooperation. Here, transitional justice appears to represent a way to legitimacy. Similar instances in other previously conflict-ridden areas such as Latin America reflect this broader impact. This may well help to explain the last decades' proliferation of transitional-justice phenomenology.

Transitional justice has become a critical element of the post-conflict security framework; its normative effects are now seen as having the potential to foster the rule of law and security on the ground. At a time when we have seen a growing number of weak and failed states, from regions ranging from Eastern Europe, to the Middle East, to Africa, it is the particular mix of assuring a modicum of security and the rule of law that, with or without other political consensus, has become a route to contemporary legitimacy.

Understanding the transformation of the categories associated with the legal regimes of war and peace illuminates the new century trend of a growing entrenchment and institutionalization of the norms and mechanisms of transitional justice. The most significant symbol of this trend is the establishment of the first freestanding, permanent International Criminal Court (ICC), mandated to apply a prevailing international consensus on the obligation to prosecute the "most serious" crimes: namely, war crimes, crimes against humanity and genocide. Further, we have seen a host of new tribunals and related developments, such as the Extraordinary Chambers in the Courts of Cambodia that were constituted to deal with the Pol Pot regime leaders who were responsible for the atrocities in the Khmer Rouge's killing fields; the special United Nations tribunals convened for Sierra Leone and Lebanon; and the return of a prosecutions policy in Argentina. Meanwhile, other non-criminal processes and institutions such as truth commissions have proliferated in their pursuits of various ways and means to deal with long-standing conflict, from Timor-Leste to Liberia.

These processes serve multiple values in the name of justice, such as nation-building, truth, reconciliation and the rule of law. By now, it is expected that the creation of such processes will be part of the necessary response to repressive prior rule. Indeed, given the many conflict-ridden areas in the world, transitional justice is no longer primarily considered to be about the normative questions regarding a state's dealing with its troubled past. Instead, the relevant questions are now considered to be part of a broader international commitment to human security. From the ICTY on, where according to its founders, establishing the truth about the conflict was seen as essential to reconciliation, similar goals have been set out in the International Criminal Court statute. Beyond, in the United Nations toolbox for dealing with post-conflict security issues, transitional justice is now viewed as an important component, so that the UN Department of Peacekeeping has reconstituted a Security Sector Reform and Transitional Justice Unit. Justice is no longer primarily about retribution, or even deterrence. Rather, these aspirations may actually give way to the demand for a kind of accountability that is suited to fostering peace and security on the ground.

Steady-state transitional justice is not always aligned in a straightforward way with transitional chronology. By now, there has been a significant normalization and entrenchment of transitional justice *within* existing legal regimes such as the human rights and humanitarian law systems. Many transitional-justice responses have become ratified in standing human rights conventions, where they have given rise to enduring and universally invoked human rights, such as the so-called "right to truth" that includes investigations, and often related prosecutions, adjudication and reparation. These rights depend for their vindication on the responses of civil society, such as NGOs devoted to the representation of human rights and its abuses. Likewise, these actors' legitimacy also draws from the emerging normativity of global transitional justice.

Indeed, wherever the issue has been kept alive, it has been as a result of the significant impetus of non-governmental actors. This has been the case, for example, in Argentina where, 30 years after junta rule, there has been a revival of human-rights-related prosecutions. Much of the impetus for this development has been an outgrowth of the interaction between the state and non-state actors in the evolution of the normativity. The significance of civil society can be observed in the role of the organization of the mothers of the disappeared, the "Mothers of the Plaza de Mayo," as well as other interest groups and the media. This underscores the ongoing repercussions of the passage of time that relates to the involvement of the state in these wrongdoings, and the often long time before the effectuation of transitional justice occurs. At present, we can see that the dynamic interaction of state and non-state actors has created a context where transitional justice is often aimed at advancing a culture of the rule of law.

Furthermore, the involvement of transnational NGOs and global civil society more broadly illustrates the wider politics of transitional justice. Reflecting on the current global politics of transitional justice may well illuminate areas of foreign-affairs controversy where claims to transitional justice change the structure of the terms of the discourse. So, for example, one might see this in the struggle over General Mladić between Serbia and the EU, where transitional justice may well end up as a chip in the bargaining regarding the status of Kosovo. It may also explain the puzzling revival of unresolved transitional justice, such as the Turkish-Armenian genocide question, where the elision of transitional justice remains critically important to the implicated peoples with extraterritorial dimensions, but where the timing of the demand indubitably shapes the structure of other questions of interstate relations, such as European accession. In another illustration, Japanese accountability for past war crimes may well affect the extent to which that country can be seen as an Asian great power with a human rights alternative to China's. Today, transitional justice discourse has a global normative reach, with effects far and wide on international affairs.

# 2    Roots

*This chapter, originally a contribution to a symposium on the 50th anniversary of the Universal Declaration of Human Rights at Columbia University, explores the evolving and arguably tightening relationship between transitional justice and international criminal law. I examine how particular trials, beginning with Nuremberg, have acquired a universal significance, shaping the political imagination of justice in times of transition.*

# 2 The Universal and the Particular in International Criminal Justice

## Introduction

The beginning of the modern moment is identified by at least one philosopher in the response to the Lisbon earthquake in 1755.[1] Rather than merely accepting the catastrophe as misfortune or fate, a new response emerged: the disaster was characterized as "injustice," a failure of human, not divine, intervention. In this about-face, the deadly consequences of the Lisbon earthquake were seen as the result of a failure of human action; the insecure architecture of the city's apartment buildings was the fault line to blame.

A similar adoption of the language of justice characterized the modern human-rights movement, which commenced in the response to World War II. This international response was noteworthy for its legal character; it emphasized criminal accountability, with its symbols the International Military Tribunal and the Nuremberg proceedings. Indeed, the ongoing legacy of the post-war response is evidenced in the contemporary moment. As we near the century's end, the recurring manifestations of the call for the protection of international human rights are persistently and overwhelmingly criminal in nature: the convening of The Hague Tribunals for the former Yugoslavia and Rwanda,[2] the entrenchment of the Nuremberg-style International Criminal Court in the Rome Statute,[3] as well as the transnational proceedings initiated against General Augusto Pinochet, the former Chilean dictator.[4] Contemporary responses to tragic atrocities identify criminal accountability in the international legal system with the rule of law.

This Article explores contemporary developments in international human rights by analyzing the emergence of international criminal law as an arch-response to atrocity in the name of human rights. A critical question that is raised by this response is: What are the aims of international criminal law in its advancement of human rights? If international criminal justice is intended to protect human rights, to what extent is its role the accurate representation of, and retribution for, past wrongs? Or, is its role to transform societal understandings in advancing the protection of human rights? And if it is the latter, how exactly are criminal processes supposed to effect the liberal transformation of transitional states emerging from authoritarian rule?

There appear to be two alternative normative paradigms that are advanced by the use of international criminal law: "politics of universalism" and "politics of difference." A universalistic politics drives the post-war paradigm, in which both principles of jurisdiction and substantive criminal law are shaped by a standard of "humanity." Challenging the historical universalist paradigm is a more contemporary paradigm, which advances an identity politics. In the politics of difference, international criminal law moves beyond the conventional role of criminal justice of isolating individual wrongdoing, to emphasizing the representation of individual victims and their persecution on the basis of group affiliation. In contemporary proceedings, international criminal law both affirms individual rights to equal protection, and through its considerations of policy, also engages the collective. As is elaborated more fully below, these alternative paradigms are in some tension with each other. This tension is apparent in how the purposes and role of international criminal law mediate the universal and the particular. Ultimately, contemporary attempts to model a coherent conception of international criminal justice culminate in a chiefly limited process-based conception of the rule of law.

What is international criminal law's potential for advancing human rights? To what extent can the difficult project of transformation, of moving to a more liberal politics, be accomplished through international criminal processes? This Article explores various paradigms of international criminal justice with an eye to achieving a better understanding of the potential of criminal law in the contemporary moment.

## The Politics of Universalism

Consider the genealogy of modern human-rights law. Historically, international criminal institutions and processes have been dedicated to representing the universal in human rights. As the prevailing scholarly accounts suggest, the beginning of the modern international human rights movements was deemed to have occurred in the post-war period, with the Universal Declaration of Human Rights following closely upon the establishment of the International Military Tribunal at Nuremberg.[5] Moreover, these understandings of human rights as universal share affinities with the constitutional developments that accompanied the beginning of the international human-rights movement.[6]

The International Military Tribunal at Nuremberg has long been a potent symbol of law's universality. The nature of the proceedings, the substantive charges brought and adjudicated, in particular "crimes against humanity" as defined in the Nuremberg Charter, and the subsequent trials all embodied understandings of universal standards of humanity.[7] A central charge at Nuremberg was "crimes against humanity," proscribing inhumane acts committed against civilians, whether or not in the context of the war.[8] Despite the enormity of the war, the Tribunal's normative legacy is one of the core concepts of universal human dignity.[9]

Though the commitment was to the advancement of "universal" values, the natural law theory animating the post-war legal responses—whether in their criminal or their constitutional form—was tempered by the various legal and political traditions prevailing in the post-war period. In part, the relevant traditions derived from the circumstances of the Allied response to Nazi Germany. Accordingly, what was deemed "universal" at the time was informed by Allied traditions and by the explicit, critical response to repressive fascism. Law's response and its turn to the universal reflected the then-reigning view that the perversion of Nazi rule derived from the moral relativism implicit in that regime's understanding of legality. The repression of the Nazi regime was associated with its putative positivist philosophy of law.[10] Thus,

the direct response to totalitarianism was the move to natural-law concepts implicated by the universal-rights violations adjudicated in the international proceedings
that were convened. This conception of universal human rights also reflected the
ascendance of the American rights traditions in postwar occupied Europe. Both
the then-emerging international human rights movement, and the wave of constitutionalism shared a common theory of rights: rights conceptualized as traditional
Anglo-American rights at law—that is, rights as norms backed by sanctions.[11]

On this account, the post-war procedures are best understood as concretiz-
ing both a particular view of rights, a conception that was a product of its times,
and the belief in modernity and law. Post-war justice was conceived of as a system
of judicially enforced rights. Whereas traditionally the predicate to enforceable
rights was a functioning nation-state, however, the post-war responses exempli-
fied the landmark uses of a new legal system by internationalizing a traditional,
domestic form of rights-protection through judicial processes. The modern
international-human-rights regime sought to construct human rights as universal
by casting individual rights and responsibilities in terms of universalizing human
characteristics. The adjudication of human rights violations in the "crimes against
humanity" proceedings in a manner that encompassed natural-law understandings
demonstrates this phenomenon.[12]

Nevertheless, it is important to recognize the extent to which the asserted universalist conception of human rights is animated by, and contingent upon, its particular
political context. Despite pretensions to universality, the wartime political context
had a pervasive and ongoing force; it operated as a substantive restrictive principle,
limiting the Tribunal's jurisdiction. Thus, prosecutions in the Nuremberg proceedings were limited to inhumane acts with a demonstrable nexus to war.[13] Even under
the rubric of universality, the understanding of human rights is limited in multiple
respects. For example, where "universal" offenses are adjudicated in the domestic
context, these adjudications are constrained by conventional jurisdictional principles such as territoriality nationality.

The post-war conception of the judicialized human rights model persists to
the present day. That protection of human rights is still thought to be attainable
through international punishment processes shows the continuing dominance of
the post-war paradigm and its central symbols. Nevertheless, such criminal proceedings have been few and far between, despite numerous genocidal campaigns and
the commission of other atrocities in this century. The adjudication of genocide has
largely been limited to the Nuremberg trial[14] and the more contemporary atrocities
relating to the Balkans conflict. Indeed, the international proceedings that were convened as a result of ethnic cleansing in Europe, the International Criminal Tribunal
for the former Yugoslavia, was the first such effort since the World War II-related

trials.[15] The sporadic application of the Genocide Convention,[16] and the failure to adjudicate cases of political genocide,[17] relate to a distinctive post-war history. The general lack of rights enforcement by means of criminal proceedings contributes to a pervasive sense that the international human rights regime is flawed, even as it also suggests that the judicial, procedural feature of the universal conception of rights retains ongoing significance today.

## The Move to Politics of Difference

The move away from the notion of a unitary, universalizing conception of human rights to a broader understanding that comprehends a more complex understanding of identity began, paradoxically, with the Cold War. The political realities of the period led to rights differentiation and the attempt to draw distinctions among rights, in particular between political and civil as opposed to economic and social rights. A debate emerged about the meaning of "real" human rights, challenging the post-war rights model. The debate reflected the existence of normative dissent not apparent at the beginning of the human rights movement. The controversy focused in particular on the conception of the state and the extent of its commitments to and agenda regarding economic security. Despite the assertion of the equivalence of political and economic rights in the Universal Declaration of Human Rights, the rights divide was stark, as seen in bitter debates in the United Nations,[18] as well as in the ultimate adoption of separate covenants to enforce political and economic rights.[19] Moreover, the dominance of the judicialized rights paradigm further obscured the comparability of these rights. Rights differentiation challenged the prevailing rights model insofar as the model had emphasized the protection, through judicial processes and apparatuses, of political norms considered universal. This challenge to the post-war rights model, raising issues of enforceability as well as the purported antinomy regarding so-called "positive" and "negative" rights, went to the very meaning of international human rights. Understandings of the justiciability and enforcement of rights ordinarily associated with domestic law played a significant role in defining rights on the international scene.[20] Ultimately, an apparent rights hierarchy emerged, with a rights conception considered so different from the first wave in the post-war period that it has been readily understood to comprise another "generation" of rights.[21]

Contemporary adjudications of international human rights violations in the courts show a more complex view of the second generation rights model. These proceedings reflect a move away from the post-war search for universal definitions and values to particularist human rights norms, understandings that are linked to particular national contexts and political conflicts. In a number of countries, the struggle over whether and how to limit the application of the concept of "universality" in the post-war human rights regime went hand in hand with related limiting jurisdictional principles based on particularist notions of identity, such as nationality and ethnicity. Whereas offenses at Nuremberg were prosecuted as "crimes against humanity" on a universalizing basis, in the subsequent national trials of the 1950s and 1960s these offenses were prosecuted in terms of the collective.[22] This change was not necessarily embraced as representative of the relevant political community.[23]

The shift to a particularized notion of rights marks a number of deliberations over adjudicating the "crime against humanity" offense within national jurisdictions throughout Europe. In the 1960s, a debate ensued in Germany over whether, and in what fashion, to continue the World War II-related trials. Once again, this debate revealed the tension in international criminal law between the universal and the particular, juxtaposing universalizing ideas of jurisdiction against more particular notions of justice as resolved in national statutes of limitations. Ultimately, the wartime-era trials were continued, but with significant limits. Indeed, the salient restrictive principles included status—for example, nationality of the parties—and motive. While jurisdictional principles are often considered largely procedural, in the international arena these principles express critical normative values; they illuminate the nature of the relation of law to politics and help explicate what norms might transcend a state's transient political consensus.

In another European trial for World War II-related atrocities, the prosecution in France of Klaus Barbie in the late 1980s for wartime deportations of civilians raised again the extent to which asserted universal human rights are reconcilable with national traditions and legal cultures. In the 1960s, France incorporated the Nuremberg definition of "crimes against humanity" into its criminal law—a domestic, national law incorporation of concepts of universality.[24] The incorporation of international standards into national law had important ramifications. Applying the principle of universal jurisdiction implied by wronging "humanity" created tension with preexisting limiting principles of jurisdiction, and therefore necessitated changing fundamental jurisdictional principles. For purposes of the "crime against humanity," the twenty-year time limit that would ordinarily have applied to all offenses in France, no matter how heinous, was tolled, allowing the prosecution of Barbie for World War II offenses to go forward in 1987. This case illustrates the extent to which prosecutions of war crimes, even years after the fact, continue to be shaped by a state's particular legal culture and the ambient political circumstances.

International jurisdiction offers a space for the representation of human rights values. Adjudicating "crimes against humanity" implies displacing the domestic law principles that would ordinarily constrain prosecution and signals an attempt to denationalize and depoliticize, and hence universalize, the relevant offenses. Yet, notwithstanding the passage of time, depoliticizing the prosecution of wartime crimes of the Vichy regime proved difficult. Despite the attempt to reconcile universal criminal justice within a national regime, crimes are adjudicated within the parameters of a distinct political context, jurisdiction, and related principles. While the adjudication of "crimes against humanity" historically implied features of normative universalism, its treatment in the Barbie trial in contemporary France ultimately represented another politics—identity politics.[25] Political differences over the trial emerged in a partisan debate in France, the broad contours of which were historical. The controversy centered around the meaning of "crimes against humanity" as incorporated in French law: namely, whether the prosecution of crimes against humanity could go beyond the atrocities committed against civilians of Jewish origin to include those committed against members of the Resistance.[26] In its review, France's High Court moved beyond the status-based conceptualization of protected classes to a more complex understanding of the scope of the "humanity" crime, focusing not on the victims' status but on the perpetrators' motives in behavior against the backdrop of state policy.[27] Yet, when policy predominated, leading to expansion of the humanity charge to include crimes against members of the Resistance, the move appeared politically motivated and was controversial in the country, opening a debate about the subjects of the humanity crime.[28] The national cases adjudicating "crimes against humanity" reinterpreted the term's meaning in the context of the changing rights regime.

The emergence of a third generation of rights, rights that protect ethnic identity, marks the more recent developments.[29] Conferring the imprimatur of international law on communities defined along ethnic and religious lines challenged the hitherto normative emphasis on the universal in human rights. The move from considerations of status to those of individual action ultimately refocuses attention on policy, linking the individual to the collective.

## Human Rights Globalization

In the contemporary moment, international human rights norms have "gone global"; their protection is envisioned as somehow autonomous, no longer bounded by international institutions or even the affected nation-states. Contemporary instantiations of international criminal justice seem to operate independent of conventional connections such as territoriality, effects, or nationality, whether of offender or victim.[30] The expansion beyond these traditional bases for jurisdiction suggests new directions for normative principles for assuming jurisdiction. On their face, rights norms appear to be developed in an unsystematic manner. Jurisdiction is often taken or assumed by states with apparently remote connections to the underlying controversy, in the name of human rights.

Accordingly, the emergence of rights globalization is highlighted not only by the ad hoc international tribunals for the former Yugoslavia and Rwanda, but also by occasional national cases, such as Spain's extradition request of General Pinochet for human rights violations perpetrated in Chile under military rule.[31] In addition, Germany indicted Dusko Tadić for commission of war crimes in the Balkans prior to turning him over to the International Tribunal.[32] The assumption of jurisdiction on the basis of "crimes against humanity" jurisdiction appears to constitute an act of solidarity. Normative instantiation, in the name of human rights, is being promoted independent of the affected states, in the name of global rule of law and justice. The contemporary globalization of rights enforcement, albeit in sporadic adjudications, challenges both the immediate post-war emphasis on international institutions as well as more particularist, local understandings of justice.

Human rights globalization through international criminal law enforcement suggests a profound change in the sources, content, and form of rights norms.[33] The enforcement of international human rights norms through judicial proceedings that occur outside the traditional spaces of contestation vividly demonstrates this change. To some extent, these adjudications signal the universal in human rights, but they also generate complex issues as the concept of universality interacts with the legal traditions and political agreements of particular countries, pointing to a changing relationship among law, politics, and justice in the international arena.

Globalization has paradoxical ramifications for international criminal justice. In some sense, it implies closer connections between countries' criminal justice systems, as reflected in the adoption of conventions and extradition treaties that facilitate transnational cooperation. At the same time, there is a change in traditional understandings of sovereignty with respect to its relation to law. As the bounds of traditional sovereignty are penetrated, expansion of criminal jurisdiction would appear to follow. Yet globalization also implies other contemporary changes that point in another direction: toward the breakdown in conventional ideas of causation, agency, and relatedly, individual responsibility.[34] Systematic repression implies more than individual responsibility; indeed, at the level of the collective and the regime, it often implies that more than one regime is responsible. Although jurisdiction over international human rights violations may well be expanded as a theoretical matter, its application is stressed by other developments. The principle of individual responsibility at the core of post-war international criminal justice cannot adequately take account of systematic repression. Accordingly, globalization in rights enforcement puts great pressure on the post-war judicial rights model, spurring the further elaboration of various restrictive principles, which delimit the potential for the construction of human rights in and through the criminal law.

## Mediating the Universal and the Particular in International Criminal Law

Let us consider the role of international criminal justice in responding to the grave political violence that has characterized much of the twentieth century. International criminal justice is thought to have a normative role in responding to illiberal identity politics—law is thought the apt response to communal violence and disorder. International criminal justice's normative potential is evident in the ongoing trials at The Hague, where criminal justice is being used both to respond to "ethnic cleansing" in the Balkans and Rwanda and to reconcile the conflicts in these areas. The new international criminal law statutes, whether the ad hoc codifications being applied in The Hague Tribunals for the former Yugoslavia and Rwanda,[35] or the statute for the proposed permanent International Criminal Court,[36] involve various constructs that attempt to bridge the universal and the particular in identity politics.

With respect to the Balkans, the goal of the tribunal was highly ambitious: to move from communal conflict to establish peace and the rule of law[37] whereby punishment under the law would hold individuals responsible in an effort to limit private vengeance. When a U.N. Commission of Experts found that there was a campaign of "ethnic cleansing,"[38] the expectation was that international criminal law would establish individual accountability to break supposed cycles of ethnic retribution. In the words of the Tribunal's prosecutor, "[a]bsolving nations of collective guilt through the attribution of individual responsibility is an essential means of countering the misinformation and indoctrination which breeds ethnic and religious hatred."[39] To that end, crimes against humanity were defined to encompass widespread and systematic inhumane acts "directed against any civilian population" including "persecutions on political, racial and religious grounds."[40] Where intent to destroy "a national, ethnical, racial or religious group" could be shown, persecution was also prosecutable as "genocide."[41]

The international proceedings at The Hague raised the question of whether the tribunals were up to the task of constructing a norm responsive to ethnic persecution. Universalist ideas were extended far beyond the post-war consensus. Thus, crimes against humanity—whether or not committed in the course of international armed conflict—were prosecuted independent of state lines. This was most vividly demonstrated in the adjudication of the attempted genocide of approximately one million Tutsi and Hutu moderates in Rwanda. The persecution was committed entirely in that country's internal conflict, and yet these crimes were adjudicated in an international forum.[42] In these proceedings, universalist norms appear to have transcended traditional limits on adjudicating international offenses.

In their conventional role, the strength of criminal proceedings is that they bring out the significance of individual action, which advances principles of liberalism. The criminal law's focus on individual responsibility represents an important liberal principle: the significance of agency and responsibility. Nevertheless, such emphasis on ascribing individual accountability in war crimes trials is of questionable value because individual proceedings ultimately obscure the profound role of systemic policy in repression. Because of their emphasis on individual accountability and because they are "bottom up," contemporary war crimes trials show a notable evasion of politics. Accordingly, international and global adjudications ultimately obscure the significance of systemic persecution. For example, since the construct of a crime against humanity highlights the universal in the offense, when persecution is adjudicated at The Hague as an offense against the entire international community, it is construed in a profoundly apolitical way. Further, where the proceedings are convened in a political vacuum, apparently independent of traditional national jurisdictions, the criminal proceedings obscure the significance of state policies and other structural causes behind these crimes.[43] In contemporary international criminal law, the constructs of "genocide" and "crimes against humanity" incorporate highly nuanced understandings of the individual and the collective. By their very definitions, these offenses link the individual and the collective. Offenses against groups incorporate a conception of cultural and ethnic identity into the definition of the offense, and individuals are prosecuted for committing such offenses. Thus, for example, the contemporary trials at the ad hoc tribunals at The Hague take note of ethnicity through principles that emphasize persecutory motive, if only to transcend it.

These contemporary criminal constructs raise again the question posed earlier in this Article of what our intuitions are regarding the appropriate purposes of international criminal law. To what extent do we expect it to simply represent past wrongdoing; or to what extent is it intended to be transformative of that past wrongdoing? In this regard, contemporary human rights proceedings risk emphasizing ethno-conscious elements of persecution that, to some extent, would affirm, and perhaps even in some small way reenact, past persecution.[44] The normative change in the rule of law is thought to be a twofold symbol of equality of protection: that is, of equal application of the law both to perpetrators and to victims—and hence all citizens in the society.

Nevertheless, the universal and the particular are somehow in tension here. While law affirms and seemingly protects individual rights, the motive principle plays a restrictive role, limiting the reach of the offense as against humanity and sharply constraining the application of international law. This results from the often crushing burden of proof, making prosecution difficult. Moreover, the insistence on proof of individual motive can be misleading, as it obscures the extent to which persecutory policy is a social and above all political construct. The parameters of this potentially universalizing construct undermine the possibility of adequately representing the extent to which the architecture of genocide is political.[45]

## Millennial Visions: Justice into the Twenty-First Century

In light of the above constraints, the question remains: What is the potential for international criminal justice in human rights? In some sense the use of criminal law to enforce human rights is a millennial vision, reaffirmed by the contemporary consensus on establishing a new international institution, the permanent International Criminal Court. The permanent International Criminal Court appears to entrench the post-war tribunal for the end of the century and the next millennium. Yet going beyond the construct at Nuremberg, the statute for the International Criminal Court reveals the dynamic tension discussed here between the politics of universalism and identity politics in international criminal justice.[46]

In the contemporary International Criminal Court, the role of international criminal justice is complex. At mid-century, the International Military Tribunal at Nuremberg articulated an understanding of the rule of law reflecting the consensus of a small number of states. Indeed, at the time, convening the International Military Tribunal was rationalized by the unavailability in occupied Europe of the ordinary nation-state rule-of-law regime. There was a lack of both sovereignty as it is conventionally understood and working judicial institutions. Whereas in the new global order, the traditional bases for jurisdiction have given way to an expansive, normative agenda. As previously discussed, the expansion of offenses for which jurisdiction is "universal" points to a similar expansion of transnational consensus. The statute for the International Criminal Court extends the reach of international criminal law; there is a pronounced move from objective approaches to jurisdiction to more subjective, policy-based principles. This is explicit in the expansion of the definition of "crimes against humanity,"[47] and the use of international criminal law both to construct international human rights violations and to represent identity politics. Thus, for example, the new codifications reflect the change afoot in the social and legal construction of rights and rights violations. The turn to international criminal law to protect a pluralist identity politics is evident in the transformation of what counts as "persecution." The Rome Statute includes, as offenses, persecution on political, racial, national, ethnic, cultural, religious, or gender grounds as a crime against humanity.[48] In addition to establishing identities, the Rome Statute's codification of "crimes against humanity" encompasses crimes of the apartheid regime as well as the repressive policies of military juntas in Latin America and Africa,[49] an eloquent recognition of profound contemporary political change.

This change is also seen in the Rome Statute's heightened protection of women from sexual violence, with the codification of rape as a crime at several places in the statute.[50] For example, the U.N. Expert's Report investigating rape and sexual assault in the former Yugoslavia concluded that several different avenues for prosecution were available to address the crime of rape or other sexual assaults.[51] The definitional requirements of additional material elements, in particular concerning intentionality, create different categories of war crimes. This raises the question of what difference it makes how the perpetrators of these atrocities are prosecuted; does the resolution of this question depend upon the perceived purpose or purposes of international criminal law? The new codifications allow for alternative adjudications of wrongdoing: rape can be prosecuted as a "war crime";[52] as a "crime against humanity";[53] or as "genocide."[54] Where rape is prosecuted as a "war crime," the offense constitutes a limit on the waging of war. Where rape is prosecuted as a "crime against humanity," it emphasizes that at war or peace women are part of "humanity." Where rape is prosecuted as "genocide," it emphasizes the intersectionality of gender-based violence with ethnic-based violence and shows how rape can serve as an instrumentality for group destruction.[55] Ultimately, the availability of alternative adjudications necessitates asking once again, what is the purpose of international criminal justice? Is it the role of prosecutions to depict accurately past wrongdoing, or is its role to transform the normative understanding so as to protect future human rights?

Developments in human rights dating back to the post-war period affirm the notion that there is a growing normative consensus in the expansion of "crimes against humanity." Though punishment may well be ex post and occasional, even this largely symbolic condemnation expresses a sense of international accord. Many of these offenses had already been recognized as human rights violations at customary international law, the most heinous known as *jus cogens*.[56] There is consensus on these most grave rights offenses, and hence universal jurisdiction. Under the new international rights regime, these offenses have been codified and ratified as conventional law, adding democratic-based legitimacy. For the first time since the immediate post-war period, there are renewed expectations of a shared international normative consensus.

International criminal law stands in fragile equipoise, balancing multiple purposes. Tension between the expression of the universal and particular is evident in contemporary institutional and statutory developments. Despite lofty universalizing goals of representation of racial, ethnic, and genderized violence, the danger is that the original construction is reaffirmed by the remedy, the equivocal representation of an illiberal politics.[57] The risk in adjudicating the discrimination-based offense, of emphasizing the racial or ethnic in the offense, is that rights adjudication could reaffirm rabid and irredentist identity politics. Such criminal proceedings would backfire, affirming only the perverse and conservative message of an illiberal state. Illiberal identity politics should be exposed for what it is: a political and social construction.

Accordingly, the International Criminal Court, established to normalize international criminal justice at the century's end by using the law to respond to a wide variety of these atrocities, ultimately raises the recurring question of what is the purpose and role of international criminal law in human rights. Undoubtedly, there is the message, albeit a thin one, of an isolated, discrete adherence to a procedural rule of law. Yet the global human rights regime constitutes a paradoxical normative order. Insofar as it attempts to represent an autonomous norm, free of national and political predicates, it is vulnerable. The sanguinary history of the twentieth century reveals that the protection of human rights is most at risk when it lacks a legal and political matrix of a rule-of-law state. But the irony is that clearly making this point necessitates the rule-of-law institutions of the working nation-state. Where there is no critical account of repressive illiberal identity politics, international criminal law can hardly serve to reconcile conflicts, nor to express the essential liberal message of transformation.

## Conclusion

How to respond to grave injustice? If the modern moment begins with a change in the understanding of the potential of human intervention in recognizing avertible tragedy, the postmodern moment implies recognition of the limits and contingency in its exercise. Yet, historically and in its more contemporary renaissance, international criminal law appears to have a role to play. The globalization of criminal law, though occasional and erratic, has a normative force. Wherever states adjudicate crimes against humanity or other universal offenses, these instantiations represent a consensus upon a rights-based limit on persecutory politics. Nevertheless, this largely symbolic and ex post normative order is lacking, removed from national contexts and thicker political constructs, international criminal processes offer only glimmerings of a transcendent rule of law. The resonance of this particular legal response in the contemporary moment derives from its potential to span universalist and particularist human rights values. Its transformative potential is in moving beyond notions of enduring ethnic conflict to express that what is at stake in the recurring and pervasive communal violence of this century are conflicts that are largely politically constructed, and, therefore, hopefully amenable to change.

## Notes

1. *See* Judith N. Shklar, The Faces of Injustice 51–54 (1990).
2. *See infra* note 35.
3. *See infra* note 7.
4. *See infra* note 31.
5. Universal Declaration of Human Rights, Dec. 10, 1948, G.A. Res. 217A, U.N. GAOR, 3d Sess., U.N. Doc. A/810 (1948); Charter of the International Military Tribunal, Aug. 8, 1945, art. 1, 59 Stat. 1544, 1546, 82 U.N.T.S. 279, 284.
6. *See* Louis Henkin, The Age of Rights 16–17 (1990) (observing that human rights began appearing in constitutions during the post-war period and that "universalization" is reflected in national constitutions).
7. *Compare* Allied Control Council Law No. 10, Punishment of Persons Guilty of War Crimes, Crimes Against Peace and Against Humanity, Dec. 20, 1945, *reprinted in* 1 Benjamin B. Ferencz, An International Criminal Court: A Step Toward World Peace 488 (1980), *with* Charter of the International Military Tribunal, *supra* note 5, art. 6(c). Article 6(c) of the Nuremberg Charter defines "crimes against humanity" as:

> "murder, extermination, enslavement, deportation, and other inhumane acts committed against any civilian population, before or during the war, or persecutions on political, racial or religious grounds in execution of or in connection with any crime within the jurisdiction of the Tribunal, whether or not in violation of the domestic law of the country where perpetrated."

Charter of the International Military Tribunal, *supra* note 5, art. 6(c).

Article 7 of the recent Rome Statute of the International Criminal Court expands the definition of "crimes against humanity" as:

> "[T]he following acts when committed as part of a widespread or systematic attack directed against any civilian population, with knowledge of the attack: (a) Murder; (b) Extermination; (c) Enslavement; (d) Deportation or forcible transfer of population; (e) Imprisonment…; (f) Torture; (g) Rape, sexual slavery…; (h) Persecution against any identifiable group or collectivity on political, racial, national, ethnic, cultural, religious, gender…grounds…; (i) Enforced disappearance of persons; (j) The crime of apartheid; and (k) Other inhumane acts of a similar character…."

Rome Statute of the International Criminal Court, U.N. Diplomatic Conference of Plenipotentiaries on the Establishment of an International Criminal Court, art. 7, U.N. Doc. A/ CONF. 183/9 (1998) [hereinafter Rome Statute].

8. *See generally* Telford Taylor, The Anatomy of the Nuremberg Trials (1992).

9. *See* Ruti Teitel, *Nuremberg and Its Legacy, Fifty Years Later, in* War Crimes: The Legacy of Nuremberg 44 (Belinda Cooper ed., 1999).

10. Though scholars of the period suggest the judiciary's philosophy of law under the Reich was considerably more complicated. *See, e.g.,* Ingo Müller, Hitler's Justice: The Courts of the Third Reich 68–81 (Deborah Lucas Schneider trans., Harvard Univ. Press 1991); Ruti Teitel, *Transitional Jurisprudence: The Role of Law in Political Transformation,* 106 YALE L.J. 2009, 2025 (1997).

11. *See* H.L.A. Hart, The Concept of Law 218 (Clarendon Press 1994) (1961).

12. *See* Judith N. Shklar, Legalism: Law, Morals, and Political Trials (2d ed. 1986).

13. For a discussion of this prudential self-limiting in the scope of the post-war trials, see Taylor, *supra* note 8, at 113–15.

14. *See* Beth Van Schaack, *The Crime of Political Genocide: Repairing the Genocide Convention's Blind Spot,* 106 Yale L.J. 2259, 2259 (1997).

15. *See infra* note 38.

16. *See* Convention on the Prevention and Punishment of the Crime of Genocide, Dec. 9, 1948, 78 U.N.T.S. 277 (entered into force Jan. 12, 1951).

17. *See* Van Schaack, *supra* note 14, at 2269–72.

18. *See generally* Seminar on the Realization of Economic and Social Rights contained in the Universal Declaration of Human Rights, at 5–13, U.N. Doc. ST/TAO/HR/31 (1967).

19. *See* International Covenant on Civil and Political Rights, *opened for signature* Dec. 19, 1966, 999 U.N.T.S. 171 (entered into force Mar. 23, 1976); International Covenant on Economic, Social and Cultural Rights, *opened for signature* Dec. 19, 1966, 993 U.N.T.S. 3 (entered into force Jan. 3, 1976).

20. *See* Maurice Cranston, What Are Human Rights? 84–85 (1962).

21. *See* Louis B. Sohn, *The New International Law: Protection of the Rights of Individuals Rather Than States,* 32 Am. U. L. Rev. 1, 32 (1982) (distinguishing the first generation of rights, civil and political rights, from economic, social, and cultural rights, which comprise the second generation).

22. In Israel, for example, Eichmann was prosecuted for commission of "crime[s] against the Jewish people." *See* Cr.C. (Jm.) 40/61 Attorney General of Israel v. Eichmann, 1961, *reprinted in* 56 Am. J. Int'l L. 805 (1962).

23. For example, for some scholars the representation in the trial of Adolf Eichmann of a more contextualized account of the wartime atrocities as committed "against the Jewish people" was incomplete. *See, e.g.,* Hannah Arendt, Eichmann in Jerusalem: A Report on the Banality of Evil 275–76 (Penguin Books 1994) (1963).

24. *See* C. Pén., arts. 211-1, 212-1 (Fr.).

25. *See* Guyora Binder, *Representing Nazism: Advocacy and Identity at the Trial of Klaus Barbie,* 98 Yale L.J. 1321, 1381 (1989).

26. *See* Fédération Nationale des Déportés et Internés Résistants et. Patriotes and Others v. Barbie, 78 I.L.R. 125, 139-40 (Fr., Cass. crim., Dec. 20, 1985).

27. *Id.*

28. *See* Alain Finkielkraut, Remembering in Vain: The Klaus Barbie Trial and Crimes Against Humanity 19-20 (Roxanne Lapidus & Sima Godfrey trans., Columbia Univ. Press 1992).

29. *See* Sohn, *supra* note 21, at 48.

30. There are traditional jurisdictional principles that connect states to criminal prosecution. *See* Restatement (Third) of Foreign Relations Law of the United States § 402 (1987). The Comment to section 402 provides that a state has jurisdiction to prescribe law under general principles of: (1) territoriality; (2) nationality; (3) effects within the territory; (4) protection of the state's security; (5) passive personality. *Id.* cmts. a-g.

31. *See In Re Pinochet*, Opinions of the Lords of Appeal for Judgment in the Cause (Jan. 15, 1999) (visited Feb. 6, 1999) <http://www.parliament.the-stationery-off...pa/ld199899/ldjudgmt/jd990115/pinoo1.htm>.

32. *See The Prosecutor v. Dusko Tadić a/k/a "Dule,"* Case No. IT-94-1-T, Opinion and Judgment, pt. I.B., PP6-9 (May 7, 1997) (visited May 11, 1999) <http://www.un.org/icty/tadic/trialc2/jugement-e/970507jt.htm>.

33. Similar developments are seen in the globalization of the civil sanctions instantiating human rights law. *See Proposals of The Hague Conference and their Effect on Efforts to Enforce International Human Rights Through Adjudication* (submitted by Int'l Assoc. of Democratic Lawyers), *in* Work Doc. No. 117, Hague Conference on Private International Law, Nov. 13, 1998.

34. *See* Samuel Scheffler, *Individual Responsibility in a Global Age, in* Contemporary Political and Social Philosophy 219, 228–29 (Ellen Frankel Paul et al. eds., 1995).

35. Statute of the International Tribunal [for the Prosecution of Persons Responsible for Serious Violations of International Humanitarian Law Committed in the Territory of the former Yugoslavia], Annex to *Report of the Secretary-General Pursuant to Paragraph 2 of Security Council Resolution 808 (1993)*, U.N. SCOR, 48th Sess., Supp. for Apr.-June 1993, at 134–38, U.N. Doc. S/25704 (1993) [hereinafter ICTY Statute].

Statute of the International Tribunal for Rwanda [for the Prosecution of Persons Responsible for Genocide and Other Serious Violations of International Humanitarian Law Committed in the Territory of Rwanda and Rwandan Citizens Responsible for Genocide and Other Such Violations Committed in the Territory of Neighbouring States], Annex to S.C. Res. 955, U.N. SCOR, 49th Sess., 3453d mtg. at 15, U.N. Doc. S/RES/955 (1994) [hereinafter ICTR Statute].

36. *See* Rome Statute, *supra* note 7.

37. The Security Council's decision to establish the International Tribunal for the former Yugoslavia (later expanded to include Rwanda) was motivated not only by an intent to punish and to prosecute, *see Final Report of the Commission of Experts Established Pursuant to Security Council Resolution 780 (1992)* ¶¶3-4, Annex to *Letter Dated 24 May 1994 from the Secretary-General to the President of the Security Council*, U.N. Doc. S/1994/674 (1994) [hereinafter *Final Report*], but also as a measure to bring about peace. *See Report of the Secretary-General Pursuant to Paragraph 2 of Security Council Resolution* 808 (1993), 48th Sess., Supp. for Apr.-June 1993, ¶¶10, 22, U.N. Doc. S/25704 (1993); S.C. Res. 808, U.N. SCOR, 48th Sess., 3175th mtg. at 28, U.N. Doc. S/RES/808 (1993). This use of judicial proceedings to bring about peace had no precedent in the post-war paradigm.

38. *See* Annex IV, *The Policy of Ethnic Cleansing* 17, 21–36, *in* Annexes to the Final Report of the Commission of Experts Established Pursuant to Security Council Resolution 780 (1992), Vol. I, U.N. Doc. S/1994/674/Add.2(Vol.I)/Annex IV (1994).

39. *See* Response to the Motion of the Defence on the Jurisdiction of the Tribunal at 23, (filed July 7, 1995), *The Prosecutor v. Dusko Tadić a/k/a "Dule,"* Case No. IT-94-IT.

40. *See* ICTY Statute, *supra* note 35, art. 5.

41 *See id.* art. 4, ¶2. *See also Final Report, supra* note 37, ¶182 (concluding that the actions perpetrated in Opština Prijedor against non-Serbs would likely be confirmed in court as constituting genocide).

42. *See* ICTR Statute, *supra* note 35.

43. On structural causes see Robert W. Gordon, *Undoing Historical Injustice, in* Justice and Injustice in Law and Legal Theory 35 (Austin Sarat & Thomas R. Kearns eds., 1996).

44. For discussion of the performative in legal responses, see Judith Butler, Excitable Speech: A Politics of the Performative 43–44 (1997).

45. *See generally* Van Schaack, *supra* note 14.

46. Rome Statute, *supra* note 7.

47. *See id.* art. 7.

48. *See id.* art. 7, ¶1(h).

49. Enforced disappearances and apartheid are now codified as "crimes against humanity." *See id.* art. 7, ¶¶1(i), 1(j).

50. "Crimes against humanity" include "rape, sexual slavery, enforced prostitution, forced pregnancy, ... or any other form of sexual violence of comparable gravity." *Id.* art. 7, ¶1(g). Under the statute, rape is also a war crime, *see id.* art. 8, ¶2(b)(xxii), and potentially a form of genocide. *See id.* art. 6(b)-(d). *See infra* notes 51-53.

51. *See* Annex II, *Rape and Sexual Assault: A Legal Study* 3, 5–9, *in* Annexes to the Final Report of the Commission of Experts Established Pursuant to Security Council Resolution 780 (1992), Vol. I, U.N. Doc. S/1994/674/Add.2(Vol.I)/Annex II (1994).

52. *See* Rome Statute, *supra* note 7, art. 8, ¶ 2(b)(xxii).

53. *See id.* art. 7, ¶1(g). *See also* The Prosecutor v. Jean-Paul Akayesu, Case No. ICTR-96-4-T, Judgment, ¶¶599-644 (Sept. 2, 1998), http://www.unictr.org/Portals/0/Case/English/Akayesu/judgement/akay001.pdf.

54. *See* Rome Statute, *supra* note 7, art. 6(b)-(d).

55. *See*, Prosecutor v. Jean-Paul Akayesu, *supra* note 53.

56. *See* Michael Akehurst, The Hierarchy of the Sources of International Law, 47 Brit. Y.B. Int'l L. 273, 281–82 (1974-75); Vienna Convention on the Law of Treaties, art. 53, *opened for signature* May 23, 1969, 1155 U.N.T.S. 331 (entered into force Jan. 27, 1980) (defining *jus cogens* as peremptory norm). For a discussion of these "peremptory norms from which no derogation by treaty is permitted," see Oscar Schachter, International Law in Theory and Practice 342–45 (1991).

57. *See generally* Butler, *supra* note 44.

*The essay that forms this chapter, originally written for a symposium on Nuremberg at Cardozo Law School, revisits the trials of the post–World War II era, above all Nuremberg, and explores their legacy for transitional justice in our own times. Today criminal responsibility for grave human rights violations is no longer just a matter of post-conflict accountability. At the same time, criminal trials have come increasingly to be viewed as an indispensable aspect of accountability. Using the criminal law as the principle site of transitional justice has important symbolic and political meanings; yet, one might ask, to what extent can trials, which are narrowly focused on proving the guilt of a particular accused, do justice to a troubled collective past, or pave the way to a liberal democratic future?*

# 3  Transitional Justice: Post-War Legacies

## Introduction

In the public imagination, transitions to liberal rule are commonly linked with punishment and the trials of the ancien regime. Thus, the trials of Kings Charles I and Louis XVI constitute enduring symbols of the English and French Revolutions, which both led to transformations from monarchic to republican rule. Similarly, more than sixty years ago, the Nuremberg Trials were convened to bring to justice the masterminds of World War II's terror, and to lay the foundation for a democratic Germany.

Even as the international community commemorates the anniversary of these trials, it is also in the midst of multiple efforts at international criminal justice. There are or have been an unprecedented number of indicted political leaders either in the dock or in the shadow of its threat: Slobodan Milošević, Saddam Hussein, Augusto Pinochet, Charles Taylor, and Alberto Fujimori. Moreover, there are war-crimes tribunals convened to prosecute violations of humanitarian law in the former Yugoslavia: one in Rwanda, for the attempted genocide; and a hybrid court in Sierra Leone, as well as the newly established standing International Criminal Court (ICC). These new tribunals once again raise the question of the ongoing legacy of the Nuremberg Tribunal, and of how it informed the aims and forms of transitional and post-conflict justice.

Nuremberg established the principle of individual criminal accountability for human-rights violations that are perpetrated against civilians in wartime: It recognized clearly that certain crimes are so heinous that they violate the "law of nations" and may be prosecuted anywhere. The twentieth century witnessed the commission of terrible atrocities: Turkey's massacre of the Armenians; Bangladesh; the Pol Pot regime in Cambodia; Iraq's brutal campaign against its Kurds; the more recent Hutu-Tutsi massacres in Rwanda; and the crimes against humanity of war-torn Yugoslavia. Yet, until recently, half a century after Nuremberg, there were few attempts to enforce international accountability for such crimes. The twentieth century's record was largely one of state persecution and impunity, keeping alive the question of: What is the meaning of rule of law when states turn on their own citizens?

There is, therefore, a puzzling dimension to our understanding of Nuremberg's significance. Intended as a precedent for the future, the trials were aimed at teaching individual responsibility for crimes of aggressive war and crimes against humanity, so as to deter their re-occurrence. Nevertheless, it would be a full half-century before another international tribunal would be convened to bring a regime to justice for human-rights abuses in times of conflict. Yet, despite the general record of failure of criminal accountability, and the Nuremberg Tribunal's anomalous nature, the Tribunal's impact has transcended its particular circumstances to contribute a guiding force for a war-driven Century.

The precedential ramifications extend well beyond the parameters of the post-war consensus to the prevailing international legal system. There continues to be a gap between international law's development of international humanitarian crimes and its enforcement of those crimes. Yet, despite its extraordinary nature, the virtue of the international legal scheme is that it contributes a normative vocabulary that somehow mediates many of the dilemmas of transitional justice. The central dilemma that is intrinsic to transition is how to move away from illiberal, often persecutory rule, and to what extent can this shift be guided by the conventional notions of the rule of law and principles of individual responsibility that are associated with established democracies. The exercise of criminal justice is thought to best undo past state injustice, and to advance the normative transformation of these times toward a rule-of-law system. Repressive regimes are often characterized by criminal behavior—such as torture, arbitrary detention, disappearance, and extrajudicial executions—that is substantially state-sponsored. Even when past wrongdoing is perpetrated by private actors, the state is nevertheless often implicated, whether in policies of persecution; by acts of omission in failing to protect its citizens; or, finally, in the cover-up of criminal acts and impunity. While the circumstances of transition, which often implicate the prior involvement of the state in criminal wrongdoing, make a compelling argument for punishment over impunity, the very transitional circumstances of the predecessor regime's implication in wrongdoing raise significant dilemmas that go to the purposes of the criminal law to advance the rule of law.

A core tension that emerges here goes to the potential use of law to advance transformation, rather than to adhere to conventional legality. To what extent is transitional criminal justice conceptualized and adjudicated as extraordinary in the relevant societies, or guided by the ordinary rule of law of established democracies? This central dilemma implies many others. Where retributive justice is sought, what principles should guide the punishment policy? These are the dilemmas over which successor societies commonly struggle. Ultimately, as the society is confronted with these dilemmas, a transitional compromise is struck, leading to the "limited criminal sanction," which, over time, frequently implied foregoing criminal justice entirely, and culminating in a symbolic form of punishment.

The gap between the international-law apparatus for thinking about justice and its mechanisms for enforcement remains a yawning chasm. Nevertheless, despite its extraordinary nature, international law contributes a normative vocabulary that mediates many of the dilemmas of transitional justice. For this reason, more than a half-century later, it is Nuremberg's legacy that continues to guide our thinking about transitional and post-conflict justice.

## Dilemmas of Transition

The key dilemma of transition is how to transform a society that has been subjected to illiberal rule. A fundamental question is the extent to which this shift is guided by conventional notions of the rule of law, and the responsibility associated with established democracies. A core tension emerges in the use of law to advance transformation, as opposed to its traditional role of adherence to and enforcement of conventional legality. Thus, we must ask: To what extent is transitional criminal justice conceptualized as extraordinary in the relevant societies or guided by the ordinary rule of law?

Until recently, the dominant force of the Nuremberg legacy lay in the way it constructed our understanding of state injustice, as well as the normative response to it. Its impact is evident in its domination of the legal culture of international human rights.

Exploring the significance of Nuremberg requires recognition of the diverse implications of the precedent it set, which may be understood in a number of ways. One might distinguish the fact of the tribunal's proceedings from their broader precedential value. Nuremberg was self-consciously styled as the foundational trial of the post-war proceedings. There was precedential value in both the convening of the international tribunal, and the standards and principles contained in the tribunal's judgment. Seen from a historical perspective, Nuremberg would be foundational in terms of the law applied, the weight of its judgment, and the related ratification of post-war doctrine. There would also be a more profound normative impact in the broader international humanitarian law discourse introduced by Nuremberg.

## Four Nuremberg Ideas

A number of features of the post-war trials continue to play an ongoing, significant role in defining the way we think about state persecution and the responses to such persecution—i.e., our sense of justice. The points of categorical change that were set in motion in these precedents can usefully be thought of in terms of a series of dualisms, which might be considered the "Nuremberg categories of justice." These categories continue to shape the structuring of successor justice.

Four central Nuremberg categories will be discussed here: first, judgment and accountability; second, conceptions of responsibility; third, the problem of sovereignty and jurisdiction and the impact of Nuremberg on military versus civilian legal order (and related developments regarding the laws of war versus laws of peace, and the relation between war crimes law and that of human rights); and fourth and finally, the sense in which Nuremberg-style accountability transcends national borders to offer a form of global justice. While there are other points to make about Nuremberg, these four features remain central because of their precedential impact.

*Judgment and Its Centrality*

To begin, the Nuremberg precedent stood for post-war judgment and the idea that warmaking was subject to judgment. The intended judgment was neither political nor moral, but legal. The central point here is the triumph of the law over the use of force as the guiding form of the rule of law in international affairs. Judgment is where the rule of law and politics meet. Therefore, the significance of Nuremberg was that the war was adjudged to be unlawful. Aggression was deemed the "supreme" crime. Moreover, the apt form of judgment was the trial, and the appropriate forum for judgment was the International Military Tribunal.

Judgment, after the war, took the form of individual accountability. The judgment at Nuremberg represents the belief that, despite the pervasiveness of a culture of totalitarian criminality, normative transformation is possible through individual accountability. As early as the St. James Declaration,[1] the intent was asserted to renounce vengeance and collective sanctions, and, instead, to pursue a policy of punishing the guilty. This punishment policy's significance is best understood in a historical light, that is, in the context of past post-war justice, as the trial at Nuremberg was convened in the shadow of post–World War I justice. Versailles's failure in not apportioning individual responsibility, together with the imposition of onerous collective sanctions, was seen as, in some fashion, to have been related to the recurrence of state aggression.

Judgment is what distinguishes the Nuremberg Tribunal's work from politics as usual. For this reason, it was critically important that the tribunal, insofar as possible, adhere rigorously to the regular procedural forms. Legality demands individual trials and specific charges that must be proven on the basis of credible evidence, with full opportunity for due process. The right to counsel was guaranteed, along with the presumption of innocence. These were not show trials, in the ordinary sense of a preordained result.

At Nuremberg, there was no difficulty establishing the necessary historical record. The evidence underlying the charges was so massive that the defenses were mainly those of law, involving the nature of the charges and the extent of individual responsibility. The trials generated a record for future proceedings, as well as for subsequent historical study. Indeed, by now, whether through trials or historical commissions, one might conclude that this record-making dimension is now concededly an independent form of accountability.

Other dimensions of the post war precedents concern the issue of legality and the resulting innovations. Though the trials largely adhered to accepted criminal procedures, they ran into problems of legality where their operation appeared to collide with adherence to the rule of law. The fundamental challenge was the charges' ex post facto nature, and the extent to which the issue of retroactivity was in tension with the tribunal's legality.[2] Retroactivity was particularly apparent in the extraordinary character of the proceedings and certain charges in the charter, such as "crimes against peace" and "crimes against humanity." No firm consensus existed on the definition of unjust war, or the distinction between such wars and others advancing political aims. Holding individuals responsible for such offenses raised questions of fundamental fairness. Codified in the post-war charter, for the first time, the notion of "crimes against humanity" aimed at distinguishing political justice from the rule of law. For the invocation of "humanity" situates the offense both outside the parameters of permissible war, and outside politics. The concept of the offense against humanity is another place where the post-war trials attempted to move beyond political justice to express a normative message.

Consider the precedential implications: the significance of judgment is seen in the degree to which punishment and the law-enforcement model continue to dominate understandings of transitional justice. This harshest form of law has become emblematic of accountability and the rule of law; yet, its impact transcends its incidence. Review of transitional periods reveals that successor criminal justice continues to raise profoundly agonizing questions for the affected societies, often resulting in punishment foregone. The debate over transitional criminal justice is marked by profound dilemmas: Whether to punish or grant amnesty? Is punishment a backward-looking exercise in retribution, or an expression of the renewal of the rule of law?

Over time, the role of judgment has revived in that it has gained greater significance. This is seen in the number of present international and hybrid tribunals that we have now seen, including the International Criminal Tribunals for the former Yugoslavia,[3] Rwanda,[4] and Sierra Leone,[5] as well as the recently established permanent International Criminal Court. Moreover, in the contemporary post–Cold-War rise of unilateralism and terrorism, these legal distinctions are all that stands between us and total war—hence, the emphasis today on the law of war and its instantiations.

While for half a century, the conception of just war had lain dormant, with the Cold War's end and the apparent potential of abjuration of force, not surprisingly, there was a call to redefine the concepts defining and enforcing aggression in ethical terms. This revival is seen in the recriminalization of "aggression," as discussed herein.[6] Any return to "just war" theory presents many issues, as the concept remains, as of yet, undefined and lacking a normative consensus.

*Reconceiving Responsibility in Transition*

Who bears responsibility for past repression? To what extent should such responsibility be ascribable to the individual, the regime, or the society?

Nuremberg presented the problem of how to prosecute the massive systemic crimes of the modern bureaucratic state. In the transitional context, what does accountability mean? Later, the question would be expanded beyond the post-war conflict. In the shadow of Versailles, Nuremberg took an important step away from the notions of collective guilt and of state responsibility—the country as a whole would not be held accountable. Instead, in a giant departure from prevailing international law, where states were the relevant subjects, responsibility was conceptualized primarily along a human measure.

A dimension of the significance of Nuremberg was its layered understanding of responsibility. The Tribunal's innovation, based on the American law of conspiracy, was in linking up individual and organizational responsibility.[7] While it later was limited, the Nuremberg conception of criminal responsibility continues to present a radical reconceptualization and expansion of the understanding of individual responsibility for state persecution.[8] Responsibility for state wrongdoing transcended prevailing understandings of official state action.[9] In this respect, Nuremberg set the tone for the many subsequent national trials of collaborators throughout the formerly occupied countries. Nuremberg's easy attribution of collective, organizational guilt would also be reflected in widespread de-Nazification policies in the post-war period.[10] Decades later, at the Cold War's end, similar lustration policies would be adopted throughout Eastern Europe.

The distinctive conception of individual responsibility was subsequently codified in the United Nations General Assembly's "Nuremberg principles."[11] The seminal conception was reflected in two principles, which operated to eliminate two central defenses to individual culpability: (1) act of state, and (2) due obedience. Removing these defenses would fundamentally transform the prevailing international-law understanding of responsibility as to both the responsibility of the prior regime and military order and its chain of command. These principles regarding individual responsibility at Nuremberg have had an enduring effect on our understanding of individual responsibility for violations of the laws of war, as demonstrated both in the follow-up trials,[12] in subsequent de-Nazification,[13] as well as in national war-crimes trials, where the defense of obedience obtained no acceptance.[14]

This idea would have legs. In post–Cold-War Germany, in another period that faced issues of transitional justice, the post-1989 border guards cases would similarly reject the defense of "following orders" and, in so doing, promote a unified rule of law for the country.[15]

Seen from a historical perspective, the Nuremberg Principles wrought a radical expansion of potential individual liability at both ends of the power hierarchy. Post-war jurisprudence signified a radical expansion in potential individual liability, without any clear stopping point. While the prosecutions commenced with the major war criminals, nothing in the charter limited the ultimate attribution of responsibility to the regime's top echelon. This potentially unbounded conception of responsibility continues to shape contemporary transitional justice, presenting the dilemma of the post-Nuremberg liability explosion. While the principles generated at Nuremberg radically expanded the potential individual criminal liability, they do not ultimately offer a basis for deciding, among all of those potentially liable, whom to bring to justice.

Therefore, the post-war expansion in potential liability raised ongoing and profound human rights dilemmas for successor regimes that are deliberating over whom to bring to trial, and for what crimes. To the extent that there is a normative guiding principle, it is the implied one of proportionality. The priority is to prosecute those "most responsible for the worst crimes"—i.e., attribution at the highest level of responsibility for the most egregious crimes.[16] Should this principle result in selective prosecution, it runs the risk of threatening the very rule of law that such processes seek to advance. Indeed, such tension is raised by the ad hoc International Criminal Tribunal for the former Yugoslavia, where only a fraction of those responsible for war crimes and atrocities will be brought to justice.[17]

For some time now, the post-war conception of responsibility has continued to be influential. These principles have had a significant impact on the broader conception of transitional justice seen in several human-rights trials held decades later, such as, for example, in Argentina during the aftermath of its military dictatorship.[18] The ongoing precedential value of the Nuremberg view of individual responsibility is evident in the contemporary international tribunals, such as the International Criminal Tribunal for former Yugoslavia, convened in The Hague, where the policy has been to indict a range of individuals all the way from the top Serbian leaders, such as Slobodan Milošević, Radovan Karadžić and Ratko Mladić, down to low-level guards and members of the paramilitary.[19] This policy is vulnerable where those who are considered most responsible for atrocities remain at large, though, to some extent, the Milošević trial has mitigated this perception.

Tensions surrounding these ideas, moreover, have been elaborated upon and expanded in the ICC in its principles regarding individual responsibility, which criminalize many forms of aid and sponsorship.[20] One direction is seen in the apparent increase in trials and indictments of political leaders in diverse causes, such as Slobodan Milošević, Saddam Hussein, Augusto Pinochet, and Charles Taylor. The challenge in the political-leader cases will be making out a demonstrable nexus between the leaders and the wrongs at stake. Wherever this is absent, the perception would be of a politicized trial at odds with the central aim of the rule of law.[21] While it is a challenge, in many ways, the present Milošević trial represents a flowering of the post-war ideas.

*Transformations in Sovereignty and Jurisdiction*

The core transitional dilemma is how to conceptualize justice in the context of a massive normative shift. Within the international legal scheme, the rule-of-law dilemma is mitigated as the framework offers a degree of continuity in law. By now, the post-war entrenchment of international legal norms affords a jurisdictional basis that transcends the limits of domestic criminal law. International law offers a way to circumvent the retrospectivity problem that is endemic to transitional justice. In this way, international standards and forums uphold the rule of law, while satisfying core fairness and impartiality concerns. The precedential and binding value of international legal action is frequently considered superior to efforts undertaken on a state-by-state basis. Heinous crimes, such as atrocities, are often defined in international law, and fit awkwardly in national law. The remaining question is: To what extent ought these principles of post-war international justice guide domestic precedents? This question had spurred ongoing deliberations concerning jurisdiction over recent decades in states debating how to deal with the question of transitional justice.[22]

Transitional justice, for some time now, has navigated the models of war and peace, of domestic and international humanitarian law. Though deploying international armed-conflict principles of responsibility may be sensible in a post-war context, because transitions often follow war, they also occur in other ways. Wherever successor trials' policy bases criminal responsibility on political status, such trials extend the logic of the analogy of war crimes to dictatorship and other forms of repressive rule. After non-democratic rule, it may well seem fair to ascribe responsibility to the top political leadership. Nevertheless, grounding transitional justice in the extraordinary international-law paradigm associated with armed conflict seems at odds with our intuitions about whether responsibility for wrongs perpetrated under repressive regimes can be fairly attributed to a state's top political echelon.

Putting into practice the above principles of accountability for grave rights-violations challenges traditional sovereignty, raising issues regarding the nature of jurisdiction. For war crimes, at Nuremberg, were not tried in military court martial proceedings, but in an international court. Convening an international tribunal was based on the legal premise that the implicated offenses were considered crimes everywhere; therefore, the Nuremberg Charter refers to "offenses" without "geographic location." The deeds were considered so overarching that they defied the ordinary criminal-jurisdiction principle of territoriality, to lay the foundation for the appropriate jurisdiction of an international military tribunal. This dimension will become more and more significant in a globalizing politics.

The post-war paradigm of justice would establish a vocabulary of international humanitarian law, which, despite its shortcomings, continues to frame the successor-justice debate. While within the national legal scheme, the problem of transitional justice seems inextricably political, from an international law perspective, the question becomes somehow divorced from national politics. Within the international legal system, the dilemmas of transitional justice fall away. International law is thought to lift the dilemmas out of their politicized national context.

Until recently, there were few instances following Nuremberg's precedent of holding individuals accountable within international jurisdiction; the most significant exceptions have been the ad hoc International Criminal Tribunals for the former Yugoslavia and Rwanda.[23] But Nuremberg as jurisdictional precedent is not synonymous with the Nuremberg Tribunal. For Nuremberg did not contemplate exclusive international jurisdiction; rather, the precedent goes beyond the proceedings convened at the Military Tribunal, because, as the charter explicitly provides, Nuremberg contemplated further national trials for similar violations.[24] Thousands of follow-up trials were held, which reflected Nuremberg's guiding view of individual responsibility for persecution.[25] War-related national trials continue to the present time throughout Europe.[26] Therefore, the Nuremberg precedent has been reconciled and is fully compatible with more traditional jurisdictional principles associated with territoriality and national sovereignty.

These precedents have given rise to a debate over which form of jurisdiction best advances transitional rule of law. Such debates are as pervasive as they are reductive, for, over time, and the experiences of the last decades of transition, it has become evident that international and national jurisdictions offer competing rule-of-law values. Deliberations over post-war trials in the former Yugoslavia, Sierra Leone, and Iraq reflect that acute tradeoffs often exist between advancing the aims of accountability versus neutrality. Indeed, these difficult choices are reflected in the compromise struck in the Rome Statute's "principle of complementarity," which makes international jurisdiction reconcilable with domestic jurisdiction so long as the domestic system is not lacking in minimum legality.[27] While the post-war tribunal was treated as presenting an exceptional situation, in a time of a great number of failed states, such potential jurisdiction has become the norm.

Perhaps the most profound dimension of the Nuremberg precedent was the nexus of the substantive rights violations to changes in jurisdiction, reflecting that state-sponsored persecution could no longer be confined to national borders. Thus, in the post-Nuremberg understanding, violations of the "law of nations" could be prosecuted by any state, under universal jurisdiction. Like the construct of the "crime against humanity," the appeal to "universality" reflected the attempt to move beyond political justice. Despite this post-war sense, the subsequent Genocide Convention neither contemplated nor provided for "universality jurisdiction."[28]

Still, the ongoing force of this dimension of universality is evident in a number of contemporary genocide and crimes against humanity cases.[29]

Relatedly, there is another important sense in which the post-war legacy has transformed our understanding of jurisdiction as it relates to our conception of criminal accountability. It is the contribution of the view, now attaining substantial consensus, that a state's persecution of its own citizens ought not be confined within national borders, but, rather, constitutes a matter of international, even universal, import.

For years, there was neither progress towards real codification of international criminal law nor progress in the establishment of an international criminal tribunal. There existed, nevertheless, a widely shared view of international accountability that, while not reflected in consistent law enforcement through prosecutions, became apparent through more pervasive exposure, censure, and through representation of human-rights issues in the media. Through the media, contemporary persecution knew no borders. Moreover, these international responses of exposure and condemnation share affinities with punishment insofar as they possess a normative force. International law's perceived advantage in creating criminal accountability, in particular, through international humanitarian law, combined with the real advances of the immediate post-war period, have rendered international criminal law the dominant language of successor justice. Though its impact is not yet evident in a record of international trials, its normative impact is evident in the demand for international accountability across state borders.

A shared language informed by the post-war precedents gives rise to a form of accountability in the identification and exposure of persecution across national borders. When states fail to protect, the leading response of the international human rights community to state persecution is in the documentation and reporting of grave abuses.[30] There has been a significant strengthening of international mechanisms aimed at investigating and publicizing claims of atrocities. Worldwide accountability occurs primarily through the exposure and public censure of state persecution. Moreover, there has been a major development, through the permanent ICC, whereby international jurisdiction is not predicated on exceptionalism, but instead, upon complementariness. Though adjudications are likely to remain exceptional, the ICC will function as an ongoing investigatory and indicting body. In this regard, there has been a significant transformation in our understanding of the meaning of international jurisdiction that builds upon the greatest legacy of the post-war precedents: that accountability would never again be confined within national borders, but, instead, would constitute a matter of international concern. Indeed, as time has passed, more and more, an international humanitarian legal discourse has developed that transcends international and domestic law, to constitute a global rule of law.

*Developments in International Humanitarian Law*

Beyond reconceptualizing accountability, the post-war precedents set the bar for the rethinking of the law of armed conflict, and its relation to the protection of human rights. This Part turns to the substantive charges at Nuremberg, to explore the ways in which these changes have defined our present understanding of the conceptions of injustice and persecution in global politics, and how they continue to shape what is currently conceived to be the rule of law.

At Nuremberg, post-war trials were intended to send a message about unjust war, and designed to vindicate Allied military policy regarding the war. Indeed, the charges reflect this concept of the unjust war. At the time, the idea of such war related to the way it was initiated and waged; therefore, at Nuremberg, the central offense was "aggression" or "crimes against the peace," centering on the injustice of the war's initiation. Aggression exists where there is no provocation or military necessity for invasion. Aggressive war was considered the "supreme" crime because of the "totality" of the charge, as the unjust war's initiation was considered to be the predicate of all other violations in the waging of the war.[31]

While the charge of aggressive war was the central and most controversial aspect of the Nuremberg judgment, over time, it turned out to have lesser precedential force. The offense of aggressive war had rarely been enforced prior to the trials; therefore, the notion of prosecuting individuals for waging aggressive war was novel, and considered a challenge to the rule of law. Insofar as aggression could be separated out from other war crimes that were prosecuted at Nuremberg, this dimension of the tribunal's judgment would be generally considered to present an issue of political justice, distinctive in its various political ramifications from that of an ordinary court. Therefore, this aspect of the precedent has hardly taken hold. In the subsequent Control Council Law No. 10 trials, individuals were tried for waging aggressive war, but war-crimes trials grounded upon this offense have been rare. Despite numerous instances of aggression recognized as such by the United Nations Security Council, military intervention has not been followed by legal action as at Nuremberg. Moreover, with technological advances, the line between aggressive wars and wars of self-defense is increasingly blurred.[32] Perhaps, not surprisingly, with the end of the Cold War there has been a return to the project of judgment of aggression and of discerning between exercises of the use of force.[33]

Still, the idea of the unjust war underlies all the offenses prosecuted at Nuremberg. The charter's second charge, violations of the "laws and customs of war," referred back to war crimes codified since the Hague Convention. Violations of the laws of war, including genocide, were considered to be related to armed conflict. As such, at Nuremberg, genocide was prosecuted as a violation of customary international law. After the war, the precedential impact of the Nuremberg concept is seen in the Genocide Convention, aimed at codifying the Nuremberg ideas. Similarly, war crimes—"willful killing, torture or inhuman treatment"—were codified as "grave breaches" of the Geneva Convention of 1949, and included mistreatment of prisoners of war and civilians.

In the International Criminal Tribunal for serious violations of humanitarian law in the former Yugoslavia, the trial's policy is being directed beyond the war, to foster ethnic reconciliation. Furthermore, genocide is being prosecuted for the first time since Nuremberg in an international tribunal, along the lines of the post-war convention, as an "act[] committed with intent to destroy, in whole or in part, a...group."[34] This imposes a difficult burden of specific intent; moreover, as at Nuremberg, the Hague Tribunal also considers the perpetration of the offense of genocide within the context of armed conflict. Nuremberg continues to cast a long shadow. Needless to say, true to the post-war precedents, the definition still excludes political genocide, a limit that, with the Cold War's end, ought to be revisited.

Perhaps the greatest influence of the Nuremberg categories over time is seen in the contemporary convergence of humanitarian law applicable in times of armed conflict, with human rights law applicable in peacetime. Many norms relating to the law of armed conflict have been extended to internal conflict and to peacetime.[35] Transitional justice appears to be more and more normalized and aimed at advancing the ongoing goals of global rule of law.

Consider the developments in humanitarian law in conditions from war to peace, in particular, as concerns the "crime against humanity," an independent charge in the charter and a statement of new positive law at Nuremberg. Though the Nuremberg Charter would have allowed prosecution of offenses occurring "before the war," the Tribunal nevertheless limited its enforcement powers to crimes against humanity committed during the war.[36] Preserving the nexus to the war was done as a prudential matter to avoid ex post facto challenges because of the sense that crimes against humanity constituted a new charge before the Tribunal.[37] Thus, despite a broader Charter conceptualization, the precedent appeared to insist that crimes against humanity required a nexus to war.

The ongoing guiding influence of the post-war precedent can be seen more than half a century later. In contemporary war crimes trials before the International Criminal Tribunal for the former Yugoslavia, the offense of "crimes against humanity" is still predicated upon a nexus to conflict. The statute regarding Yugoslavia specifically contemplates "armed conflict," either "international" or "internal" in character.

Finally, perhaps the most significant feature of the conceptualization of crimes against humanity codified at Nuremberg was their definition as crimes that could be committed by a state against its own citizens. These violations were defined as "murder, extermination, enslavement, deportation and other inhumane acts committed against any civilian population" or persecutions on political, racial or religious grounds "whether or not in violation of the domestic law of the country where perpetrated."[38] While apparently unremarkable today, the central change after Nuremberg was the rethinking of the offense of state persecution, rendering a state's treatment of its own citizens an international matter. This transformed conception would spur subsequent prosecutions in other countries by successor regimes for attacks committed by the prior regime against its own civilians. A concerted effort is now underway to expand and normalize the post-war understandings of state persecution. Contemporary developments in international humanitarian law reflect an understanding that the offense of wartime persecution extends beyond the international response to actions within the state.[39] These developments are also reflected in the jurisdiction assumed of the ad hoc international war crimes tribunals regarding the former Yugoslavia and the genocide in Rwanda. In these more contemporary instances, a dynamic understanding of "crimes against humanity" has evolved beyond the predicated nexus to armed conflict, to become virtually synonymous with persecution whether at war or at peace.[40]

Most significant was that pursuant to this legacy, the law of humanity would penetrate internal sovereignty, imposing a limit—even if honored more in the breach—upon the behavior of states towards their citizens, standing for a principle against persecution. This understanding of global rights protection at the level of the human would become a significant part of the normative understanding of liberalization at the century's turn.

## Conclusion

For decades, Nuremberg's precedent has been honored largely in its breach. Until the last two decades, no similar war-crimes tribunals had been convened. After more than sixty years, a permanent international criminal court has been established. Yet the impact of Nuremberg extends far beyond these facts, to the way we think of accounting for state injustice. The force of the legacy can be seen in the many ways in which the Nuremberg ideas have constructed our understanding of and responses to state wrongdoing in this century. The Nuremberg paradigm created fundamental changes in the relation of law to politics; in our view of the rule of law as accountability; in the reconceptualization and shift of responsibility from the collective to the individual; in the reconceptualization of sovereignty and jurisdiction; and, finally, in the reconceptualization of international humanitarian law, from a law of war to an ongoing rule of law for war and for peacetime. One might say that, over time, the force of the Nuremberg legacy has only increased, transcending its particular engendering circumstances to play a constitutive role in contemporary international human rights. Nuremberg has had a powerful influence on the human-rights order, giving us nothing less than a new vocabulary for thinking and talking about responsibility for state wrongdoing. Perhaps its greatest legacy is that the question of accountability for atrocities and persecution within a state would never again be confined within national borders, but would reach beyond such boundaries to become a matter of international human-rights import. The challenges for the future are the dilemmas raised by the conceptualization of the humanitarian law order as a global rule of law.

## Notes

1. The St. James Declaration was signed in 1942 in London by nine Nazi-occupied countries, the United States, the United Kingdom, and the Soviet Union, and announced Allied intentions to punish crimes against civilians following the war.

2. The dilemma raised at Nuremberg relating to the rule of law catalyzed a debate on the nature of international norms and the extent to which these could be considered consistent with positive law. Ultimately, Nuremberg would imply a move away from support of positivist principles of interpretation and toward an endorsement of natural law principles. For an exploration of this issue, see Quincy Wright, *Legal Positivism and the Nuremberg Judgment*, 42 AM. J. INT'L L. 405 (1948).

3. See Statute of the International Criminal Tribunal for the Prosecution of Persons Responsible for Serious Violations of International Humanitarian Law Committed in the Territory of the former Yugoslavia Since 1991, May 25, 1993, 32 I.L.M. 1192 [hereinafter International Criminal Tribunal for the former Yugoslavia].

4. *See* Statute of the International Criminal Tribunal for Rwanda, Nov. 8, 1994, 32 I.L.M. 1602.

5. *See* Statute of the Special Court for Sierra Leone, Aug. 14, 2000, http://www.icrc.org/ihl/INTRO/605?OpenDocument.

6. The ICC Charter includes "aggression" as one of the substantive offenses under its jurisdiction, yet the offense continues to lack a definition. *See* Rome Statute of the International Criminal Court art. 5(2), July 17, 1998, U.N. Doc. A/CONF.183/9, 37 I.L.M. 999 [hereinafter Rome Statute]; Jennifer Trahan, *Defining "Aggression": Why the Preparatory Commission for the International Criminal Court Has Faced Such a Conundrum*, 24 LOY. L.A. INT'L & COMP. L. REV. 439 (2002).

7. For discussion of the approach at Nuremberg to the responsibility of Nazi organizations, see Robert H. Jackson, *The Law Under Which Nazi Organizations Are Accused of Being Criminal*, 19 TEMP. L.Q. 371 (1946).

8. Control Council Law No. 10 provided the legal basis for the subsequent American trials. It delineated the crimes that could be prosecuted under the heading crimes against peace, war crimes, and crimes against humanity.

9. Compare articles 6(a), (b), and (c) of the Nuremberg Charter. Charter of the International Military Tribunal at Nuremberg art. 6, Aug. 8, 1945, art. 6 (a)-(c), 59 Stat. 1546, 1547, 82 U.N.T.S. 279 [hereinafter Charter of the International Military Tribunal].

10. Thus, in part, denazification occurred in Germany through the U.S.-imposed "Law of Liberation." For an account, see JOHN HERZ, FROM DICTATORSHIP TO DEMOCRACY: COPING WITH THE LEGACIES OF AUTHORITARIANISM AND TOTALITARIANISM (1983).

11. *See* Affirmation of the Principles of International Law Recognized by the Charter of the Nuremberg Tribunal, G.A. Res. 95(I), at 188, U.N. Doc. A/64/Add.1 (Dec. 11, 1946).

12. *See* TELFORD TAYLOR, THE ANATOMY OF THE NUREMBERG TRIALS: A PERSONAL MEMOIR (1992).

13. *See* Law for Liberation from National Socialism and Militarism (1946) (German legislation), *available at* http://digicoll.library.wisc.edu/cgi-bin/History/History-idx?type=tur n&entity=History004201870056&isize=M.

14. *See* ADALBERT RUCKERL, THE INVESTIGATION OF NAZI CRIMES, 1945-1978: A DOCUMENTATION (Derek Rutter trans., 1980).

15. *See* RUTI TEITEL, TRANSITIONAL JUSTICE 18–20 (2000) (discussing the border guards decisions).

16. *See, e.g.,* Richard Dicker & Elise Keppler, *Beyond the Hague: The Challenges of International Justice, in* HUMAN RIGHTS WATCH WORLD REPORT 2004: HUMAN RIGHTS AND ARMED CONFLICT (2004), *available at* http://hrw.org/wr2k4/10.htm.

17. *See* Ruti Teitel, *Bringing in the Messiah Through the Law, in* HUMAN RIGHTS IN POLITICAL TRANSITION: GETTYSBURG TO BOSNIA 177 (Carla Hesse & Robert Post eds., 1999).

18. *See Federal Criminal and Correctional Court of Appeals, Buenos Aires: Conviction of Former Military Commanders,* 8 HUM. RTS. L.J. 368 (1987).

19. *See* Press Release, International Criminal Tribunal for the former Yugoslavia, Milan Martic, Radovan Karadžić and Ratko Mladić Indicted Along with 21 Other Accused (July 25, 1995) (see also statement by Justice Richard Goldstone, Apr. 24, 1995).

20. *See* Rome Statute, *supra* note 6, art. 25, at 1016 (Individual Criminal Responsibility).

21. Indeed, the reliance on "joint criminal enterprise" in the trial of Slobodan Milošević has raised these issues. Prosecutor v. Milošević, Case No. IT-02-54-T, Decision on Motion for Judgment of Acquittal, ¶142 (June 16, 2004), http://www.un.org/icty/milosevic/trialc/judgement/index.htm.

22. Indeed, most recently, this question would be debated concerning the trials relating to Saddam Hussein in Iraq, and the extent to which these should be convened instead offsite, and with a significant international dimension, instead of the national model the IST adopts. Though even this formulation is too simple for, while the proceedings are national, the conception of the charges is international. *See* Statute of the Iraqi Special Tribunal, Dec. 10, 2003, 43 I.L.M. 231; *see also* Ruti Teitel, *The Law and Politics of Contemporary Transitional Justice,* 38 CORNELL INT'L L.J. 837, 843–44, 848 (2005).

23. *See supra* notes 3, 4 and accompanying text.

24. According to the Nuremberg Charter, Article 6: "Nothing in this Agreement shall prejudice the jurisdiction or the powers of any national or occupation court established or to be established in any allied territory or in Germany for the trial of war criminals." Agreement for the Prosecution and Punishment of the Major War Criminals of the European Axis art. 6, Aug. 8, 1945, 59 Stat. 1544, 1545, 82 U.N.T.S. 279, 282; *see also* Article 10 of the Charter, providing for follow-up trials in national, military or occupation courts. Charter of the International Military Tribunal, *supra* note 10, art. 10, 59 Stat. at 1548, 82 U.N.T.S. at 290.

25. Thus, Control Council Law No. 10 was the basis for war crimes trials held at Nuremberg after the International Military Tribunal.

26. *See* TEITEL, *supra* note 5, at 63–65. The subsequent French trial of non-national Klaus Barbie was based on a "scene of the crime," or territoriality principle of jurisdiction.

27. *See* Rome Statute, supra note 6, art. 1, at 1003.

28. *See* Convention on the Prevention and Punishment of the Crime of Genocide, Dec. 9, 1948, 102 Stat. 3045, 78 U.N.T.S. 277.

29. The leading example remains the trial of Adolf Eichmann in Jerusalem. *See* HANNAH ARENDT, EICHMANN IN JERUSALEM: A REPORT ON THE BANALITY OF EVIL 258–59 (Penguin Books 1994) (1963).

30. *See* TEITEL, *supra* note 15, at 69–117 (reviewing various forms of official and unofficial record-making as pursuit of "historical justice").

31. *See* TAYLOR, *supra* note 12, at 575.

32. *See* MICHAEL WALZER, JUST AND UNJUST WARS 74–85 (1977).

33. *See supra* note 6.

34. *See* International Criminal Tribunal for the former Yugoslavia art. 4, *supra* note 3, at 1193.

35. Consider that the International Tribunal for the former Yugoslavia was convened during, and not after, the conflict, raising difficult questions about the relationship of law to the use of force. *See generally* Theodor Meron, *International Criminalization of Internal Atrocities*, 89 AM. J. INT'L L. 554 (1995).

36. *Compare* the following language within Article 6(c) of the Nuremberg Charter. Article 6(c) provided that persecution was punishable only if perpetrated "in connection with any crime within the jurisdiction of the Tribunal," but also refers to acts committed "before or during the war." Charter of the International Military Tribunal, *supra* note 9, art. 6(c), 59 Stat. at 1547, 82 U.N.T.S. at 288.

37. *See* Judgment of the International Military Tribunal for the Trial of German Major War Criminals 41 (1946). For discussion, see TAYLOR, *supra* note 12, at 583 (citing to Nuremberg Tribunal's Judgment).

38. *See* Charter of the International Military Tribunal, *supra* note 9, art. 6(c), 59 Stat. at 1547, 82 U.N.T.S. at 288 (emphasis added).

39. *See* Prosecutor v. Tadić, Case No. IT-94-1-A, Judgment in Sentencing Appeals, ¶¶ 65-66 (Jan. 26, 2000).

40. *See* Rome Statute, *supra* note 7, art. 7, at 1004 (crimes against humanity).

# 3    Narratives

*After articulating in* Transitional Justice (2000) *the concept of transitional justice as both legal and political, and as revelatory about the nature of the rule of law as such, I undertook a new project of exploring the genealogy of transitional justice practices and discourses. The genealogy includes an intellectual history of the concept of "transitional justice." From perspectives both backward-looking and forward-looking, I saw that the conception of transitional justice was informed by the nature of the political repression and the degree of commitment to political repression.*

*The genealogy frames the last decades of transitional justice by offering three phases of transitional justice that reflect changes in the fundamental conception of justice. These phases appear to have been long-acting, as the genealogy has been widely cited. It is now more apt than ever, as its framework can help us understand the phenomena of transition of recent years. In particular, there is the move from post-war internationalism to a stage of local justice. The second stage was aimed at societal transformation and often conceived in terms of collective restoration and reconciliation, with less emphasis on the singleminded punishment of perpetrators.*

*The third, global stage continues today. Transitional justice has become an established discourse that appears to be more and more disconnected from a nexus to political transition and where weak states transition hence depends on the involvement of outside supranational institutions. This is a situation where there is more than one constituency for transitional justice, where victims accessing legal institutions have entrenched one face of transitional justice in terms of victims' justice, and where these processes are often in tension with other political decision-making.*

*This raises the current issue of what is the normative relation between law and politics as to the location of a site or space for justice?*

# 4  Human Rights in Transition: Transitional Justice Genealogy

## Introduction

This chapter articulates a genealogy of transitional justice.[1] Transitional justice can be defined as the conception of justice associated with periods of political change,[2] characterized by legal responses to confront the wrongdoings of repressive predecessor regimes.[3] The genealogy presented in this Article traces the historical pursuit of justice in periods of political flux, reviewing the political developments of the last half-century and analyzing the evolution of the conception of transitional justice.[4] This Article contends that a genealogy of transitional justice demonstrates, over time, a close relationship between the type of justice pursued and the relevant limiting political conditions. Currently, the discourse is directed at preserving a minimalist rule of law identified chiefly with maintaining peace.

The genealogy is structured along critical cycles that divide along three phases.[5] This chapter begins by briefly describing the phases, and then elaborates upon each phase, as well as upon the critical dynamic interrelationships of the three phases within the genealogy.[6] The genealogy presented in this chapter is structured along the lines of, and situated within, an intellectual history.[7] Accordingly, the genealogy is organized along a schematic of the development of ideas associated with the three phases of transitional justice. These phases ultimately reflect the genealogy's link with the broader intellectual trend toward an increased pragmatism in, and politicization of, the law.[8]

The origins of modern transitional justice can be traced to World War I.[9] However, transitional justice becomes understood as both extraordinary and international in the post-war period after 1945. The Cold War ends the internationalism of this first, or post-war, phase of transitional justice. The second, or post–Cold War, phase is associated with the wave of democratic transitions and modernization that began in 1989. Toward the end of the twentieth century, global politics was characterized by an acceleration in conflict resolution and a persistent discourse of justice throughout law and society. The third, or steady-state, phase of transitional justice is associated with contemporary conditions of persistent conflict which lay the foundation for a normalized law of violence.

Phase I of the genealogy, the post-war phase, begins in 1945. Through its most recognized symbol, the Allied-run Nuremberg Trials,[10] this phase reflects the triumph of transitional justice within the scheme of international law. However, this development was not enduring, due to its association with the exceptional political conditions of the post-war period: Germany's diminished sovereignty formed the basis for international nation-building. These political conditions were unique, and would neither persist nor recur in the same manner. Accordingly, this first phase of transitional justice, associated with interstate cooperation, war crimes trials, and sanctions, ended soon after the war. Beginning in the 1950s, the Cold War and a relatively stable bipolar balance of power led to a general political equilibrium and an impasse on the question of transitional justice. Nevertheless, the legacy of the post-war trials that criminalized state wrongdoing as part of a universal rights scheme far exceeds the actual force of historical precedent, and this legacy forms the basis of modern human rights law.[11]

Phase II is associated with a period of accelerated democratization and political fragmentation that has been characterized as a "third wave" of transition.[12] Over the last quarter of the twentieth century, the collapse and disintegration of the Soviet Union led to concurrent transitions throughout much of the world. Withdrawal of Soviet-supported guerrilla forces in the late 1970s fueled the end of military rule in South America.[13] These transitions were rapidly followed by post-1989 transitions in Eastern Europe, Africa, and Central America.[14] While these changes are often described as isolated developments or as a series of civil wars, many of these conflicts were fostered or supported by international power politics[15] and were therefore affected by the Soviet collapse, which ended the Cold War period of political equilibrium.[16]

While the post–Cold War wave of transition theoretically raises the possibility of a return to Phase I international transitional justice, the form of transitional justice that in fact emerges is associated with the rise of nation-building.[17] Moreover, rather than understanding the rule of law in terms of accountability for a small number of leaders, the Phase II transitional model tends to rely upon more diverse rule-of-law understandings tied to a particular political community and local conditions.[18] However, this move toward more local or even privatized justice stands in tension with the potential of a broader conception of justice associated with transnational politics.

By the end of the twentieth century, the third steady-state phase of transitional justice emerges. This third phase is characterized by the fin-de-siècle acceleration associated with globalization and typified by conditions of heightened political instability and violence.[19] Transitional justice moves from the exception to the norm, to become a paradigm of rule of law. In this contemporary phase, transitional jurisprudence normalizes an expanded discourse of humanitarian justice constructing a body of law associated with pervasive conflict, which contributes to laying the foundation for the emerging law of terrorism.

## Phase I: Post-War Transitional Justice

The first phase of a genealogy of transitional justice encompasses the post–World War II model of justice. However, the history begins earlier in the century, following World War I. During the inter-war period, the central aim of justice was to delineate the unjust war and the parameters of justifiable punishment by the international community. Questions confronted in this context included whether and to what extent to punish Germany for its aggression, and what form justice should take: international or national, collective or individual. Ultimately, the decision to convene international proceedings reflected the prevailing political circumstances, particularly the limits upon national sovereignty and the conceded international governance of that period.

A genealogical perspective situates post-war transitional justice in its own historical context, specifically the transitional justice of World War I,[20] and reveals the extent to which this preceding conception informs the critical response of post–World War II justice.[21] At least two critical responses emerge regarding World War II transitional justice. First, national justice was displaced by international justice. The administration of the post–World War I model of transitional punitive justice, characterized by failed national trials, was left to Germany.[22] Seen with the hindsight of history, it was clear that the post–World War I national trials did not serve to deter future carnage. In an evident critical response to the past, post–World War II transitional justice began by eschewing national prosecutions,[23] instead seeking international criminal accountability for the Reich's leadership.[24]

The second critical response concerned the post–World War I collective sanctions levied against Germany.[25] Seen through the lens of genealogy, these transitional responses clearly failed and came to be identified as a basis for the sense of economic frustration and resentment that fueled Germany's role in World War II.[26] Onerous sanctions and their crude undifferentiated impact raised profound normative questions.[27] After World War II, this approach gave way to the critical response and to the liberal focus on individual judgment and responsibility.

While the asserted aim of the transitional justice norm in this first phase was accountability, a striking innovation at the time was the turn to international criminal law and the extension of its applicability beyond the state, to the individual. Moreover, through changes in the law of war and its principles of criminal responsibility, the international legal order imposed enabled holding accountable the Reich's higher echelons for the offenses of aggression and persecutory policy. While claims are made about the forward-looking nature of deterrence, it is clear that the Nuremberg prosecution was primarily intended to justify and legitimate Allied intervention in the war.[28] This use of transitional justice recurs in Phase III.[29]

The period immediately following World War II was the heyday of international justice. The critical turn away from prior nationalist transitional responses, and toward an internationalist policy, was thought to guarantee the rule of law. However, whether deterrence would necessarily be better advanced by international accountability was debatable. Whereas international justice is commonly thought to incorporate the impartiality associated with the rule of law,[30] other rule-of-law values, such as nexus, are seen as deriving from the local accountability associated with domestic justice.[31] Moreover, following World War II, the application of international justice involved legal irregularities that raised tensions for the rule of law, especially given its stated liberalizing aim.[32] Ultimately, the Phase I model would offer a very limited precedent. With the Cold War bifurcation, it became eminently clear that this model could not be readily exported. While a form of international justice does recur in Phase III,[33] this more contemporary internationalism has been transformed by the ongoing developments caused by globalization.[34]

The post-war turn to international law also reflected the sense that the relevant subject of transitional justice was an international legal response governed by the law of conflict. Over the years, this legacy has been mixed: the force of the precedent has hardly been reflected in other instances of international justice,[35] although this is arguably changing given the creation of the permanent International Criminal Court.[36] The post-war legacy's ongoing force has been evident in developments in international law, where dimensions of the precedent establishing international accountability for wartime abuses were entrenched in international conventions soon after World War II, such as the Genocide Convention.[37] Moreover, dimensions of the post-war precedent, such as its preeminent commitment to individual rights, have also informed domestic and comparative law, as evidenced in the heightened wave of related constitutionalism.[38] In the post-war phase, the exportation of forms of transitional justice occurred through legal transplants of treaties, conventions, and constitutionalism. The post-war period was also the heyday of the belief in law and development, and, more generally, in the belief in law as a tool for state modernization.[39]

The international justice associated with the post-war period returns in a new form in contemporary post-conflict circumstances, revealing transitional justice's critical dynamic. International justice recurs but is transformed by past precedents and a new political context. The subject and scope of transitional justice have expanded to transcend its operative action upon states, and to operate upon private actors. Transitional justice has also extended beyond its historic role in regulating international conflict, to regulate intrastate conflict as well as peacetime relations, comprising a threshold rule of law in globalizing politics.[40] The significance of these developments will be discussed further in Phase III.

## Phase II: Post–Cold War Transitional Justice

The last two decades of the twentieth century have been characterized as a veritable wave of political transitions. The collapse of the Soviet Union, the end of the bipolar balance of power, and the attendant proliferation of political democratization and modernization ushered in the post–Cold War phase of transitional justice.[41]

The decline and eventual collapse of the Soviet Empire sparked a wave of liberalization that began with the transitions in the Southern Cone of South America in the late 1970s and early 1980s, and continued throughout Eastern Europe and Central America.[42] While these regional developments are generally represented as independent of one another, a genealogical perspective illuminates the connection between these political transitions and illustrates how many local conflicts were supported by United States/Soviet bipolarism.[43] The end of this historical schematic does not imply that such conflict has also ended, as there remain numerous interconnected insurgency movements.[44]

When political transitions occurred in the 1980s, the questions confronted by successor regimes were whether and to what extent to adhere to the Phase I model of transitional justice.[45] In the new democracies that emerged in South America following the collapse of repressive military juntas, it was unclear whether trials of leaders in the style of Nuremberg could be successfully followed in the Americas.[46] This question was first posed in Argentina after the Falklands/Malvinas War,[47] where the successor regime attempted to distinguish the context from that of international post-war justice and called for domestic trials.[48] Throughout Latin America, nascent democratic governments struggled with national militaries over the chosen justice policy.[49] This provided a haunting reminder of the post–World War I period and again raised the question whether the administration of criminal justice advanced the rule of law. In Phase II, modernization and the rule of law were equated with trials by the nation-state to legitimate the successor regime and advance nation-building.

Phase II manifests a similarly limited transferability to political contexts of radically different sovereignty as the Phase I model.[50] However, despite the general absence of international trials in Phase II, a review of the transitional jurisprudence demonstrates that international law can play a constructive role, providing an alternative source of rule of law to guide national trials in a transitional society.[51] In this regard, international legal norms serve to construct a perception of continuity and consistency in the rule of law.[52] The profound and permanent significance of the Nuremberg model is that by defining the rule of law in universalizing terms, it has become the standard by which all subsequent transitional justice debates are framed. Whereas the Phase I justice policy simply assumed the legitimacy of punishing human rights abuses, in Phase II the tension between punishment and amnesty was complicated by the recognition of dilemmas inherent in periods of political flux.

Transitional justice in its second phase reflected that the relevant values in the balance were hardly those of the ideal rule of law. Where the aim was to advance legitimacy, pragmatic principles guided the justice policy and the sense of adherence to the rule of law. Transitional jurisprudence was linked to a conception of justice that was imperfect and partial. What is fair and just in extraordinary political circumstances was to be determined from the transitional position itself.[53] Accordingly, multiple conceptions of justice emerged in Phase II.

The deliberations over justice in transition are best understood when they are situated in the actual political realities and in the transitional political context, which included the features of the predecessor regime as well as political, juridical, and social contingencies. The feasibility of pursuing justice and its ability to contribute to transitional rule of law depended upon the scale of prior wrongdoings, as well as the extent to which they were systemic or state-sponsored. The attempt to impose accountability through criminal law often raised rule-of-law dilemmas, including retroactivity in the law, tampering with existing laws, a high degree of prosecutorial selectivity, and a compromised judiciary.[54] Therefore, to whatever extent imposing transitional criminal justice included such irregularities, it risked detracting from the contribution that justice can make to reestablishing the rule of law.[55] In fledgling democracies, where the administration of punishment can pose acute rule-of-law dilemmas, the contradictions regarding the uses of the law may become too great.[56] These profound dilemmas were recognized in the deliberations preceding the decisions in many countries to forgo prosecutions in favor of alternative methods for truth-seeking and accountability.[57]

Given the tensions present in the administration of transitional justice in its second phase, the principles of justice associated with Phase I were increasingly questioned. In a critical response to the Phase I post-war justice project, Phase II moved beyond retributive justice as historically understood. The transitional dilemmas at stake in Phase II were framed in terms more comprehensive than simply confronting or holding accountable the predecessor regime, and included questions about how to heal an entire society and incorporate diverse rule-of-law values, such as peace and reconciliation, that had previously been treated as largely external to the transitional justice project. Accordingly, the move away from judgment associated with international justice reflected a shift in the understanding of transitional justice, which became associated with the more complex and diverse political conditions of nation-building.

The post–Cold War phase stands in a critical position relative to Phase I transitional justice. In the Phase II context of a heightened wave of democratic transition and nation-building, transitional justice involved crucial rule-of-law compromises. Therefore, whereas Phase I transitional justice initially appeared to assume its potentially limitless and universal extension in the law, by its second phase transitional justice was more concededly contextual, limited, and provisional. Ultimately, the primary focus on local responsibility in post–Cold War transitions offered a partial, distorted perspective of the historically broader bipolar conflict. While the Phase II reliance on local or national justice constituted a critical response to Phase I, the post–Cold War model was ultimately not appropriate for later globalizing politics, in which national and international factors became interdependent contributors to political change.

## Juxtaposing Truth with Justice

This Part elaborates upon the link between the chosen form of transitional justice response and political context. In Phase II, the central transitional dynamic responded to post-war transitional justice, while also differentiating itself from that period. Transitional justice responses in the second phase moved away from post-war international transitional justice toward alternative strategies. This was illustrated by the surge of hybridized law and the move to law and society responses.

The leading model in this phase is known as restorative. In this phase, the main purpose of transitional justice was to construct an alternative history of past abuses. A dichotomy between truth and justice therefore emerged. Thus, the Phase II paradigm largely eschewed trials, to focus instead upon a new institutional mechanism: the truth commission. A truth commission is typically an official body, often created by a national government, to investigate, document, and report upon human-rights abuses occurring within a country over a specified period of time. While first used in Argentina,[58] the investigatory model is associated with the response adopted in post-apartheid South Africa in the 1990s.[59] Truth and reconciliation commissions of various types have since been proposed or convened throughout the world and often garner significant international support.[60]

The appeal of the model is its ability to offer a broader historical perspective, rather than mere judgments in isolated cases.[61] Truth commissions are most popular where the predecessor regime disappeared persons or repressed information about its persecution policy, as was typical in Latin America.[62] In contrast, truth commissions have been of less interest in post–Communist Europe, where the use of history by various governments was itself a destructive dimension of Communist repression.[63] Accordingly, in Eastern Europe, the main critical response by the successor regime was not to create official histories, but rather to guarantee access to the historical record.[64]

The second-phase model did appear to advance some of the rule-of-law aims of criminal justice in transitional societies, in which legal institutions were functioning under stressed transitional conditions. Seen in a genealogical perspective, the primary aim of truth commissions was not justice, but peace. This raised the question of the expected relationship between peace and furthering the rule of law and democracy. While proponents of the South African model argued that peace was a necessary precondition to democracy,[65] building democratic institutions was not their primary goal.[66] It is not at all evident that short-term approaches to conflict management would further the rule of law.[67] Nevertheless, often a truth commission's purposes are deemed analogous to those of criminal justice, as both trials and truth commissions can be understood as primarily animated by deterrence.[68] Indeed, such commissions' mandates often include recommendations to prevent the recurrence of rights abuses.[69]

The Phase II response transcended the singleminded focus on individual accountability, in favor of a more communitarian conception. Nevertheless, this phase's aim was hardly a full-scale social justice project.[70] Instead, transitional justice's aims in this phase shifted from the earlier goal of establishing the rule of law through accountability to the goal of preserving peace.[71] This change in emphasis redefines the understanding of the purposes of transition.

Moreover, in this phase, the modality of transitional justice often became a private matter. Even when vested with government authority, transitional justice through truth commissions often became primarily a vehicle for victims to reconcile and recover from past harms, in consultation and with the assistance of various nonstate actors. Transitional justice became a form of dialogue between victims and their perpetrators. There was a move away from the Phase I focus on universalizing judgment toward a focus on rebuilding political identity,[72] through the rule of law, premised on local understandings of legitimacy.

The problem of judgment gave rise to other responses, primarily national investigatory commissions that had the advantage of being able to inquire more systematically into a state's wrongdoings.[73] Despite the move away from the international criminal justice associated with the first phase, the Phase II response did incorporate the post-war model's human rights rhetoric, albeit in a broader, societal, restorative approach. The central dilemma associated with this phase was often framed in human-rights terms, such as whether victims had rights to truth, and whether the state had a duty to investigate in order to reveal truth.[74] Within this framework, the core dynamic of "truth versus justice" suggested that there existed necessary conflicts among justice, history, and memory. This dynamic formulation is best understood as a critical response to the prior post-war model. However, the attempt to accommodate the international human rights rhetoric to a variety of broader social aims raises a number of contradictions and risks its likely misappropriation.[75]

However limited, transitional justice in its second phase enabled a form of preservative justice. The Phase II response allowed for the creation of a historical record, while also leaving open the possibility of future judicial resolution. The emphasis on preservation conceded the existing constraints upon political sovereignty that are associated with modern democratization, globalizing political fragmentation, and other limiting political conditions at the core of contemporary transitional justice.

*Trading Justice for Peace*

A dynamic discourse that juxtaposed and even sacrificed the aim of justice for the more modest goal of peace emerged in Phase II.[76] This Part elaborates upon that discourse and reflects upon its place in the genealogy, largely in terms of its critical dynamic with the Phase I justice model. This Part ultimately contends that the Phase II model expanded the category of transitional justice, with implications for its future normalization.[77]

A jurisprudence of forgiveness[78] and reconciliation[79] is associated with the Phase II model. The truth and reconciliation project incorporated much of its normative discourse from outside the law, specifically from ethics, medicine, and theology.[80] Its purpose was not merely justice, but peace for both individuals and society as a whole.[81] The problem of transitional justice was reconceived across moral and psychological lines to redefine identity. The evident mix of legal, political, and religious language reflected both the conceit and the limits of the law. Phase II had its roots in Phase I, and constituted a critical response to the broader post-war justice project. Whereas in its first phase the problem of transitional justice was framed in terms of justice versus amnesty, with amnesty considered exceptional to general adherence to the rule of law, the second phase adopted a broader amnesty policy with the aim of reconciliation.[82] The exception became generalized and reflected an explicit attempt to incorporate both mercy and grace into the law.

Both political activism and scholarship sought to move outside contemporary politics and history to represent conflict in timeless and universal terms.[83] Phase II did not resist the universalizing impetus associated with Phase I.[84] There was some continuation of the Phase I norm of the deployment of universal rights as part of the justifying structure of Phase II. The form of law adopted offers a universalizing language about the aims of forgiveness and the possibility of political redemption.[85] While law as conventionally understood had almost disappeared, the alternative model was said to have universal applications and claimed general diffusion around the world.[86] Consider the extent to which the transitional justice being exported in the post–Cold War paradigm is a secularized religion without law.[87]

In Phase II, there was an apparent conflation of the realm of ethics, generally considered to involve the private sphere rather than public choices,[88] and the realm of the political. This signaled the breakdown and interconnection of the private and the public spheres, a phenomenon associated with globalization.[89] Further, in the second phase, the relevant political actors changed from those with legal and political authority, to those with moral authority in civil society. Whereas, in its first phase, justice was chiefly the purview of the successor regime and courts of law, in the second phase many of the relevant actors and institutions lay outside law and politics, and included churches, NGOs, and human rights groups that incorporated a variety of alternative forms of conflict resolution.[90]

Moreover, the Phase II model adhered only tenuously to conventional legal processes. This was illustrated by the move from the courtroom to the hearing room, and the turn to discursive confessional testimonials. The choice of language had significant juridical and political implications. An ethical-religious discourse injected a moral basis into transitional justice. Yet the truth and reconciliation movement tended to eschew judgment and instead aimed to move beyond legal notions of guilt and responsibility. It contributed a political theology,[91] building a discourse that incorporated moral imperatives and had the potential to threaten the parameters of legitimate political discourse in liberalizing states, which conceive of the public sphere as a realm of free contestation.[92] Nevertheless, the truth commission was also associated with critical responses to globalization, where the perceived democratic deficit has led to the pursuit of a universalizing and legitimizing discourse.[93]

The evolution of the transitional-justice discourse in the second phase highlighted a complex interaction between the dimensions of the universal, the global, and the local. While framing the problem in universalizing human rights terms suggested a form of justice that is abstracted from the interests and needs of societies, even the Phase II approach assumed conditions that are not formally present in many countries, with often dubious restorative results. Genealogical review illuminates the historical and political contingencies in the policy choices. It also shows the extent to which the Phase II juridical regime incorporated rule-of-law ideas that related closely to the legitimacy of local institutions, thus addressing the multiple aims associated with periods of political flux.

The politics associated with the post–Cold War transitional response are illustrative. The asserted aim of transitional policy was said to be the threshold goal of peace, rather than that of democracy. The turn to alternative strategies, whether theological or therapeutic, was animated by the forward-looking aim of reconciliation. Forgiveness became a distinctive form of political apology,[94] understood as an act of contrition in a realm of unity politics.[95] A variety of conciliatory mechanisms emerged in many transitional societies, with the ostensible aim of stabilizing internal politics. These policies became the signs of an age of restoration of the rule of law in a global politics.

Nevertheless, there may well be long-term negative consequences to this type of reconciliation politics. For example, instigation of the settlement of claims can have conservative ramifications. The focus may subvert broader political reform[96] and generally cannot assist in laying the basis for development of democracy.[97] Moreover, as the responses discussed here have mostly implied national political resolutions, they often missed the broader structural causation associated with the bipolar balance of power. The Phase II discourse was being renegotiated at the same time as the debate on globalization reform. This appears to be more than historical coincidence. Even as the disparities between rich and poor that are associated with the free market economy have grown,[98] the impetus has been to resort increasingly to the transitional justice discourse, and a project that is to some extent backward-looking and limited to restoration.[99] Presently, the extent to which transitional justice has displaced other justice projects signals chastened political expectations responding to the failed experiments of a not-so-distant past.

### Fin-de-Siècle Transitional Justice and the Passage of Time

This Part examines transitional justice over time. It explores the degree to which the discourse of transitional justice has become ever-present in politics. With apparently ongoing processes of transitional justice delayed, the very meaning of the category of transition has expanded over time to become a persistent trope.[100]

The developments described above have implications for human historical self-understanding. By the end of the twentieth century, it seemed that all justice had become transitional, ex post, and backward-looking. Among some theorists of the period, the post-Soviet dynamics and the related wave of transitions were expected to lead to political stabilization and, according to Francis Fukuyama, "the end of history."[101] Other theorists suggested that the Communist collapse left few political choices, and that therefore, politics was past and all that remained was history. Thus, Jacques Derrida wrote about Marxism as a "ghost" to be mourned.[102] And while Derrida and Fukuyama shared little in the way of politics, they represented a broad span of political writers whose work at century's end clearly memorialized a time when politics involved a pronounced revolutionary project.[103] However, these conclusions forecasting the end of history or the end of politics certainly seem inapposite.[104] Existing scholarship has not yet captured the prevailing dynamic of transitional justice or its nexus with ongoing political change.

The discourse of transitional justice persisted through the final years of the twentieth century. There were persistent calls for apologies, reparations, memoirs, and all manner of account-settling related to past suffering and wrongdoing.[105] Examples of claimmaking and settlements abounded, including those related to assets and property lost during World War II,[106] reparations for slave labor,[107] and even more ancient injustices such as colonization, the Inquisition, and the Crusades.[108]

As a genealogical perspective illustrates, interest in the pursuit of justice does not necessarily wane with the passage of time.[109] This may be because transitional justice relates to exceptional political conditions, where the state itself is implicated in wrongdoing and the pursuit of justice necessarily awaits a change in regime. In recent years, this has been characterized by some as the "Scilingo Effect," so-called for a confession given two decades after junta rule ended in Argentina that reopened the question of justice for crimes committed during the Dirty War.[110] Transitional justice implies a nonlinear approach to time. This phenomenon is reflected in legal responses that are taken, often in the form of delayed litigation, to extend the span of transitional-justice, case-by-case.[111] In the international sphere, this dilemma was resolved by the adoption of the U.N. Convention on the Non-Applicability of Statutory Limitations to War Crimes and Crimes Against Humanity, although this measure did not necessarily resolve the attendant political tensions.[112]

There is a complicated relationship among transitional justice, truth, and history. In the discourse of transitional justice, revisiting the past is understood as the way to move forward.[113] There is an implied notion of progressive history. As a matter of intellectual historiography and human self-understanding, this notion is under siege.[114] However, transitions are rare periods of rupture which offer a choice among contested narratives. The paradoxical goal in transition is to undo history. The aim is to reconceive the social meaning of past conflicts, particularly defeats, in an attempt to reconstruct their present and future effects.[115]

Transitions present a threshold choice. By definition, they are times of contestation in historical narratives. Transitions thus present the potential for counter-histories. The question is posed anew after the passage of time, which underscores the threshold challenge of remaining in history, as well as the limits to transformation. Indeed, the possibility of some minimal amelioration is often juxtaposed with the countervailing resistance to working within historical and political parameters for the possibility of change. The notion of a threshold choice following massive tragedy appears in works chiefly addressing responses to the Holocaust.[116] In this context, there is often resistance to the very idea of a transition, which would raise the possibility of political change. The problem concerns the propriety of further engagement after massive catastrophe, whether in the form of giving testimony, taking political action, or contributing scholarship.[117]

In the post–Cold War phase, historical production was fundamental to building a state's political identity,[118] and control over construction of an alternative history could lie with multiple actors, including historians, lawyers, journalists, and victims.[119] This raised the normative question of who should write the history of the transition. In this regard, Phase II transitional justice moved from a project dependent upon the leading role of the state to a process that often elided it. The devolution of state power reflected the broader political conditions associated with post–Cold War transitions and globalization. Given the fact that predecessor regimes were frequently implicated in past wrongdoing, the diminished role for political authority in Phase II managed to avoid many of the dilemmas associated with the more ambitious Phase I justice project.

This transforming context increased the possibility of various alternative and even competing transitional justice resolutions involving international, transnational, national, or private settlements. In Phase II, there were a host of new political actors[120] and a distinct privatization of the transitional response. The trend toward privatization took a number of forms, from its devolution to civil society to its relegation to private citizens via litigation.[121] These processes were partially related to globalization, and raised the question of the extent to which normative principles were available to guide transitional decision-making. The second phase policy reflected a struggle between local and global resolutions, even as globalization increased the interconnectedness of political decision-making. Genealogical, interdisciplinary, and comparative review reveals highly divergent approaches to the rule of law,[122] which in turn reflect different legal and cultural perspectives.[123] A profound normative question was raised concerning the interaction of transitional justice, globalization, and sovereignty: whether and to what extent the response to a harm should rightly remain under the control of the state where the harm occurred. In Phase II, actions related to transitional justice were increasingly taken independent of state actors. This unsettled earlier determinations, as illustrated in the landmark extradition case of General Augusto Pinochet.[124] Moreover, this case also demonstrated the expansion of transitional justice in time.[125] In a world that is increasingly economically, technologically, politically, and legally interdependent, profound questions arise at the intersection of the principles of jurisdiction and sovereignty. Given the ongoing processes of globalization, this phenomenon will likely accelerate.[126] This seems to portend an expanded category of transitional justice.

The association of post–Cold War transitional justice with a globalizing politics acutely reflected the constructivist dimension of the more limited Phase II approaches. Whereas the first phase conceived of the rule of law in universalizing terms associated with accountability for humanity, the Phase II model was instead concerned with advancing an opposing idea of the rule of law associated with the legitimacy of a country's national jurisdiction and sovereignty. This Phase II narrowing of the relevant scope of inquiry illuminated the political construction that correlated with this form of transitional justice, specifically responses that implicated local, rather than international, actors, and those lower, rather than higher, in the echelon of political responsibility and power. This signaled the Phase II response's constructive force and also showed the extent to which the Phase II model was amenable to politicization and ultimately depended upon promoting alternative values, besides universal rights and accountability, underlying the rule of law.

To the extent that the second phase moved away from traditional legal remedies, it challenged whether any threshold remained regarding what constitutes the predicate transitional rule of law.[127] These changes illustrate the normative implications of deploying a discourse of justice. The discourse can influence the legitimacy of the response by giving it the provenance, and hence the democratic accountability, of the successor regime, and by imputing the administration of the transitional response with the legality traditionally associated with judicial proceedings.[128] The question remains whether there are any transitional-justice baselines or any threshold minimum beyond which historical, psychological, or religious inquiry ought to be characterized as justice-seeking. This genealogy suggests that the relevant inquiry is not a metaphysical enterprise, but rather must be understood in its historical and political context. Still, there is an independent basis for critique which influences the nature of the emerging discourse and affects whether it is likely to simply assist in the immediate aim of conflict resolution, or also contribute to the goals of democracy, nation-building, and the advancement of liberal political aims.[129]

## Phase III: Steady-State Transitional Justice
### *Transitional Justice All the Time*

The present phase can be characterized as steady-state transitional justice. The discourse has now moved from the periphery to the center. As discussed above, the new millennium appears to be associated with the expansion and normalization of transitional justice. What was historically viewed as a legal phenomenon associated with extraordinary post-conflict conditions now increasingly appears to be a reflection of ordinary times. War in a time of peace,[130] political fragmentation, weak states, small wars, and steady conflict all characterize contemporary political conditions.[131] These contemporary developments have spurred the attempted normalization of transitional justice, leading ultimately to ambivalent consequences. As a jurisprudence associated with political flux, transitional justice is related to a higher politics of the law and to some degree of compromise in rule-of-law standards.

The most recognized symbol of the normalization of transitional jurisprudence is the entrenchment of the Phase I response in the form of the International Criminal Court ("ICC"), the new international institution established at the end of the twentieth century.[132] This court was preceded by the ad hoc international criminal tribunals convened to respond to genocidal conflicts in the Balkans and Rwanda.[133] Half-a-century after World War II, the ICC symbolizes the entrenchment of the Nuremberg Model: the creation of a permanent international tribunal appointed to prosecute war crimes, genocide, and crimes against humanity as a routine matter under international law.[134] The threshold global rule of law presently appears to be based upon an expansion of the law of war.[135] Indeed, the move back to international humanitarian law incorporates the complex relationship between the individual and the state as a legal scheme which enables the international community to hold a regime's leadership accountable and condemn a systematic persecutory policy, even outside the relevant state.[136] Further, this particular form of international justice offers the potential for regime delegitimation that can support, or even instigate, transition.[137] Nevertheless, there are also many dilemmas and limits raised by the turn to the law of war in relative peacetime, as well as by the preference for international legal regimes. A dynamic tension emerges among adjudicatory fragmentation, the attendant potential for universal jurisdiction associated with transitional justice,[138] and the attempted centralization of accountability in the ICC.[139]

The normalization of transitional justice currently takes the form of the expansion of the law of war, as illustrated by the rise of humanitarian law.[140] Contemporary developments involve an appropriation of the discourse of the humanitarian-law regime with twofold significance. The establishment of humanitarian law as the present rule of law constrains not only the conduct of war,[141] but also appears to expand the humanitarian regime to address broader aspects of the law of war, including the justification of its possible initiation. Further, the use of the international humanitarian regime to justify the NATO intervention in Kosovo appears to have established a precedent for expanding the legitimate bases for intervention, specifically a humanitarian basis for just war.[142] A juridical scheme in which the law of war forms the basis for international criminal justice resonates more deeply and offers a more thorough justificatory structure. Whether unilaterally or multilaterally, the expanded humanitarian law enables recognition of lapses in state action, but also appears to enforce state respect for human rights. This demonstrates the potential for sliding from a normalized transitional justice to the campaign against terrorism. The use of human-rights law and the law of war has shifted after the move away from modern state theory to the period of globalization. The contemporary conflation of human rights law, criminal law, and the international law of war implies a pronounced loss for those seeking to challenge state action. Through the use of the transformed law of war and its rights-enforcement scheme as a basis for intervention, the expanded humanitarian regime introduces new human rights dilemmas that bring to the surface the tension in the aims of justice and peace.

Under the label of "preemptive self-defense," a related discourse of continuing war is being appropriated to legitimate the next stage in the war on terrorism.[143] The rhetoric attempts to eviscerate the distinctions between war and peace, and between law and its exception. The notion of Phase III steady-state transitional justice is evident in the deployment of the humanitarian regime, which has expanded and merged with the law of human rights.[144] The appeal to a language of universal morality in humanitarian legal discourse resonates with recent developments in transitional justice. The apparent normalization of transitional justice is also evident in the toleration of greater political discretion,[145] politicization in the uses of justice, the rise of highly irregular procedures, and explicit departures from prevailing law,[146] all justified in humanitarian terms.[147]

The expansion of the transitional justice discourse to the issue of terrorism proves problematic due to the inadequacy of the analogies between terrorism and war or political crisis. Transitional justice tends to look backward in responding to the last conflict, and therefore, it does not adapt easily to use as a template to guarantee prospective security. Any attempt to generalize from exceptional post-conflict situations in order to guide politics as a matter of course becomes extremely problematic.

Resisting the normalization of transitional justice is difficult. There is a significant loss in vocabulary from which to make any critique, since in the expanded discourse of transitional justice, the law of war has merged with the law of human rights. Only time will tell whether and to what extent these developments pose a serious challenge to the rule of law or are associated with the present cycle of contemporary politics.

## Transitional Justice: Discontinuity Versus Continuity

The remaining question that follows, given current trends in normalization, is what a genealogical perspective of transitional justice might convey about the conception of justice in ordinary times. To what extent is there continuity, and to what extent discontinuity, both descriptively and normatively? In recent years the question has been controversial, sparking a proliferation of scholarly writing. A number of scholars have challenged any conceptualization of transitions as exceptional in political life, claiming that the aspiration during transitional periods ought to be based on a general theory about the rule of law.[148]

This genealogy suggests that this is a false dichotomy. Two political dimensions determine what signifies the rule of law in periods of transition: the transitional context, specifically the circumstances relating to political and legal conditions associated with periods of political change, and other political factors, such as local context. Beyond the dimension of transition, local factors also affect the legitimacy of transitional responses. Thus, the mere exportation of ideal rule-of-law models does not provide sufficient guidance. While there is no clear boundary between ordinary and transitional periods, justice-seeking in periods of transition is differentiated by the rule of law associated with limited conditions of political flux. The central dilemma of transitional justice relates to the recurring issues that, even if not sui generis, are largely associated with the legal and political factors common to unstable periods of liberalizing political transformation.[149] To the extent that these political conditions are present in a successor regime, the circumstances will present rule-of-law challenges that are peculiar to, or arise more frequently in, the transitional context. Therefore, while in the abstract it might be desirable to insist that justice-seeking projects in transitional times emulate those of established liberal democracies, this exhortation will ultimately be of limited normative guidance. The rule-of-law capacity of transitional societies cannot be expected to function at the same level as that of states that have a consolidated liberal juridical apparatus.

Transitional periods, depending on the political and legal conditions in the relevant society, will fall somewhere along the continuum of the rule-of-law's established democracies. This observation should have implications for the impetus to entrench any particular form of transitional rule of law. To some extent, the dilemmas of transitional justice in its contemporary phases raise issues that resonate more generally with the efforts to establish rule of law in a globalizing world. These include how to shape law reform and justice projects in light of growing global interdependence, and to what extent to accommodate local structures to outside forces.[150]

## Conclusion

This chapter provides a genealogy of transitional justice over the arc of the past half-century. The genealogical perspective situates transitional justice in a political context, challenging essentializing approaches and thereby illuminating the dynamic relationship between transitional justice and politics over time.

The genealogical inquiry highlights the relationship between juridical and political conditions during periods of political transformation. This inquiry indicates that transitional justice, while contingent upon local conditions and culture, also displays dimensions commonly associated with periods of political flux.

The genealogical approach contributes a needed perspective on the post-war model's enduring dominance in the field of transitional justice. It also illuminates the critical move in Phase II toward local, alternative approaches associated with nation-building, and highlights the Phase II privatization and hybridization of the law, which also reflects trends in globalization. The post–Cold War focus on alternative methods for changing political identity was a strategy that responded critically to the post–World War II movement to internationalize and universalize the rule of law, but the strategy was also closely related to the particular national politics of the immediate post–Cold War moment. Change was therefore inevitable: roughly fifteen years after the end of the Cold War, we are now witnessing the normalization of transitional justice, as seen in the current expansion of humanitarian law to ordinary peacetime contexts.

Finally, transitional justice is an important part of broader political developments in recent international history. Thus, in Phase I, transitional justice adhered to juridical rights-enforcement associated with liberal ideals of rule of law. However, as time passed, those normative assumptions were challenged, and similar trends emerged in both transitional justice and also in the broader discussion of the concept of the rule of law. Just as postmodernist challenges generally offer better critiques than practical strategies,[151] in moving the discourse away from universalizing rule of law, the contemporary transitional-justice model reflects a limited critical response. The genealogical method is no exception: it yields ongoing critical cycles, rather than a progressive history of transitional justice.

## Notes

1. For a comprehensive analysis of transitional justice, see RUTI G. TEITEL, TRANSITIONAL JUSTICE (2000).

2. *See* GUILLERMO O'DONNELL & PHILIPPE C. SCHMITTER, TRANSITIONS FROM AUTHORITARIAN RULE: TENTATIVE CONCLUSIONS ABOUT UNCERTAIN DEMOCRACIES 6 (1998) (defining transition as the interval between one political regime and another).

3. For a helpful compilation, see TRANSITIONAL JUSTICE: HOW EMERGING DEMOCRACIES RECKON WITH FORMER REGIMES (Neil J. Kritz ed., 1997).

4. *See* TEITEL, *supra* note 1; Ruti Teitel, *Transitional Jurisprudence: The Role of Law in Political Transformation*, 106 YALE L.J. 2009 (1997).

5. The use of the term "phases" here should be considered primarily as an heuristic, to help understand the periodization of the various political and legal periods. This is not to say that there are entirely well-defined separations dividing these phases. Indeed, there are overlaps among the three phases proposed here.

6. On the "critical" responses of transitional justice to predecessor political repressions, see TEITEL, *supra* note 1, at 216, 220–25.

7. Regarding genealogy, see Michel Foucault, *Nietzche, Genealogy, History* (Donald F. Bouchard & Sherry Simon trans.) *in* THE FOUCAULT READER 80 (Paul Rabinow ed., 1984). On genealogical politics, see WENDY BROWN, POLITICS OUT OF HISTORY, 91–120 (2001); MICHAEL CLIFFORD, POLITICAL GENEALOGY AFTER FOUCAULT: SAVAGE IDENTITIES 149–70 (2001).

8. On pragmatism, see Marion Smiley, *Democratic Justice in Transition*, 99 MICH. L. REV. 1332 (2001) (discussing pragmatic views of transitional justice and reviewing Ruti Teitel's *Transitional Justice*). *See also* Jack Snyder & Leslie Vinjamuri, *Principles and Pragmatism in Strategies of International Justice* (presented at the Olin Institute National Security Seminar at Harvard University, December 2001) (on file with author).

9. For historical examples, see TEITEL, *supra* note 1, at 31, 39–40. For earlier precedents, see also MICHAEL WALZER, REGICIDE AND REVOLUTION: SPEECHES ON THE TRIAL OF LOUIS XVI (Michael Walzer ed., Marion Rothstein transl., 1992) (providing a historical account).

10. On the post-war period, see FROM DICTATORSHIP TO DEMOCRACY: COPING WITH THE LEGACIES OF AUTHORITARIANISM AND TOTALITARIANISM (John H. Herz ed., 1983). Of course, there are earlier examples in the century, but these are smaller-scale responses. *See* PHILLIPE C. SCHMITTER, TRANSITIONS FROM AUTHORITARIAN RULE: COMPARATIVE PERSPECTIVES (Guillermo O'Donnell et al. eds., 1986).

11. On the impact of the Nuremberg precedent, see Ruti G. Teitel, *Nuremberg and Its Legacy, Fifty Years Later, in* WAR CRIMES: THE LEGACY OF NUREMBERG 44 (Belinda Cooper ed., 1999). For an example of the impact of the post-war precedents in human rights law, see HENRY STEINER & PHILIP ALSTON, INTERNATIONAL HUMAN RIGHTS IN CONTEXT: LAW, POLITICS, MORALS (2000).

12. *See* SAMUEL P. HUNTINGTON, THE THIRD WAVE: DEMOCRATIZATION IN THE LATE TWENTIETH CENTURY (1991).

13. On the Latin American transitions, see PHILIPPE C. SCHMITTER ET AL., TRANSITIONS FROM AUTHORITARIAN RULE: LATIN AMERICA (1986); JAIME MALAMUD-GOTI, GAME WITHOUT END: STATE TERROR AND THE POLITICS OF JUSTICE (1996); LAWRENCE WESCHLER, A MIRACLE, A UNIVERSE: SETTLING ACCOUNTS WITH TORTURERS (1998); *see also* TRANSITION TO DEMOCRACY IN LATIN AMERICA: THE ROLE OF THE JUDICIARY (Irwin P. Stotsky ed., 1993).

14. See *supra* note 12.

15. On Latin America see LARS SCHOULTZ, NATIONAL SECURITY AND UNITED STATES POLICY TOWARDS LATIN AMERICA (1987) (discussing Latin America and the global balance of power); *see also* DAVID GREEN, THE CONTAINMENT OF LATIN AMERICA: A HISTORY OF THE MYTHS AND REALITIES OF THE GOOD NEIGHBOR POLICY (1971); WITH FRIENDS LIKE THESE: THE AMERICAS WATCH REPORT ON HUMAN RIGHTS AND U.S. POLICY IN LATIN AMERICA (Cynthia Brown ed., 1985).

16. This is, of course, not to offer an unicausal theory, but rather to clarify shared factors in the multiple transitions that occurred in approximately the last quarter of the last century. For disciplinary reasons, scholarship in each area tends to be isolated.

17. There are exceptions in the turn to international justice regarding the conflicts in the Balkans and in Rwanda. *See infra* text accompanying note 133.

18. *See infra* text accompanying notes 53-73.

19. *See infra* text accompanying notes 128-145.

20. *See* NIALL FERGUSON, THE PITY OF WAR: EXPLAINING WORLD WAR I (2000).

21. Regarding the post-war Allied Trials program, see TELFORD TAYLOR, THE ANATOMY OF THE NUREMBERG TRIALS: A PERSONAL MEMOIR (1992); SHELDON GLUECK, WAR CRIMINALS: THEIR PROSECUTION AND PUNISHMENT (Kraus Reprint Co., 1976) (1944).

22. For an account see Geo. Gordon Battle, *The Trials Before the Leipsic Supreme Court of Germans Accused of War Crimes*, 8 VA. L. REV. 1 (1921).

23. On the history of the deliberations, see ROBERT I. CONOT, JUSTICE AT NUREMBERG (1983).

24. However, the subsequent Control Council Ten trials would be convened on a national basis. *See* GOV'T PRINTING OFFICE, TRIALS OF THE MAJOR WAR CRIMINALS BEFORE THE NUREMBERG MILITARY TRIBUNALS UNDER CONTROL COUNCIL LAW NO. 10 (1953) (commonly known as the "green books").

25. The Versailles Treaty at Article 231 provides: "The Allied and Associated Governments affirm and Germany accepts the responsibility of Germany and her Allies for causing all the loss and damage to which the Allied and Associated Governments and their nationals have been subjected as a consequence of a war imposed upon them by the aggression of Germany and her Allies." According to the Treaty's "war-guilt" clause, all responsibility for the war was to be borne by Germany. *See* Treaty of Versailles, June 28, 1919, art. 231, pt. VIII, Consol. T.S. 225; *see generally* NANA SAGI, GERMAN REPARATIONS: A HISTORY OF THE NEGOTIATIONS (Dafna Alon trans., 1980).

26. *See* FERGUSON, *supra* note 20.

27. The uses of economic sanctions in the contemporary moment have raised similar concerns. On the U.S. sanctions debate, see Audie Klotz, *Norms Reconstituting Interests: Global Racial Equality and U.S. Sanctions Against South Africa*, 49 INT'L ORG. 451 (1995).

28. Transitional justice was used as a norm to distinguish between justified and unjustified military intervention. *See* TAYLOR, *supra* note 21, at 22–42 (discussing the Nuremberg ideas regarding whether launching an aggressive war should be considered a crime under international law).

29. *See infra* text accompanying notes 133-137.

30. *See* TEITEL, *supra* note 1, at 30–39; Stotsky, *supra* note 13.

31. These are discussed *infra* at Part II, notes 53-57, 58-73 and accompanying text. *See* TEITEL, *supra* note 1 at 36–40; *see generally* Stotsky, *supra* note 13.

32. *See* DAVID LUBAN, LEGAL MODERNISM 336 (1994).

33. *See* Teitel, *Transitional Jurisprudence, supra* note 4.

34. *See infra* text accompanying notes 132-137.

35. *See* Teitel, *supra* note 11, at 44. The World War II-related prosecutions are still the largest precedents in criminal accountability. For a bibliography of war crimes trials, see WAR CRIMINALS AND WAR CRIMES TRIALS: AN ANNOTATED BIBLIOGRAPHY AND SOURCE BOOK (Norman E. Tuterow ed., 1986). *See* Symposium, *Holocaust and Human Rights Law: The Sixth International Conference,* 12 B.C. THIRD WORLD L.J. 191 (1992).

36. *See infra* notes 132-134 (regarding the Rome Statute).

37. *See* Affirmation of the Principles of International Law Recognized by the Charter of the Nuremberg Tribunal, G.A. Res. 95(1), U.N. GAOR, Doc. A/64/Add.1 (1946). For a discussion of the codification process and efforts of the International Law Commission, see M. Cherif Bassiouni, *The History of the Draft Code of Crimes Against the Peace and Security of Mankind, in* NOUVELLES ETUDES PENALES, COMMENTARIES ON THE INTERNATIONAL LAW COMMISSION'S 1991 DRAFT CODE OF CRIMES AGAINST THE PEACE AND SECURITY OF MANKIND 11 (M. Cherif Bassiouni ed., 1993); Convention on the Prevention and Punishment of the Crime of Genocide, Dec. 9, 1948, 78 U.N.T.S. 277 (entered into force Jan. 12, 1951); The Universal Declaration of Human Rights, G.A. Res. 217A (III), 71 U.N. Doc. A/810 (1948). For

broader discussion of these post-war developments, see Ruti G. Teitel, *Human Rights Genealogy*, 66 FORDHAM L. REV. 301 (1997).

38. This is evidenced in the constitution-making of the post-war period. *See* LOUIS HENKIN, THE AGE OF RIGHTS (1990). On the emerging right to democracy, see Thomas M. Franck, *The Emerging Right to Democratic Governance*, 86 AM. J. INT'L. L. 46, 53 (1992).

39. John Henry Merryman, *Law and Development Memoirs II: SLADE*, 48 AM. J. COMP. L. 713 (2000). *See* John Henry Merryman, *Comparative Law and Social Change*, 25 AM. J. COMP. L. 457, 483 (1977); *see also* THOMAS CAROTHERS, AIDING DEMOCRACY ABROAD: THE LEARNING CURVE (1999).

40. *See infra* notes 128-140 and accompanying text.

41. Other works refer to this development as the "third wave" of democratization. *See, e.g.*, HUNTINGTON, *supra* note 12.

42. *See supra* notes 14-15; WALTER LEFEBER, INEVITABLE REVOLUTIONS: UNITED STATES AND CENTRAL AMERICA (1984).

43. For a review of this third wave of transition, see HUNTINGTON, *supra* note 12. *See also* SCHOULTZ, *supra* note 15, at 112–204 (discussing geopolitics and human rights regarding U.S. policy in Central America).

44. This was made very clear after the terrorist attacks on September 11, 2001. *See* AHMED RASHID, JIHAD: THE RISE OF MILITANT ISLAM IN CENTRAL ASIA (2002); *see also* Harold Hongju Koh, *A United States Human Rights Policy for the 21st Century*, 46 ST. LOUIS U. L.J. 293 (2002); *infra* notes 130-131 and accompanying text.

45. For a leading advocate of the "Nuremberg Model," see Aryeh Neier, *What Should Be Done About the Guilty?*, N.Y. REV. BOOKS, Feb 1, 1990; *see also* ARYEH NEIER, WAR CRIMES: BRUTALITY, GENOCIDE, TERROR, AND THE STRUGGLE FOR JUSTICE (1998).

46. *See* Ruti G. Teitel, *How Are the New Democracies of the Southern Cone Dealing with the Legacy of Past Human Rights Abuses?*, in Kritz, *supra* note 3; Jaime Malamud-Goti, *Transitional Governments in the Breach: Why Punish State Criminals?*, 12 HUM. RTS. Q. 1 N.1 (1990). Other aspects of the precedent, such as reparations, were taken up later in the phase.

47. The war resulted in a crushing defeat of the country's military junta and allowed the transition to go forward. For discussion of the Argentine trials policy, see CARLOS SANTIAGO NINO, RADICAL EVIL ON TRIAL (1996); *see also* Carlos S. Nino, *The Duty to Punish Past Abuses of Human Rights Put into Context: The Case of Argentina*, 100 YALE L.J. 2619 (1991).

48. *See* Nino, *supra* note 47.

49. *See* Alice H. Henkin, *Conference Report, in* STATE CRIMES: PUNISHMENT OR PARDON, PAPERS AND REPORT OF THE CONFERENCE, NOV. 4-6, 1988, WYE CENTER, MARYLAND 1 (1989).

50. *See* TEITEL, *supra* note 1, at 36–39.

51. *See id.*, at 20–23 (identifying and evaluating numerous instances where alternative rule of law values are drawn from international law and incorporated within the national law of transitional societies).

52. *See* Alvarez, *infra* note 56; Schabas, *infra* note 56.

53. *See* TEITEL, *supra* note 1, at 234.

54. Where prosecutorial strategy singles out individuals, it often fails to adequately express condemnation of the system that defines the modern repressive regime, potentially defeating a core purpose of transitional justice. *See* Jon Elster, *On Doing What One Can: An Argument Against Post-Communist Restitution and Retribution, in* Kritz, *supra* note 3, at 566–68. On selective trials, *compare* Teitel, *Transitional Jurisprudence, supra* note 4 (presenting selective trials as a limit in transitional punishment policy), *with* Payam Akhavan, *Justice in The Hague, Peace in the former Yugoslavia? A Commentary on the United Nations War Crimes Tribunal,* 20 HUM. RTS. Q. 774, 774–81 (1998) (arguing for selective trials for their "truth-telling impact"), *and* Diane F. Orentlicher, *Settling Accounts: The Duty to Prosecute Human Rights Violations of a Prior Regime,* 100 YALE L.J. 2537 (1991) (offering an argument in favor of selective trials as on balance contributing to the rule of law).

55. *See* TEITEL, *supra* note 1, at 2016–30 (discussing rule of law dilemmas).

56. *See* TEITEL, *supra* note 1, at 36–39, 46–51. *See generally* Ruti G. Teitel, *Persecution and Inquisition: A Case Study, in* Stotsky, *supra* note 13, at 141. Failed trials in fledgling democracies such as Rwanda demonstrate the conflicts between the processes of national reconciliation and criminal justice. For an analysis of the Rwandan judicial system and the debate over U.N. Security Council Resolutions to create an international criminal tribunal in Rwanda, see NEIL J. KRITZ, U.S. INST. OF PEACE, SPECIAL REPORT, RWANDA: ACCOUNTABILITY FOR WAR CRIMES AND GENOCIDE (A REPORT ON A UNITED STATES INSTITUTE FOR PEACE CONFERENCE) (1995) *available at* http://www.usip.org/publications/ rwanda-accountability-war-crimes-and-genocide (last visited Jan. 11, 2003). *See also* William Schabas, *Justice, Democracy and Impunity in Post-Genocide Rwanda: Searching for Solutions to Impossible Problems,* 7 CRIM. L.F. 523, 551–52 (1996) (citing S.C. Res 955, U.N. SCOR, 49th Sess., 3453rd mtg., U.N. Doc. S/RES/995 (1994)). Compare the international solution; *see* Jose Alvarez, *Crimes of State/Crimes of Hate: Lessons from Rwanda,* 24 YALE J. INT'L L. 365 (1999) (discussing the limits of international criminal tribunals).

57. South Africa is a prominent example. For a discussion of the state of the South African judiciary as a factor in South Africa's transitional amnesty agreement, see Paul Van Zyl, *Dilemmas of Transitional Justice: The Case of South Africa's Truth and Reconciliation Commission,* 52 J. INT'L AFF. 647 (1999). For a comprehensive analysis of the historical role of the judiciary under apartheid, see STEPHEN ELLMANN, IN A TIME OF TROUBLE: LAW AND LIBERTY IN SOUTH AFRICA'S STATE OF EMERGENCY (1995); David Dyzenhaus, *Transitional Justice,* 1 INT'L J. CONST. L. 163 (2003).

58. Argentina established the first official transitional commission of inquiry in the modern period. While it was a truth commission, it was not aimed at reconciliation. Indeed, the "Nunca Mas" commission inquiry was the first stage in Argentina's post-junta justice following the collapse of the military regime after the Falklands war defeat. For an account, see NINO, *supra* note 47. *See also* NUNCA MAS: THE REPORT OF THE ARGENTINE NATIONAL COMMISSION ON THE DISAPPEARED (Farrar et al. trans, 1986).

59. *See* TRUTH AND RECONCILIATION COMMISSION OF SOUTH AFRICA REPORT (Truth and Reconciliation Comm'n eds., 1999); Promotion of National Unity and Reconciliation Act, No. 34 (1995) (S. Afr.) (establishing the Truth and Reconciliation Commission). For an in-depth account of this history from a biographical perspective, see ALEX BORAINE, A COUNTRY UNMASKED (2000).

60. For a comprehensive discussion of truth commissions, see PRISCILLA B. HAYNER, UNSPEAKABLE TRUTHS: CONFRONTING STATE TERROR AND ATROCITY (2001). For a discussion of the South African Model, see BORAINE, *supra* note 59. For a critical interpretation of the truth commissions project, see TEITEL, *supra* note 1, at 77–88.

61. *See* TEITEL, *supra* note 1, at 70 (discussing Foucauldian "truth regimes" and their inevitable association with a political regime).

62. *See* Teitel, *supra* note 46. *See also* THE REPORT OF THE CHILEAN NATIONAL COMMISSION ON TRUTH AND RECONCILIATION (Phillip E. Berryman trans., 1993), *available at* http://www.usip.org/sites/default/files/resources/collections/truth_commissions/Chile90-Report/Chile90-Report.pdf. (last visited Jan. 11, 2003).

63. On East Germany and its post-transition treatment of official file archives, see TINA ROSENBERG, THE HAUNTED LAND: FACING EUROPE'S GHOSTS AFTER COMMUNISM 261–394 (1996). *See also* TIMOTHY GARTON ASH, THE FILE: A PERSONAL HISTORY (1998).

64. Many countries in the region have enacted laws allowing victims and others access to the files. *See* TEITEL, supra note 1, at 95–103; *see also* Ruti Teitel, *Preface, in* TRUTH AND JUSTICE: THE DELICATE BALANCE: THE DOCUMENTATION OF PRIOR REGIMES AND INDIVIDUAL RIGHTS (1993).

65. *See* BORAINE, *supra* note 59; Margaret Popkin & Naomi Roht-Arriaza, *Truth as Justice: Investigatory Commissions in Latin America*, LAW AND SOC. INQUIRY, VOL. 20 (WINTER 1995); KADER ASMAL ET AL., RECONCILIATION THROUGH TRUTH: A RECKONING OF APARTHEID'S CRIMINAL GOVERNANCE 12–17 (1997) (describing the Truth and Reconciliation Commission as "achieving justice through truth").

66. *See* GEORGE BIZOS, NO ONE TO BLAME: IN PURSUIT OF JUSTICE IN SOUTH AFRICA 229–39 (1998) (discussing the African National Congress' debate over the goals to be achieved by a South African truth commission).

67. For a related argument, see HUMAN RIGHTS IN POLITICAL TRANSITIONS: GETTYSBURG TO BOSNIA 13–31 (Carla A. Hesse & Robert Post eds., 1999); *see also* Ruti Teitel, *Millennial Visions: Human Rights at Century's End, id.* 339–42.

68. *See* TEITEL, *supra* note 1, at 81. The establishment of the truth commissions does not necessarily imply that their investigative inquiries will be the government's complete and exclusive response to past injustices. For discussion of the Argentine process, see NUNCA MAS, *supra* note 58. In El Salvador and South Africa, Truth and Reconciliation Commission confessions were traded for amnesties. *See* The Truth Commission for El Salvador, *From Madness to Hope: The 12-Year War in El Salvador*, U.N. SCOR, Annex to letter dated 29 March 1993 from Boutros-Boutros Ghali to President of Security Council, U.N. Doc. S/25500 (1993), *available at* http://www.usip.org/sites/default/files/file/ElSalvador-Report.pdf (last visited Jan. 11, 2003); Thomas Buergenthal, *The United Nation's Truth Commission for El Salvador,* 27 VAND. J. TRANSNAT'L L. 497 (1994). A counter example would be Argentina, whose transition commenced with a truth commission, which then led to the formation of criminal justice policy, and finally to prosecutions. On the Latin American agreements see WESCHLER, *supra* note 13. Regarding the South African arrangement, see Promotion of National Unity and Reconciliation Act, *supra* note 59. On amnesty adjudication in South Africa, see TRUTH AND RECONCILIATION COMMISSION, AMNESTY DECISION TRANSCRIPTS, *available at* http://www.doj.gov.za/trc/amntrans/index.htm (last visited Jan. 11, 2003). For further remarks on the

reconciliation process, see Abdullah Omar, *Truth and Reconciliation in South Africa: Accounting for the Past*, 4 BUFF. HUM. RTS. L. REV. 5 (1997).

69. *See* Popkin & Roht-Arriaza, *supra* note 65.

70. Of course, there are exceptions. When the South African transition first began, the African National League sought a broader redistributive program.

71. *See* Ruti Teitel, *Bringing the Messiah Through the Law*, in HESSE & POST, *supra* note 67, at 177–93 (discussing the conflict between the political business of peacemaking and the assertion of law in the International Criminal Tribunal for the former Yugoslavia).

72. There are a variety of related aims implied in this shift, including remembering, mourning, and recovering. There is a growing literature on the alternatives to punishment. *See, e.g.*, THE POLITICS OF MEMORY: TRANSITIONAL JUSTICE IN DEMOCRATIZING SOCIETIES (Alexandra Barahona de Brito et al. eds., 2001); GARY JONATHAN BASS, STAY THE HAND OF VENGEANCE: THE POLITICS OF WAR CRIME TRIBUNALS (2000); BORAINE, *supra* note 59; JOHN BORNEMAN, RULE OF LAW, JUSTICE AND ACCOUNTABILITY IN POST-SOCIALIST EUROPE (1997); HAYNER, *supra* note 60; Jennifer J. Llewellyn & Robert Howse, *Institutions for Restorative Justice: The South Africa Truth and Reconciliation Commission*, 49 U. TORONTO L.J. 355 (1999); MAHMOOD MAMDANI, WHEN VICTIMS BECOME KILLERS: COLONIALISM, NATIVISM, AND THE GENOCIDE IN RWANDA (2001); A. JAMES MCADAMS, JUDGING THE PAST IN UNIFIED GERMANY (2001); THE (UN) RULE OF LAW & THE UNDERPRIVILEGED IN LATIN AMERICA (Juan E. Mendez et al. eds., 1999); MARTHA MINOW, BETWEEN VENGEANCE AND FORGIVENESS: FACING HISTORY AFTER GENOCIDE AND MASS VIOLENCE (1998); MARK OSIEL, MASS ATROCITY, COLLECTIVE MEMORY, AND THE LAW (1997); Popkin & Roht-Arriaza, *supra* note 65; MARGARET POPKIN, PEACE WITHOUT JUSTICE: OBSTACLES TO BUILDING THE RULE OF LAW IN EL SALVADOR (2000); TRUTH V. JUSTICE: THE MORALITY OF TRUTH COMMISSIONS (Robert I. Rotberg & Dennis Thompson eds., 2000); DESMOND IMPILO TUTU, NO FUTURE WITHOUT FORGIVENESS (1999); RICHARD A. WILSON, THE POLITICS OF TRUTH AND RECONCILIATION IN SOUTH AFRICA: LEGITIMIZING THE POST-APARTHEID STATE (2001).

73. For a comprehensive account of recent truth commissions and for an argument advocating investigation, see HAYNER, *supra* note 60; *see also* Kritz, *supra* note 3.

74. *See* Popkin & Roht-Arriaza, *supra* note 65, at 79; *see also* Rotberg & Thompson, *supra* note 72. Certainly there is no necessary conflict between investigation and justice, as is reflected in the first truth commission, convened during Argentina's 1983 political transition. *See* NUNCA MAS, *supra* note 58, preface.

75. For an argument that there is such an obligation, see Velásquez Rodríguez, Inter-Am. C.H.R. 35, at ¶166, OEA/ser. L/V/III.19, doc. 13 (1988) ("[T]he state must prevent, investigate and punish any violation of the rights recognized by the convention and…restore the right violated and provide compensation as warranted."). *See also* Torture Victim Protection Act, 28 U.S.C. § 1350 (1992).

76. *See* TEITEL, *supra* note 1, at 51.

77. *See* discussion *infra* at Part III.

78. *See* TUTU, *supra* note 72, at 260; MINOW, *supra* note 72; JACQUES DERRIDA, ON COSMOPOLITANISM AND FORGIVENESS 55–59 (Mark Dooley & Michael Hughes trans., 2001).

79. For a thoughtful philosophical justification of restorative justice, see Elizabeth Kiss, *Moral Ambitions Within and Beyond Political Constraints: Reflections on Restorative Justice, in* Rotberg & Thompson, *supra* note 72, at 68.

80. For a discussion of the turn to therapeutic language, see MINOW, *supra* note 72, at 21–22; Kenneth Roth & Alison Desforges, *Justice or Therapy?*, BOSTON REV., Summer 2002, *available at* http://bostonreview.mit.edu/BR27.3/rothdesforges.html. For a historical account of the turn to moral and religious language, see *infra* note 87; ASMAL ET AL., *supra* note 65, at 25.

81. On the uses of justice to advance peace, see Teitel, *supra* note 71, at 177–93. The Truth and Reconciliation Commission confronted "crucial questions of moral and political responsibility." ASMAL ET AL., *supra* note 65, at 25. *Compare* Popkin & Roht-Arriaza, *supra* note 65 (truth as route to peace), *with* Akhavan, *supra* note 54 (trials as route to peace). *See* HAYNER, *supra* note 60, at 134–35 (discussing complicated results of truth commissions for the aim of individual healing).

82. Most of the amnesties are pursuant to legislation, as in much of Latin America's Southern Cone. *See* Teitel, *supra* note 46. Others, as in South Africa, are handled on an individual basis but still pursuant to a broader transitional amnesty project. *See supra* note 59.

83. For example, there is an explosion of writing on the subject of evil. *See, e.g.*, ALAN BADIOU, ETHICS: AN ESSAY ON THE UNDERSTANDING OF EVIL (2001); SUSAN NEIMAN, EVIL IN MODERN THOUGHT: AN ALTERNATIVE HISTORY OF PHILOSOPHY (2002); JOHN KEKES, FACING EVIL (1990).

84. *See* STEINER & ALSTON, *supra* note 11 (discussing Nuremberg and the development of the universal human rights movement); *see also* HENKIN, *supra* note 38.

85. Indeed, this aim is made clear in the Truth Commission Reports. *See* TEITEL, *supra* note 1, at 69–72.

86. *See* BORAINE, *supra* note 59.

87. On the link between the corruption of political and legal authority and the move to moral and religious authority, see BORAINE, *supra* note 59, 340–78; *see also* LOOKING BACK, REACHING FORWARD: REFLECTIONS ON THE TRUTH AND RECONCILIATION COMMISSION OF SOUTH AFRICA (Charles Villa-Vicencio & Wilhelm Verwoerd eds., 2000) (discussing the religious character of South Africa's Truth and Reconciliation Commission).

88. On the broader developments at this time toward an ethically driven public discourse, see THE TURN TO ETHICS (Marjorie B. Garber et al. eds., 2000); *see also* ZYGMUNT BAUMAN, POSTMODERN ETHICS (1993).

89. *See* DAVID HELD, GLOBAL TRANSFORMATIONS: POLITICS, ECONOMICS, AND CULTURE (1999); ULRICH BECK, WHAT IS GLOBALIZATION? (Patrick Camiller trans., 2000).

90. *See infra* notes 120, 123.

91. On political theology, see CARL SCHMITT, POLITICAL THEOLOGY: FOUR CHAPTERS ON THE CONCEPT OF SOVEREIGNTY (George Schwab trans., 1985). On the relationship of religion and violence, see HENT DE VRIES, RELIGION AND VIOLENCE: PHILOSOPHICAL PERSPECTIVES FROM KANT TO DERRIDA (2002); *see also* JACOB TAUBES, DIE POLITISCHE THEOLOGIE DES PAULUS (Aleida Assman et al. eds., 1993). For a related argument, see HANNAH ARENDT, THE HUMAN CONDITION 38–78 (U. Chi. Press 2d ed. 1998) (1958) (exploring the distinctions between the public and the private realms).

92. *See* Jürgen Habermas, the Theory of Communicative Action: Reason and the Rationalization of Society (1985).

93. The emergence of this form of transitional justice discourse at this time reflects its association with the politics of globalization, and the related challenges to the maintenance of a robust public sphere.

94. For a discussion of some of the philosophical and sociological implications of forgiveness, see Nicholas Tavuchis, Mea Culpa: A Sociology of Apology and Reconciliation (1993); *see also* Jeffrie G. Murphy & Jean Hampton, Forgiveness and Mercy (1990); Michel Rolph-Trouillot, *Abortive Rituals: Historical Apologies in the Global Era, in* Interventions: Righting Wrongs, Rewriting History, vol. 2(2), at 171–86 (H. Bhabha & R. S. Rajan, eds., 2000).

95. On the role of forgiveness in the political sphere, see Arendt, *supra* note 91, at 236–43. On South Africa, see Boraine, *supra* note 59, 340–78, at 340–78 (discussing the need for "facing up to collective responsibility"). On the expected role of the South African Truth and Reconciliation Commission, see Asmal Et Al., *supra* note 65, at 143.

96. *Compare* Robert Meister, *The Politics and Political Uses of Human Rights Discourse: A Conference on Rethinking Human Rights* (paper presented at conference at Columbia, Nov. 8-9, 2001) (focusing on the model's effect upon the revolutionary project, rather than the democracy building project), *with* Jung & Shapiro, *infra* note 97.

97. In South Africa, the politics of reconciliation was associated with the politics of consociationalism. *See* S. Afr. Const. ch. 15, § 251 (1993) (the "National Unity and Reconciliation" provision); Courtney Jung & Ian Shapiro, *South Africa's Negotiated Transition: Democracy, Opposition, and the New Constitutional Order*, 23 Pol. & Soc. 269 (1995).

98. For a discussion of current tensions in the globalization of the market, see Joseph E. Stiglitz, Globalization and its Discontents (2002).

99. For a discussion of some of the contradictions, see Meister, *supra* note 96.

100. On the normalization of transitional justice, see *infra* Part III(A) and notes 130-147.

101. *See* Francis Fukuyama, the End of History and the Last Man (1992).

102. *See* Jacques Derrida, Specters of Marx: The State of the Debt, the Work of Mourning, and the New International (Peggy Kamuf trans., 1994) (discussing the remains of Marxism after the fall of communism).

103. *But see* Eric Hobsbawm, on the Edge of the New Century 95–107 (Allan Cameron trans., Antonio Polito ed., 2000) (discussing the changes in the meaning of the political discussion of left and right and in particular "progressive" politics).

104. Indeed, there is an evident post-Soviet fragmentation and disaggregation. For an argument that the contemporary world today appears more violent, see Ken Jowitt, New World Disorder (1992). For discussion of the role of law in circumstances of apparent perpetual conflict, see Ruti Teitel, *Humanity's Law: Rule of Law in the New Global Politics*, 35 Cornell Int'l L.J. 352 (2002).

105. *See generally* John Torpey, *Making Whole What Has Been Smashed: Reflections on Reparations*, 73 J. Mod. Hist. 333, 334 (2001) (discussing the global spread of "reparations politics"); Sharon K. Hom & Eric K. Yamamoto, *Symposium, Race and the Law at the Turn of the Century: Collective Memory, History, and Social Justice*, 47 U.C.L.A. L. Rev. 1747 (2000).

106. On the Holocaust as a standard and globalized model, see Torpey, *supra* note 105, at 338–42. *See also* Farmer-Paellmann v. FleetBoston Financial Corp., No. CV-02-1862 (E.D.N.Y. filed Mar. 26, 2002); Anthony Sebok, *Prosaic Justice*, LEGAL AFF., Sept.-Oct. 2002, at 51–53; Anthony Sebok, *The Brooklyn Slavery Class Action: More than Just a Political Gambit* (Apr. 9, 2002), *available at* http://writ.news.findlaw.com/sebok/20020409.html (FindLaw's Legal Commentary); WHEN SORRY ISN'T ENOUGH: THE CONTROVERSY OVER APOLOGIES AND REPARATIONS FOR HUMAN INJUSTICE (Roy L. Brooks ed., 1999).

107. Declaration of the World Conference Against Racism, Racial Discrimination, Xenophobia and Related Intolerance, Durban, South Africa (31 August-8 September 2001), *available at* http://www.unesco.org/most/migration/full_dec_wcr.htm.

108. For historical discussion, see, *e.g.*, ELAZAR BARKAN, THE GUILT OF NATIONS: RESTITUTION AND NEGOTIATING HISTORICAL INJUSTICES (2002); JUSTICE DELAYED: THE RECORDS OF THE JAPANESE AMERICAN INTERNMENT CASES (Peter Irons ed., 1989); *see generally* ERIC YAMAMOTO ET AL., RACE, RIGHTS, AND REPARATION: LAW AND THE JAPANESE AMERICAN INTERNMENT (2001).

109. *Compare* Jeremy Waldron, *Superseding Historic Injustice*, 103 ETHICS 4, n.1 (1992) (arguing for "succession" of claims) *with* TEITEL, *supra* note 1, at 138–39 (discussing the paradox of the passage of time as concerns transitional justice, which generally involves state wrongdoing).

110. *See* MARGUERITE FEITLOWITZ, A LEXICON OF TERROR (1988) (discussing Argentina's "Scilingo Effect" of justice delayed).

111. *See infra* note 124 (regarding the Pinochet litigation).

112. Convention on the Non-Applicability of Statutory Limitations to War Crimes and Crimes Against Humanity G.A. Res. 2391, U.N. GAOR, 23rd Sess., Supp. No. 18, at 40, U.N. Doc. A/7218 (1968).

113. Indeed, this notion appears throughout the truth commission literature. In South Africa, the role of the Truth and Reconciliation Commission was envisioned as a "bridge" between the past and the future. *See* S. AFR. CONST. ch. 15, § 251 (1993) (the "National Unity and Reconciliation" provision).

114. For the most part such notions of history are associated with now largely passé perfectionist projects such as Marxism. For a later critical presentation, see Walter Benjamin, *These on the Philosophy of History, in* ILLUMINATIONS: ESSAYS AND REFLECTIONS 253–64, at 257 (Hannah Arendt ed., 1968) (opposing progressive historical thought); *see also* FOUCAULT, *supra* note 7 (distinguishing genealogy from progressive histories).

115. On the notion of "working through history" or "vergangenheitsbewältigung," see Marc Silberman, *Writing What—for Whom? 'Vergangenheits Gewältigung' in GDR Literature*, 10 GERMAN STUD. REV. 527, n.3 (1987); Richard Evans, *The New Nationalism and the Old History: Perspectives on the West German Historikerstreit*, 59 J. OF MOD. HIST. 761, 785 n.4 (1987); *see also* Gordon Craig, *The War of the German Historians*, N.Y. REV. BOOKS, Jan. 15, 1987, at 16–19; CHARLES MAIER, THE UNMASTERABLE PAST (1988).

116. *See* JEAN AMERY, AT THE MIND'S LIMITS: CONTEMPLATIONS BY A SURVIVOR ON AUSCHWITZ AND ITS REALITIES (Stella P. Rosenfeld & Sidney Rosenfeld trans., 1980).

117. On the problem of post-Holocaust representation, in scholarly writing in particular, see PROBING THE LIMITS OF REPRESENTATION: NAZISM AND THE FINAL SOLUTION (Saul Friedlander ed., 1992).

118. *See* TEITEL, *supra* note 1, at 77–92.

119. On victims' testimony, see LAWRENCE L. LANGER, HOLOCAUST TESTIMONIALS: THE RUINS OF MEMORY (1993); MINOW, *supra* note 73.

120. On the growing role of transnational networks, see Martha Finnemore & Kathryn Sikkink, *International Norms Dynamic and Political Change*, 52 INT'L ORG. 887, 907 (1998); MARGARETH KECK & KATHRYN SIKKINK, ACTIVISTS BEYOND BORDERS: ADVOCACY NETWORKS IN INTERNATIONAL POLITICS (1998).

121. This is seen in the contemporary proliferation of lawsuits against multinationals. *See Developments in the Law—International Criminal Law: II. The Promises of International Prosecution*, 114 HARV. L. REV. 1957 (2001). On the problem of the relationship between state and individual responsibility, see STATE RESPONSIBILITY AND THE INDIVIDUAL: REPARATIONS IN INSTANCES OF GRAVE VIOLATIONS OF HUMAN RIGHTS (Albrecht Randlezhofer & Christian Tomuschat eds., 1999); Guillermo A. O'Donnell, *Democracy, Law, and Comparative Politics*, 36 STUD. COMP. INT'L DEV. 7 (2001).

122. Whereas the U.S. approach tends to delegate resolution of controversies to case-by-case litigation, the European approach generally focuses on rulemaking through legislation. For a comparative discussion of illustrations of transitional rule of law, see TEITEL, *supra* note 1.

123. One illustration of these differences in transitional justice is post-war litigation, chiefly regarding the Holocaust, which has occasioned a reaction against the supposed export of the "American" approach to injury abroad.

124. *See* Regina v. Bow St. Metro. Stipendiary Mag., *ex parte* Pinochet Ugarte (No. 3) 1 A.C. 147 (2000).

125. For discussion of the relation of transitional justice to the passage of time, see *supra* text accompanying note 109.

126. For commentary on the potential of universal jurisdiction, see *infra* note 138; *see generally* HUMAN RIGHTS WATCH, 2001 WORLD REPORT, *available at*: http://www.hrw.org/wr2k1/ index.html (last visited Jan. 13, 2003).

127. *See* TEITEL, *supra* note 1, at 213–28 (promoting an explicitly transitional rule of law that is not merely symbolic).

128. *See* H. L. A. HART, THE CONCEPT OF LAW (2nd ed. 1997); *see also* HENKIN, *supra* note 38, at 31–41.

129. On the evolution of transitional justice, see TEITEL, *supra* note 1, at 223–28.

130. *See* DAVID HALBERSTAM, WAR IN A TIME OF PEACE: BUSH, CLINTON, AND THE GENERALS (2001).

131. For a more thorough discussion of law and politics in the post–September 11 political context, see Teitel, *supra* note 104.

132. Rome Statute of the International Criminal Court, U.N. Doc. A/CONF.183/9 (1998) *reprinted in* 37 I.L.M. 999 (1998) [hereinafter Rome Statute].

133. *See Statute of the International Tribunal for the Prosecution of Persons Responsible for Serious Violations of International Humanitarian Law Committed in the Territory of the former Yugoslavia since 1991*, U.N. Doc. S/25704/Annexes (1993); *Statute of the International Criminal Tribunal for the former Yugoslavia*, U.N. SCOR, 48th Sess., 3217th Mtg., U.N. Doc. S/RES/827 (1993), *amended by* U.N. SCOR, U.N. Doc. S/RES/1166 (1998); *Statute of the International Tribunal for Rwanda*, U.N. SCOR, 49th Sess., 3453rd Mtg., U.N. Doc. S/RES/955 (1994), *annexed to* U.N. Doc. S/IN-F/50 (1996). For discussion of the expectations of the *ad hoc* international criminal

tribunals, see Teitel, *supra* note 71. For discussion of these tribunals' constraints, see Alvarez, *supra* note 56 (discussing the limits on international tribunals).

134. *See* Rome Statute, *supra* note 132, Preamble, at 1002 (affirming that "the most serious crimes of concern to the international community as a whole must not go unpunished.").

135. *See United Nations Diplomatic Conference of the Plenipotentiaries on the Establishment of an International Criminal Court*, 17 July 1998, Annex 11, U.N. Doc. A/CONF. 183/9, *reprinted in* 37 I.L.M. 999 (1998), *available at* http://legal.un.org/icc/statute/finalfra.htm.

136. *See supra* text accompanying notes 27-28.

137. *See* Teitel, *supra* note 71 (discussing the limited normative potential of such off-site tribunals); *see also* Christopher Rudolph, *Constructing an Atrocities Regime: The Politics of War Crimes Tribunals*, 55 INT'L ORG. 655, 684–85 (2001). Indeed, this was the theory for the Milošević trial, in light of the Kosovo Commission's conclusion that the NATO intervention in the conflict was "illegal but legitimate." THE INDEPENDENT INTERNATIONAL COMMISSION ON KOSOVO, THE KOSOVO REPORT (2001), *available at* http://reliefweb.int/sites/reliefweb.int/files/resources/F62789D9FCC56FB3C1256C1700303E3B-thekosovoreport.htm.

138. Certainly it is the legacy of Phase I post-war justice that is amplified in the globalizing context where greater international interconnectedness allows for the pursuit of offenders regardless of status or citizenship. *See* PRINCETON UNIVERSITY PROGRAM IN LAW AND PUBLIC AFFAIRS, THE PRINCETON PRINCIPLES ON UNIVERSAL JURISDICTION (2001); Kenneth C. Randall, *Universal Jurisdiction under International Law*, 66 TEX. L. REV. 785 (1988). On the effect of universal jurisdiction, *compare* Andrea Bianchi, *Immunity versus Human Rights: The Pinochet Case*, 10 EUR. J. INT'L L. 237 (1999), *with* Curtis A. Bradley & Jack L. Goldsmith, *Pinochet and International Human Rights Litigation*, 97 MICH. L. REV. 2129 (1999).

139. On the prospective role of the ICC and its likely interaction with domestic transitional justice, see Leila Nadya Sadat & S. Richard Carden, *The New International Criminal Court: An Uneasy Revolution*, 88 GEO. L.J. 381 (2000); Gwen K. Young, *Amnesty and Accountability*, 35 U.C. DAVIS L. REV. 427 (2002). On a related point regarding the Pinochet precedent, see Richard J. Wilson, *Prosecuting Pinochet: International Crimes in Spanish Domestic Law*, 21 HUM. RTS. Q. 927 (1999) (discussing implications of universality).

140. For elaboration of this current development, see Teitel, *supra* note 104.

141. On this distinction between *jus in bello* and *jus ad bello*, which has given rise to modern humanitarian law, see STUDIES AND ESSAYS ON INTERNATIONAL HUMANITARIAN LAW AND RED CROSS PRINCIPLES IN HONOUR OF JEAN PICTET (Christophe Swinarsky ed., 1984). On *jus ad bello*, see MICHAEL WALZER, JUST AND UNJUST WARS: A MORAL ARGUMENT WITH HISTORICAL ILLUSTRATIONS 21 (1977).

142. *See* THE INDEPENDENT INTERNATIONAL COMMISSION ON KOSOVO, *supra* note 137.

143. *See* RICHARD TUCK, THE RIGHTS OF WAR AND PEACE 22–25 (1999) (discussing the historical justifications for preemptive attacks in the law of empire).

144. On this development, see Teitel, *supra* note 104.

145. This is seen in the lack of precise definition of the "enemy," other than in terms of executive discretion. *See* Detention, Treatment and Trial of Certain Non-Citizens in the War Against Terrorism, at § 1(e), 66 Fed. Reg. 57,833, 57,834 (2001) (military order of Nov. 13, 2001).

146. *See* DUNCAN KENNEDY, A CRITIQUE OF ADJUDICATION (1997). Compare with discussion of characteristics of rule of law in transition, *see* TEITEL, *supra* note 1, at 11–26.

147. On the general decline in adherence to the rule of law during this period, see Ruti G. Teitel, *Empire's Law: Foreign Relations by Presidential Fiat, in* SEPTEMBER 11TH: TRANSFORMATIVE MOMENT? CULTURE, RELIGION AND POLITICS IN AN AGE OF UNCERTAINTY (Mary Dudziak ed., 2003).

148. *See* Martin Krygier, *Transitional Questions about the Rule of Law: Why, What and How?*, Presented before the Conference of the East Central Europe Institute for Advanced Study, Budapest (L'Europe du Centre Est. Eine wissenschaftliche Zeitschrift at Collegium Budapest) (Feb. 15-17, 2001); Dyzenhaus, *supra* note 57.

149. *See* TEITEL, *supra* note 1, at 11–18, 33–36.

150. *See* STIGLITZ, *supra* note 98. For discussion of globalization's effect on the Third World, *see* Tina Rosenberg, *Globalization*, N.Y. TIMES MAG., Aug. 18, 2002, § 6, at 28.

151. On postmodernism as a source of critical theory, *compare* POSTMODERNISM & SOCIAL THEORY: THE DEBATE OVER GENERAL THEORY (Steven Seidman & David G. Wagner eds., 1992) (discussing the postmodern critique) *with* Jacques Derrida, *Force of Law: Mystical Foundation of Authority*, 11 CARDOZO L. REV. 919 (1990).

*The context of the essay below is the establishment by the U.N. Security Council of the the Ad Hoc International Criminal Tribunal for the former Yugoslavia. The innovation here was using international criminal justice to address an ongoing conflict, rather than simply for purposes of post-conflict accountability. The essay evaluates the role of the ICTY, reflecting on some of its challenges and constraints, which arise from having to operate while the conflict continues and in a location far removed from the site of the offenses and the peoples implicated in the conflict.*

# 5     Bringing the Messiah Through the Law

THE INTERNATIONAL CRIMINAL tribunal for the former Yugoslavia (ICTY) was convened in 1993 in The Hague to prosecute war crimes committed in the course of the conflict in the Balkans.[1] It is the first international legal body authorized to adjudicate war crimes since the court in Nuremberg about a half-century ago.

Although the tribunal in The Hague was consciously patterned after Nuremberg, it was created in utterly distinct political circumstances. The trials after World War II represented "victors' justice": They were conducted after peace had been achieved, and they sought to give legal expression to the victors' outrage at Germany's initiation of an unjust war.

The ICTY, by contrast, was established in the midst of a bloody conflict. Its mandate was not to shape the meaning of a peace that had already been achieved, but instead to bring individuals who were responsible for atrocities to justice in an effort to establish peace.

The ICTY, therefore, prompts us to investigate the connection between international criminal justice and peace. The mandate handed by international law to the ICTY—to impose justice before peace, and as a means to achieve peace—has no precedent. How can justice in a courtroom wrapped in tempered glass in The Hague, isolated from a raging conflict on the ground in war-torn Yugoslavia, contribute to peace?

In this essay, I shall explore the relationship between the messy and political business of peacemaking, and the assertion of law in a distant and antiseptic vacuum. The essential mission of the ICTY is to transform the conflict in the Balkans into one of individual crimes answerable to the rule of law, and so to achieve peace and reconciliation. But the efforts of the ICTY to accomplish this mission serve primarily to underscore the dependence of the rule of law on the supporting matrix of national and international politics. Stripped of this matrix, deprived of political authority and constituency, the transformative potential of the ICTY must rely on the proffer of a thin and inadequate image of liberal identity.

## Punishment, Truth, and Peace

The mission of the ICTY must be understood in the context of its origins in the Balkans conflict. In the spring of 1992, Bosnian Serbs, with the assistance of the Yugoslavia army, began a drive to "ethnically cleanse" all non-Serb inhabitants from large stretches of Bosnia. Their tactics included widespread and systematic persecution, torture, murder, rape, beatings, harassments, discrimination, and forced displacements. With the fall of the U.N. safe havens of Srebrenica and Zepa in April and July 1995, Bosnian Serb forces virtually completed the "ethnic cleansing" of eastern Bosnia. It is estimated that their campaign of terror killed close to a quarter of a million persons; it produced tens of thousands of refugees.

Almost three years before, however, in the fall of 1992, the U.N. Security Council had received reports of mass expulsion, civilian deportations, mass killings, torture, imprisonment, and atrocities in detention camps.[2] It therefore set up a commission to investigate atrocities committed in the region. It was the first such commission created since World War II, and it was modeled on the 1943 Allied War Crimes Commission. By February 1993, the "Commission of Experts" had concluded that there had been willful killing, organized massacres, torture, rape, pillage, and destruction of civilian property,[3] all in a campaign of "ethnic cleansing" to "render an area ethnically homogeneous using force and intimidation to remove persons of given groups from the area."[4] In eastern Bosnia, ethnic cleansing appeared to constitute part of a much larger attempt by Bosnian Serb forces to commit genocide against Bosnian Muslims and other non-Serbs.[5]

By early spring 1993, the United Nations was confronted with the question of how to respond. Though ethnic cleansing and other violations of humanitarian law in the Balkans were declared to threaten "international peace and security," allied humanitarian intervention was not marshalled to stop the atrocities. Instead, operating under its Chapter 7 powers, the Security Council established the ICTY as "a measure to maintain or restore international peace and security." According to prevailing conventions codified after the postwar period, the atrocities exposed in the Balkans could be punished as war crimes.[6] Bringing individuals to justice, the Security Council said, would contribute to the restoration and maintenance of the peace.

The international community failed to respond to the terrible abuses in the Balkans by organizing military interventions forcefully to prevent further atrocities. It chose instead to create and empower a tribunal capable of enforcing the rule of law. The international community asserted that peace and proper governance could be restored to the region through the politics of punishment.

Historically, however, justice has followed war. Post-war trials have been used to establish the nature of an antecedent war, to determine whether it had been an "unjust" or a "just" war.[7] The Treaty of Versailles, for example, was an example of "victors' justice," avenging Germany's unjust war. And again, after World War II, the Allies attempted to punish Germany for waging aggressive war. Unlike Nuremberg, however, the ICTY was no post-war tribunal. The ICTY would attempt to dispense justice before peace, and without the clarification of military victory. It would therefore lack the authority and power of traditional victors' justice. The difference was plainly visible in the ICTY's frustrating inability to seize custody of defendants or to command access to evidence.

The difficulties of the ICTY were compounded by its double mission. The tribunal was created not merely to dispense justice, but also to achieve reconciliation in the region. It was explicitly established by the Security Council as a "peacemaking" measure.[8] No doubt this political mission was grafted onto the ICTY in part to compensate for the glaring failure of the international community to take the political and military steps necessary to stop the slaughter. But there are rather obvious tensions between criminal law and peacemaking.

So, for example, when the tribunal declared its intention to indict Bosnian Serb leaders Radovan Karadžić and General Ratko Mladić, the indictments themselves appeared to endanger the peace. Although the parties to the Dayton Peace Accords had pledged full cooperation with the tribunal,[9] and although the accords obligated signatories to support the tribunal and to hand over suspected war criminals, these obligations lacked explicit enforcement mechanisms.[10] There was no unambiguous assignment of responsibility for the apprehension and arrest of indicted war criminals, and in fact these powers were said to lie outside the mandate of the NATO-led Implementation Force (IFOR). Tension caused by the refusal of the Bosnian Serbs to honor persistent calls for the arrests of Radovan Karadžić and Ratko Mladić had certainly proved a thorn in the side of the peace process.

The pivotal question posed by the ICTY, therefore, is how the dispensation of international criminal justice can be joined to the establishment of peace. Deterrence might be one such connection. Holding war crimes trials during conflict might be said sometimes to deter crimes. French trials of German soldiers during World War I,[11] and Allied threats of punishment issued during World War II, were both predicated on the notion that they would discourage the commission of further atrocities.[12] But the prosecutions of the ICTY have been far too sparse and ineffectual to hold much promise of actual deterrence, and indeed massacres continued well after the tribunal's establishment.

The blunt and unpleasant fact is that the ICTY has been forced to seek criminal punishment within a political vacuum. In contrast to the victors' justice confidently meted out at Nuremberg over a vanquished enemy, the ICTY is fragile. Seated in the Netherlands, far from the Balkans, it lacks both custody over the accused and control of the evidence necessary to establish individual wrongdoing. Most of those responsible for war crimes remain at large.

More to the point, the ICTY is without the political resources to remedy these gross inadequacies. In a speech to the United Nations General Assembly, the tribunal's president, Antonio Cassesse, compared the ICTY to "a giant who has no arms and no legs. To walk and work, he needs artificial limbs. These artificial limbs are the State authorities; without their help the Tribunal can not operate."[13] Like Gulliver among the Lilliputians, the ICTY has been paralyzed by the international community.

The ICTY has responded to these limitations by seeking justice largely within the framework of judicial processes of inquiry and indictment. Because the ICTY statute, unlike the Nuremberg Charter, forbids trials and convictions in absentia, the tribunal has, to date, been forced to focus on indicting those whom the ICTY is powerless to apprehend to stand trial. ICTY indictments, the so-called "super-indictments," have consequently become elaborate proceedings, involving both recitation of offenses and presentation of evidence. The proceedings are public and even televised; Court TV covered the Karadžić and Mladić indictments "live." The proceedings offer the drama and testimony of living witnesses.[14] In outward form they are similar to trials in absentia, although there can be no judgment in the absence of the accused.[15]

These super-indictment proceedings are like "show trials." This is not because their results are foreordained, but because their main purpose is to tell a story. It is largely through the proceedings of these public indictments that the ICTY establishes and condemns wrongdoing. Following the indictments, an international warrant of arrest is issued, the evidence published, and the accused publicly branded as an international fugitive from justice. These indictments and the resulting stigmatization will often be the tribunal's only sanction.

From this we may conclude that the ICTY's mission of achieving a peaceful reconciliation in the region is less dependent on the actual infliction of punishment than on the use of super-indictment proceedings to construct truthful narratives of past abuses. It has almost become dogma in contemporary foreign policy that establishing the "truth" about a state's repressive past can lay the foundation for national reconciliation. National truth commissions in Argentina, Chile, and South Africa have been touted as prerequisites for successful political transitions. In advocating the establishment of the ICTY, Madeline Albright asserted before the U.N. Security Council that "the only victor that will prevail in this endeavor will be the truth."

The promise of such a reconciliation-based-in-truth was symbolized by the ICTY's appointment of Chief Prosecutor Richard Goldstone, known for his leadership in South Africa's peaceful transition from apartheid. Indeed, at the first super-indictment proceeding, Goldstone likened public indictments to national truth commissions, declaring that the "public record will assist in attributing guilt to individuals and be an important tool in avoiding the attribution of collective guilt to any nation or ethnic group."[16]

There can be no doubt that, through its indictments, the ICTY has helped to make known the terrible atrocities perpetrated in the Balkans, and that public knowledge of these facts may well have contributed toward shaping the peace. At Dayton, for example, ICTY indictments of Serbian leaders Radovan Karadžić and General Ratko Mladić for genocide, murder, rape, and other offenses significantly affected resolution of the question of political representation in the region. The peace accords banned indicted war criminals from holding future political office.[17]

Nevertheless, there remains a rather large gap between these contributions and the achievement of that reconciliation to which Goldstone and the founders of the ICTY aspired. Even indicted perpetrators of genocide remain free and continue to wield political power. Although Bosnian Serb leader Radovan Karadžić may have been forced, after his indictment, to resign as head of his political party, he does not seem also to have been deprived of his considerable political influence.

ICTY indictments are thus not functionally equivalent to convictions and imprisonments. The difference emphasizes the distinction between institutions that seek to establish the truth after a transfer of power and shift in regimes, as in South Africa, and institutions like the ICTY that hope to use a new collective truth as a basis to establish reconciliation. Ordinarily, official truth investigations are convened to secure a peace that has already been achieved through military and political means. Their narratives carry the full retrospective authority of victors' justice. But the ICTY must attempt to uncover a historical "truth" that is so abstractly convincing as to be in itself capable of establishing a peace. In the absence of a Bosnian political constituency, it is not clear what such a "truth" might be.

There is considerable tension, moreover, between the ICTY's efforts to construct truthful narratives to achieve reconciliation and the ICTY's fundamental obligation to dispense criminal justice. Although criminal proceedings may well establish some sense of truth about individual wrongdoing, as Hannah Arendt observed of the Eichmann trial, historical inquiry implies a broader lens than that of individual trials.[18] This observation has particular application to the Balkans, where a truthful account would require working through the region's history of complex and conflictual politics.

Conversely, by conflating the production of historical narratives with criminal processes, fundamental norms of due process may be endangered. The prime focus of a criminal proceeding is to ascribe individual responsibility for past wrongdoing. This is the foundation of the presumption of innocence, the significance of which is that criminal judgments should not be used merely as a means to other ends, even the end of truth. Although indictments are not convictions, they do have important legal consequences, and it would be improper to use indictments in a merely instrumental fashion.

## From Communal Conflict to International Justice

If the ICTY's lack of political authority undermines its efforts to achieve pacification through deterrence and to accomplish reconciliation through the creation of historical narratives, perhaps the relationship of the ICTY to peace might be conceptualized along different lines. Those who created the ICTY spoke feelingly of the expectation that international criminal justice would establish a form of individual accountability that would break "old cycles of ethnic retribution" and thus advance ethnic "reconciliation." They propounded a traditional account of liberal legalism, in which the punishment of the law would hold individuals responsible, so as to limit and displace private vengeance.[19] This was a central justification that was advanced for prosecuting atrocities associated with the conflict. "Absolving nations of collective guilt through the attribution of individual responsibility is an essential means of countering the misinformation and indoctrination which breeds ethnic and religious hatred."[20]

In the eyes of the international community, the conflict in the Balkans became defined by its "ethnic cleansing." Responding to ethnic persecution became the crux of the project of international criminal justice. The ICTY reaffirmed Nuremberg's central principle that responsibility for war crimes should be borne by individuals, and it sought to highlight individual responsibility for ethnic persecution. It chose to prosecute ethnic cleansing—the purposeful policy employed by one group to purge by terror the civilian population of another ethnic group from defined geographic areas—as a series of "crimes against humanity," as "inhumane acts" discrete but nevertheless "widespread and systematic," "perpetrated on any civilian population, on an ethnic basis."[21]

At The Hague, for the first time since the trials of World War II, ethnic persecution would also be prosecuted as "genocide." By the spring of 1992, the Final Report of the Commission of Experts had concluded that mass murder, torture, and rape committed in the area of Opština Prijedor in northwestern Bosnia, against civilians both in and out of detention camps, unquestionably constituted crimes against humanity and that a court of law would find it to be genocide.[22] The distinctive patterns of Bosnian Serb ethnic cleansing, massacres, and systematic rapes displayed a genocidal intent to destroy ethnic and religious groups. The ICTY found that "the Muslim population of the enclave of Srebrenica [previously designated a U.N. 'safe area'] virtually was eliminated by Bosnian Serb Military personnel…under the command and control of Radovan Karadžić and Ratko Mladić," so that there was prima facie evidence that the facts "disclose above all, the commission of genocide."

The ICTY actually expands the scope of international criminal jurisdiction. Whereas the Nuremberg tribunal's jurisdiction over atrocities was ultimately tied to the conduct of an unjust war,[23] the jurisdiction of the ICTY was extended to crimes against humanity that are committed in the course of an armed conflict, whether or not that conflict is international. Ethnic persecution is prosecuted as an "international" offense even if it occurs wholly within a state.[24]

This represents a major expansion of traditional international justice, from wrongs committed by foreign occupiers, to wrongs committed by states against their own citizens. Underlying the expansion is the notion that victims of ethnic persecution, even if citizens, are rendered "aliens" and pariahs within their own homeland. They are protected by neither state nor law. International criminal justice is for them. State persecution of its citizens will never again rest immune within national boundaries, but will potentially be accountable to the international community.

The creators of the ICTY hoped that this vision of international law and accountability would create the foundation of a lasting peace in the Balkans. The vision evokes the twin ideas of individual responsibility and the rule of law, yet it fails to fully capture the nature and political purpose of the violence in the region.

The concept of individual responsibility that emerges from the ICTY is complex, and merits close attention. Historically, post-war trials have posited limits to state sovereignty, but they have not displaced it. The ICTY, however, stands entirely apart from national institutions, and it seeks to enforce a strange deracinated form of individual accountability that is answerable to a global order. In its landmark decision affirming jurisdiction under the U.N. Charter, the tribunal justified its jurisdiction over the crimes at issue by asserting that they "cannot be considered political offenses, as they do not harm a political interest of a particular state," and that the "norms prohibiting them have a universal character." In this way, the tribunal figured ethnic persecution as a profound and apolitical offense against the entire international community, indeed, against humanity itself. The ICTY embraces a project of transformative justice that will enforce these universal human norms.

But prosecuting ethnic persecution this way—stripped of its political context and purpose—poses a real challenge. For this use of law seemed, perhaps unwittingly, only to support the notion that the conflict in the Balkans is a story of ancient and intractable ethnic enmity.[25] Pursuant to this characterization of the violence in the region, which is popular in media representations, as well as in the diplomatic community, contemporary atrocities in the Balkans are only the latest round of a violence that is portrayed as inevitable and natural to the region. Insofar as the ICTY merely counterposes a portrait of ahistorical atrocities, committed by atomized individuals within a political vacuum, it risks confirming the notion that these atrocities were inevitable, a fate foretold. But this representation undermines the project of establishing individual accountability, and even appears to justify international neglect.

The tribunal risks using the law to construct a lesson about eternal atrocities, without victors or heroes. The abstract tales of individualized horror produced by the ICTY may efface questions about political responsibility—both national and international responsibility—for the crimes perpetuated in the Balkans. A more historical and political understanding of atrocities in the region would question the role of the United Nations and the international community at the time when the atrocities were being committed. It was the United Nations that created the "safe areas" that drew Muslims and Croats into the concentrated enclaves for protection. It was the passivity of the United Nations and of the international community that allowed the massacres. After Nuremberg, international criminal responsibility extends even to acts of omission by those possessing relevant elements of authority and control.

Arguably, the United Nations itself had such authority over its "safe" areas, yet has remained immune from criminal responsibility.

The United Nations and the entire international community thus have deep self-regarding interests in constructing a narrative of the massacres that stresses individual responsibility, rather than policy and political will. So it is that the absence from the courtroom of defendants who were leaders and policymakers, and especially the continued apparent disinterest among NATO allies in their arrest, serves to affirm a craven international neutrality. The very neutrality that was thought to render the proceedings at The Hague superior to past war crimes trials, and impervious to charges of "victors' justice," can itself be seen to raise grave issues of international moral responsibility and, by association, of the tribunal's own authority.

The challenge of "tu quoque," of "unclean hands," was also leveled at Nuremberg, loudly so with respect to the Soviet judges; but the bold new jurisdictional initiatives of the ICTY paradoxically make this challenge particularly apt to the proceedings in The Hague. There is considerable tension in the attempt to condemn atrocities in the Balkans as international injustice, and yet simultaneously to seek to cabin ICTY indictments so as not also to inculpate the international community that allowed the atrocities to be perpetuated. Precisely to the extent that the ICTY seeks to internationalize "crimes against humanity," to subject them to universal jurisdiction. For there is a sense in which there are victims here of a broader international injustice. The ICTY claims that ethnic persecution and genocide give rise to a universal jurisdiction that transcends national borders. And, if that is so, then why, we may ask, should international responsibility to respond to persecution be triggered only *after* the massacres?

The concept of individual responsibility advanced by the ICTY also bears a complex relationship to the question of identity at play in the Balkans. Indeed, the very offenses prosecuted by the ICTY—"genocide" and "crimes against humanity"—embody a highly nuanced relationship between individual and group identity. Both offenses connect individuals to group identities through the element of motive; i.e., through the persecutory policy.[26] This means that responsibility is best conceptualized in ways that bridge and connect individuals and collectivities.

More fundamentally, however, the offenses spring from the supposed understanding that what has transpired involves terrible ethnic persecution, so that the project of ascribing individual responsibility must somehow be reconciled with these contemporary constructions of ethnic identity. The strain of this reconciliation is apparent in the prosecution's strategy, which is affirmatively ethno-conscious in order to achieve its conciliatory purpose of diffusing ethnic tension in the region. The ICTY takes note of ethnicity ostensibly in order to transcend it.

The Tribunal's transformative mandate is to express the message that individuals bear responsibility for persecution. The idea is therefore to construct a plausible account of persecution in the region,[27] and this has been thought to require an "exemplary cases" strategy.[28] Thus, the ICTY has attempted to prosecute atrocities selected to include a representative sample of those committed against Muslims, Croats, and Serbs. Defendants are also expected to be ethnically representative.[29] Victims, even participating jurists, are identified by their ethnic origin.[30]

Gender also plays a complex role in ethnic cleansing. Most of those massacred were men, while the mass rapes were largely perpetrated against women. Although not separate charges at Nuremberg, sex crimes, such as rape, are prosecutable as crimes against humanity in The Hague.[31] In the Balkans, mass rape and forced pregnancies were tools of destruction and genocide that were positioned at the interface of sex and ethnic persecution.

The strategy of prosecuting "exemplary cases" also has important implications for the ICTY's construction of the intersection between individual responsibility and corporate accountability. The strategy is evident in the indictments that have been issued so far, ranging from those leveled against Karadžić and Mladić for genocide and crimes against humanity, to those issued against Bosnian Serb and Croat officials and civilians for atrocities committed in the camps. The ICTY's aim has apparently been to prosecute perpetrators at all levels of the power echelon—from the architects of the persecution policy, to its lowest level agents, as well as to reach both the military and civilian sectors of society.[32]

The strategy of exemplary prosecutions appears to make practical sense, so much so that it is easy to miss just how deeply it challenges core principles of the rule of law. Fundamental to the rule of law is the notion that the law applies with equal force and obligation to all. Thus, the Nuremberg trials were merely the first of thousands of subsequent prosecutions.[33] By contrast, the highly selective prosecutions of the ICTY seem to circumscribe the very rule of law that it is designed to instantiate. The policy of selective prosecutions thus underscores the elusive quality of the transformative project of the ICTY, a project that only gestures toward a liberal rule of law that the project can bring itself at most merely to symbolize.

Symbols, however, have their uses. Created pursuant to international peace accords, the tribunal's mandate was ambitious, and, in the context of the ongoing commission of brutal atrocities in the region, nothing short of messianic. The Hague was assigned the mission of transforming the course of the conflicts in the region so as to lead to conciliation. In this context, the image of the rule of law, shimmering at the horizon, serves unambiguously positive purposes.

The Balkans have long brooded over an ever-present sense of terrible injustice. Although it is often thought that a primary function of human rights law is to expose and condemn heinous wrongs, such an apprehension of injustice already permeates the Balkans.[34] False allegations of preemptive genocide perversely appear to have sparked the most recent wave of horror. However, a full understanding of the political causes of the ongoing injustice and its future direction remains elusive.

The ICTY symbolizes the possibility of change in the region. It offers the potential of moving from persecutory violence to the rule of law. Within the rule of law, past wrongs cannot serve to justify the ongoing perpetration of massacres and atrocities. By seeking to forestall revenge, the tribunal reaffirms its purpose as forward-looking, rather than backward-looking. Its aims are less to offer retributive justice for past wrongs than to prepare the region to embrace equal protection under the law. Yet, this message can only be limited and partial—when justice does not clarify the particular politics that derogate from the rule of law in the region. For there to be meaningful change in societies driven by racial, ethnic, and religious conflict, "identity politics" should be exposed for what it is—political construction. Ethnic politics has no place in the liberal state. What needs construction is the liberal response to injustice.

Because the ICTY cannot itself fully embody the rule of law, it must represent the rule of law in a transitional form, as an image of the possibility of liberal justice. But what is the point of such an image? As a practical matter, the tribunal's proceedings are located at a venue that is so remote and insulated from the Balkans that it is difficult to relate its trials and indictments to the actual conflict that is at issue. In the international proceedings of the ICTY, defendants and victims are frequently absent, particularly women in the rape cases. For this reason, trials at The Hague commonly lack confrontation, an integral element of the catharsis and healing that are ordinarily offered by the criminal process. More fundamentally, the ICTY is foreign to the Balkans, so that its legal pronouncements, its enactment of the forms of liberal legalism, do not carry sufficient local political authority or weight there.

These limitations serve to underscore the salient conditions and circumstances of meaningful reconciliation. Although international criminal justice offers some degree of individual accountability, and hence affirms the liberal response to wrongdoing, it lacks the supportive national structures that are necessary for the true realization of reconciliation and the rule of law. And these limitations are also apparent at the level of the individual, for the risk of such justice is that persons may come to identify with the role of perpetrator or victim, rather than with that of citizen.

The proceedings in The Hague fall short because they cannot offer the thick form of reconciliation that is necessary for truly reconstructing a community inhabited by citizens. But the foreign status and international authority of the ICTY does offer one single advantage. By intervening unambiguously from outside the region, the ICTY operates beyond the political circumstances that trap participants within the

Balkans. Although the ICTY can offer to substitute for this context only a thin and procedural symbol of the rule of law, it is nevertheless a symbol that is full of potential. As a symbol, the tribunal points to a conceivable future. It thus represents a form of justice that is distinctly associated with transitional periods.[35] It offers an instance of transitional justice associated with extraordinary political circumstances—when the full rule of law is unavailable. In such transitional circumstances, perhaps the best that can be brought into view is the image, rather than the reality, of the liberal state.

## Notes

1. United Nations, Security Council, *United Nations Security Council Resolution 827 on Establishing An International Military Tribunal for the Prosecution of Persons Responsible for Serious Violations of International Humanitarian Law in the Territory of the former Yugoslavia Since 1991,* S/Res/827 (1993).

2. See United Nations, Security Council, *Resolution 764,* S/Res/764, 1992, reprinted in 31 I.L.M. at 1465 (1992); United Nations, Security Council, *Resolution 771,* S/Res/771, 1992, reprinted in 31 I.L.M. at 1470 (1992).

3. See United Nations, Secretary-General, *Final Report of the Commission of Experts Established Pursuant to Security* Council *Resolution 780* (1994); *Available in Letter Dated 24 May 1994 From the Secretary-General to the President of the Security Council,* Annex 1, S/1994/674. (Hereafter referred to as *Final Report of the Commission of Experts.*)

4. See United Nations, Secretary-General, S/25274 at 16, para. 55(1993).

5. *Ibid.* at para. 355–56.

6. This was true under the post–World War II Geneva and Genocide Conventions.

7. On this distinction, see Michael Walzer, *Just and Unjust Wars: A Moral Argument with Historical Illustrations* (New York: Basic Books, 1977).

8. United Nations. Secretary-General, *Report of the Secretary-General Pursuant to Paragraph 2 of Security Council Resolution 808 (1993),* s/25704, 1993, reprinted in 31 I.L.M. 1159 (1993). (Hereafter referred to as *Report of Secretary-general.*)

9. *Bosnia and Hersegovina-Croatia-Yugoslavia: General Framework Agreement for Peace in Bosnia and Herzegovina,* Art. *9,* reprinted in 35 I.L.M. 89, 90 (1996). (Hereafter referred to as *Dayton Accords.*)

10. *Ibid.* at Art. 9, 10. See also *ibid.* at Annex 4 referring to Article 11(8) of the new Bosnia and Herzegovina Constitution which provides: "All competent authorities in Bosnia and Herzegovina shall cooperate with and provide unrestricted access to…the International Tribunal for the former Yugoslavia." The Constitution also affirms the state's commit "to fully complying with orders issued pursuant to Art. 29 of the statute of the Tribunal." The statute contemplates cooperation with the Tribunal in investigation and prosecution, which would include Tribunal orders concerning the production of evidence or the surrendering of those accused.

11. See Jacques Dumas, *Les Sanctions penales des crimes allemands* (Paris: Librairie Arthur Rousseau, 1916).

12. See *Declaration of German Atrocities,* Nov. 1, 1943, 3 Bevans 816, 834, Dep't St. Bull., Nov. 6, 1943, at 310–11.

13. See *Address of Antonio Cassese, President of the International Criminal Tribunal for the former Yugoslavia to the General Assembly of the United Nations,* Nov. 7, 1995, p.4.

14. United Nations, International Military Tribunal for the Prosecution of Persons Responsible for Serious Violations of International Humanitarian Law in the Territory of the former Yugoslavia Since 1991, *Rules of Procedure and Evidence,* Art. 61, reprinted in 33 I.L.M. 484, 519 (1994).

15. We can expect the public recitatives of these "super-indictments" to continue, for as of September 29, 1998, there were twenty-six suspects in custody out of the eighty pending indictments. For Tribunal updates, see International Criminal Tribunal for the former Yugoslavia, Bulletin No. 20, III (1998).

16. See "Opening Statement by Justice Goldstone," para. 12, Rule 61 Hearing (Oct. 9, 1995).

17. See *Dayton Accords,* at Annex 4, referring to the Constitution of Bosnia and Herzegovina, Art. 9, which provides: No person who is serving a sentence imposed by the International Tribunal for the former Yugoslavia, and no person who is under indictment by the Tribunal and who has failed to comply with an order to appear before the Tribunal, may stand as candidate or hold any appointive, elective, or other public office in the territory of Bosnia and Herzegovina."

18. See Hannah Arendt, *Eichmann in Jerusalem* (1964).

19. See Immanuel Kant, *The Metaphysics of Morals,* trans. Mary Gregor (Cambridge, UK: Cambridge University Press, 1991), 183.

20. See "Prosecutor's Response to the Defense's Motions filed on 23 June 1995," at 23. Dusko Tadić Case No. IT-94-IT.

21. See *Final Report of the Commission of Experts,* at Annex 4, "The Policy of Ethnic 'Cleansing,'" at 21.

22. See *Final Report of the Commission of Experts,* para. 182, at 43.

23. See *Agreement for the Prosecution and Punishment of the Major War Criminals of the European Axis, Charter of the International Military Tribunal,* Aug. 8, 1945, Art. 6(c), 82 U.N.T.S. 279.

24. United Nations, Secretary-General, *Statute of the International Tribunal for the Prosecution of Persons Responsible for Serious Violations of International Humanitarian Law in the Territory of the former Yugoslavia),* Art. 5, Annex to *Report of Secretary-General.* This point was illuminated when the Tribunal's mandate was expanded to include prosecution of those who masterminded the genocide of approximately one million Tutsis and Hutu moderates in Rwanda. Although this persecution was committed entirely in that country's internal conflict, it was nevertheless brought for the first time before an international forum. See United Nations, Security Council, *United Notions Security Council Resolution 955 Establishing the International Tribunal for Rwanda,* S/Res/955, 1994, reprinted in 33 I.L.M. 1598 (1994).

25. See Robert D. Kaplan, *Balkan Ghosts* (New York: St. Martin's Press, 1993); *Playing the Communal Card: Communal Violence and Human Rights* (Human Rights Watch, 1995) (discussing the role of the media, U.N. officials, and European and U.S. government policymakers in framing the Bosnian conflict in these terms).

26. See *Convention on the Prevention and Punishment of the Crime of Genocide* (1948) entered into Force, Jan. 12, 1951, 78 U.N.T.S. 277 (defining "genocide" in terms of acts committed "with intent to destroy, in whole or in part, a national, ethnical, racial or religious group, as such"). Regarding the recognition of crimes against humanity, see *Agreement for the Prosecution and Punishment of the Major War Criminals of the European Axis, Charter of the International Military Tribunal,* Aug. 8, 1945, Art. 6(c), 82 U.N.T.S. 279.

27. See International Criminal Tribunal of the former Yugoslavia, Office of the Prosecutor, press release, July 25, 1995 ("Full Picture of OTP's Strategy"), p. 3. See also, "Statement by Justice Richard Goldstone," April 24, 1995.

28. The abuses represented are to cover the entire time period, from 1991 through the fall of the safe havens in 1995, and to include the full spectrum of war crimes and crimes against humanity committed in the region, including the setting up and implementation of detention camps; Serb military takeover of towns; campaigns of terror; firing of rockets into cities; deportation of civilians; shelling of civilian gatherings; plunder of property; destruction of sacred sites; sniping campaigns against civilians in Sarajevo; targeting of peacekeepers and their use as human shields.

29. It is a matter of public knowledge that, to date, the overwhelming number of the indicted are Serb nationals. See, e.g., *Bulletin, International Criminal Tribunal for the former Yugoslavia,* No. 15/16 10-III-1997 (referring to Celebici trial as the first where Bosnian Serbs are victims of crimes charged).

30. See, e.g., *Bulletin, International Criminal Tribunal for the former Yugoslavia,* No. 15/16 10-III-1997.

31. See United Nations, Secretary-General, *Statute of the International Tribunal for the Prosecution of Persons Responsible for Serious Violations of International Humanitarian Law in the Territory of the former Yugoslavia),* Art. 5, Annex to *Report of Secretory-General,* Art. 5(g) (citing "rape" as a "crime against humanity").

32. Because the ICTY has not been able to obtain custody of most defendants, those most responsible for the persecution policy have been largely absent from The Hague. Indeed, the very first trial in 1996, for murder, torture, and sexual mutilation committed in the Omarska death camp, was of a civilian café owner, Duskan Tadić. Commencing international justice with the trial of a civilian has been challenged for its failure to capture the impetus and scope of the region's ethnic cleansing policy. To seek to demonstrate the fundamental proposition that ethnic cleansing was itself a deliberately-executed policy without prosecuting the policymakers, seems impotent, perhaps even incoherent.

33. For an account, see Telford Taylor, *The Anatomy of the Nuremberg Trials* (New York: Knopf, 1992).

34. See Judith N. Shklar, *The Faces of Injustice* (New Haven, CT: Yale University Press, 1990), 93.

35. For discussion elaborating on this conception, see Ruti Teitel, "Transitional Jurisprudence: The Role of Law in Political Transformation," *Yale Law Journal* 106 (1997): 2009.

*This essay was written the summer before September 11th for an interdisciplinary art theory conference on transitional justice, which was part of the major contemporary art event 'Documenta 11'. The setting was New Delhi, and part of the inspiration was Mahatma Gandhi, as well as forms of narrative associated with the contemporary art movement. As I build on the conclusions drawn in my 2000 book,* Transitional Justice, *this essay seeks to keep alive the appreciation of the complex normativity of transition, an even greater challenge today provided the tendency to bureaucratize transitional justice, severing or attenuating its connection to the political.*

# 6    Transitional Justice as Liberal Narrative

## Introduction

In recent decades, societies across much of the world—Latin America, Eastern Europe, the former Soviet Union, Africa—have been engaged in transition: post-colonial changes, and the overthrowing of military dictatorships and totalitarian regimes with hopes for greater freedom and democracy. In these times of massive political movement away from illiberal rule, a burning question recurs: How should societies deal with their evil pasts? What, if any, is the relation between a state's response to its repressive past, and its prospects for creating a liberal order?

The point of departure in the transitional-justice debate is the presumption that the move toward a more liberal, democratic political system implies a universal norm. Instead, my remarks here propose an alternative way of thinking about the law and political transformation. In exploring an array of experiences, I will describe a distinctive conception of justice in the context of political transformation.

The problem of transitional justice arises within the distinctive context of a shift in political orders, or, more particularly today, of change in a liberalizing direction. Understanding the problem of justice in this context requires entering into a discourse that is organized in terms of the profound dilemmas characteristic of these extraordinary periods. The threshold dilemma arises from the situation of justice in times of political transformation: Law is caught between past and future, between backward-looking and forward-looking, between retrospective and prospective. Transitional justice is the justice associated with these circumstances. To the extent that transitions imply paradigm shifts in the normative conception of justice, the role of law at these moments appears deeply paradoxical. In ordinary times, law provides order and stability, but in extraordinary periods of political upheaval, law is called upon to maintain order, even as it enables transformation. Accordingly, the ordinary intuitions and predicates about law simply do not apply in transitional situations. These dynamic periods of political flux generate a sui generis paradigm of transformative law.

The conception of justice that emerges is contextualized and partial: It is both constituted by, and constitutive of, the transition. What is "just" is contingent, and informed by prior injustice. As a state undergoes political change, legacies of injustice have a bearing on what is deemed transformative. Indeed, at some level it is the legal responses to these legacies that create the transition. In these situations, the rule of law is historically and politically contingent, elaborated in response to past political repression that had often been condoned. While the rule of law ordinarily implies prospectivity, transitional law is both backward- and forward-looking, as it disclaims past illiberal values and reclaims liberal norms.

## I. Punishment or Impunity

The core debate in the prevailing view of transitional justice is the so-called "punishment or impunity" debate, the debate over whether or not to punish the predecessor regime. The contemporary wave of transitions away from military rule throughout Latin America and Africa, as well as from communist rule in Central Europe and the former Soviet bloc, has revived the debate over whether to punish. While trials are thought to be foundational, and to enable the drawing of a bright line demarcating the normative shift from illegitimate to legitimate rule, the exercise of the state's punishment power in circumstances of radical political change raises profound dilemmas. Transitional trials are emblematic of accountability and the rule of law, yet their representation far transcends their actual exercise; they are few and far between, particularly in the contemporary period, and their low incidence reveals the real dilemma in dealing with systemic wrongdoing by way of criminal law. In transitional contexts, conventional understandings of individual responsibility are frequently inapplicable, and have spurred the emergence of new legal forms: partial sanctions that fall outside conventional legal categories.

The agonizing questions raised by successor-regime criminal justice include whether to punish or to grant amnesty. Is punishment a backward-looking exercise in retribution, or an expression of the restoration of the rule of law? Who properly bears responsibility for past repression—does it lie with the individual or perhaps with the collective, the regime, the entire society?

## *The Legacy of Nuremberg*

Since World War II, international justice has been dominated by the legacy, the myth, of the Nuremberg trials. The significance of Nuremberg is best understood, in its full political context, by returning to the period after World War I, and to the policies set at Versailles and the failed national trials. The national prosecution policies were seen as hopelessly political, and their failures are said to explain the subsequent resurgence of German aggression. This view had repercussions for the rest of the century: the Nuremberg trials shifted the paradigm of justice from that of national to that of international processes. It is this shift that has framed both the successor-justice debate and the dominant scholarly understanding of transitional justice over the last half-century.

While there are many dilemmas associated with the application of criminal justice in the national arena, within the international legal system these dilemmas appear to fall away. In the abstract, the dilemmas of successor justice are seemingly best resolved by turning to an autonomous legal system. Within the national legal scheme, the question of justice may seem inextricably political, but international justice is thought, by comparison, to be neutral and apolitical.

A number of dilemmas recur in the deployment of law in political transition, most basically the question of how to conceptualize justice in the context of a massive political shift. But this problem is mitigated within international law, as the international legal system offers a degree of continuity. The postwar entrenchment of international legal norms affords a jurisdictional basis that goes beyond the limits of domestic criminal law. International law seemingly offers a way to circumvent problems that are endemic to transitional justice: international standards and forums appear to uphold the rule of law while also satisfying core concerns of fairness and impartiality.

Another dilemma of transitional justice is how to ascribe criminal accountability for offenses that implicate the state in a policy of repression. Here, too, international law offers a standard, in the Nuremberg Principles, a turning point in the conceptualization of responsibility for state crime. These principles for the first time attributed responsibility to individuals for atrocities under international law. In rejecting traditional defenses against such charges, Nuremberg dramatically expanded potential individual criminal liability under law. While, historically, heads of state had enjoyed sovereign immunity, under the Nuremberg Principles, public officials could no longer avail themselves of a "head of state" defense based on their official positions. Instead, they could be held criminally responsible. Moreover, while, under the traditional military rule applicable in a command structure, "due obedience" to orders was a defense, under the Nuremberg Principles even persons acting under orders could be held responsible. By eliminating the "head of state" and "superior orders" defenses, the Nuremberg Principles pierced the veil of diffused responsibility that characterized the wrongdoing perpetrated under totalitarian regimes.

With the Nuremberg Principles, international humanitarian law came to offer a normative framework and language for thinking about successor justice. The wrongdoing of a political regime could now be conceptualized under the rubric of the law of war. Mediating the individual and the collective, the Nuremberg Principles—and World War II itself—left our understanding of individual responsibility permanently altered. The Nuremberg Principles wrought a radical expansion of potential individual criminal liability, at both ends of the power hierarchy. The post-Nuremberg liability explosion has profound ramifications that have not yet been fully absorbed. The massive contemporary expansion in potential criminal liability raises real dilemmas for successor regimes that are deliberating over whom to bring to trial, and for what: the priority was to target those at the highest level of responsibility for the most egregious crimes. These dilemmas continue to appear in contemporary international criminal proceedings.

Developments in the ad hoc tribunals, the ICTY and ICTR, expand on the post-war understandings of state persecution to include nonstate actors. This is seen in those developments in international humanitarian law in which the understanding of the offense of wartime persecution extends beyond the international realm, to action within the state. It is also seen in the jurisdiction of the ICTY, as well as of the International Criminal Court. In these contemporary instances, a dynamic understanding of "crimes against humanity" moves beyond a predicated nexus of armed conflict to persecution, and becomes virtually synonymous with the enforcement of equality of the law. Though the strength of national law may not be evident in the record of international trials, one might see the normative force in current international discourse, where it stands for what rule of law exists in global politics.

## The Transitional Limited Criminal Sanction

Despite the call for criminal justice in the abstract, the history of the last half-century reveals recurring problems of justice within the norm shifts that characterize political transitions. Under such conditions, there are limits on the exercise of the power to punish, and justice is often compromised. These real rule-of-law dilemmas help explain why, despite dramatic expansions of criminal liability in the abstract, enforcement lags far behind. Indeed, transitional practices reveal a pattern of criminal investigations and prosecutions followed by little or no penalty. While punishment is ordinarily conceptualized as a unitary practice that includes both the establishment and the penalizing of wrongdoing, in transitional criminal law the elements of establishing and sanctioning have become somewhat detached from one another. It is this partial process, which I term the "limited criminal sanction," that distinguishes criminal justice in transition.

The limited criminal sanction constitutes compromised prosecution processes that do not necessarily culminate in full punishment. Depending on just how limited the process is, investigations may or may not lead to indictments, adjudication, and conviction. If conviction does ensue, it is often followed by little or no punishment. In situations of political transition, the criminal sanction may be limited to an investigation establishing wrongdoing.

The constraints on the limited criminal sanction are well-illustrated historically, in, for example, the aftermaths to World Wars I and II, the postmilitary trials of Southern Europe, the contemporary successor criminal proceedings in Latin America and Africa, and the wave of political change in Central Europe following the collapse of the Soviet Union. Although the specific history is often repressed, post–World War II successor justice well illustrates the limited criminal sanction. Even in the midst of trials mounted by Allied Control Council No. 10 after the war, the International Military Tribunal began a reversal of the Allied punishment policy, and between 1946 and 1958, a process of reviews and clemency culminated in the mass commutation of war criminals' sentences. A similar sequence unfolded in Germany's national trials, in which, out of more than 1,000 cases that were tried between 1955 and 1969, fewer than 100 of those convicted received life sentences, and fewer than 300 received limited terms. Years later, a similar sequence unfolded in Southern Europe with Greece's trials of its military police, which culminated largely in suspended or commutable sentences. In the 1980s in Latin America, soon after the Argentine junta trials, limits on follow-up trials were imposed, and pardons were ultimately extended to everyone convicted of atrocities, even the junta leaders. In fact, amnesties became the norm throughout much of the continent, including in Chile, Nicaragua, and El Salvador.

The story has repeated itself since the communist collapse. Ten years after the revolution, the story is the transitional limited criminal sanction. In unified Germany's border-guards trials, suspension of sentences is the norm. This was also true of the few prosecutions in the Czech Republic, Romania, Bulgaria, and Albania. History repeatedly reflects a limiting of the final phase of punishment policy. Sometimes, the limiting of the criminal sanction is used strategically, as an incentive to achieve other political goals, such as cooperation in investigations or in other political projects; in Chile, a law exempting its military from prosecution was conditioned on officers' cooperation in criminal investigations relating to past wrongdoing under military rule. In post-apartheid South Africa, penalties were dropped upfront on condition of confession to wrongdoing, as crimes deemed "political" were amnestied on condition of full disclosure to the Truth and Reconciliation Commission. This left a window open for investigations into past wrongs, a practice that could also be understood as a limited prosecutorial process.

Other contemporary legal responses, such as the ad hoc international tribunals established to adjudicate genocide and war crimes in Yugoslavia and Rwanda, reflect similar developments. The general absence of custody over the accused—currently, only thirty-eight are in custody in the case of the former Yugoslavia—as well as the lack of control over the evidence and the many other constraints relating to war-crimes prosecutions, have left little choice but to investigate, indict, and go no farther. In Rwanda, there has been resort to traditional criminal proceedings, which also reflect a form of limited criminal sanction.

The limited criminal sanction offers a pragmatic resolution of the core dilemma of transition; namely, that of attributing individual responsibility for systemic wrongs perpetrated under repressive rule. The basic transitional problem is whether there is any theory of individual responsibility that can span the move from a repressive, to a more liberal, regime. Indeed, the emergence of the limited sanction suggests a more fluid way to think about what punishment does. In fact, there has been a rethinking of the theory of punishment: wrongdoing can be clarified and condemned without necessarily attributing individual blame and penalty. In effect, punishment is justified as inherent in the stages of the criminal process.

The transitional sanction, in other words, points to an alternative sense of the retributivist idea. Although the sanction is limited in character, it suggests that core retributive purposes of the recognition and condemnation of wrongdoing are vindicable by diminished—even symbolic—punishment. The recognition and condemnation of past wrongdoing themselves have transformative dimensions; the public establishment of which liberates the collective. Mere exposure of wrongs, moreover, can stigmatize their agents, and can disqualify them from entire realms of the public sphere, relegating them to a predecessor regime. In the extraordinary circumstances of radical political change, some of the purposes that ordinarily are advanced by the full criminal process can be advanced instead by the sanction's more limited form.

The limited criminal sanction may well be the crucial mediating form of transitional periods. The absence of traditional plenary punishment during these shifts out of repressive rule suggests that they may allow more complex understandings of criminal responsibility to emerge through the application of criminal justice to the principle of individual responsibility in the distinct context of systemic crimes. Yet this perspective on punishment does not account well for its role in times of radical political flux, where the transitional criminal form is informed by values related to the project of political change. Ordinarily, criminal justice is theorized in starkly dichotomous terms, as animated by either a backward-looking concern with retribution, or a forward-looking, utilitarian concern with deterrence. In transitions, however, punishment is informed by a mix of retrospective and prospective purposes: the decision whether to punish or to amnesty, to exercise or to restrain criminal justice, is rationalized in overtly political terms. Values such as mercy and reconciliation, commonly treated as external to criminal justice, are explicit parts of the transitional deliberation. The explicit politicization of criminal law in these periods challenges ideal understandings of justice, yet turns out to be a persistent feature of jurisprudence in the transitional context.

The limited criminal sanction is an extraordinary form of punishment, for it is directed less at penalizing perpetrators than at advancing the normative shift of a political transformation. It is well-illustrated historically, not only in policy after World War II, but also in the punishments following more recent cases of regime change. Performing important operative acts—via formal public inquiries into, and clarifications of, the past, and indictments of past wrongdoing—the sanction has advanced the normative shift that is central to the liberalizing transition. Even in its most limited form, it is a symbol of the rule of law, and, as such, has enabled the expression of a critical normative message.

This use to construct normative change is what distinguishes transitional criminal measures, even despite the varying application from country to country. Where the prior regime was sustained by a persecutory policy that was rationalized within a legal system, transitional legal responses express the message that the policy was man-made and is therefore reformable. In that their procedures of inquiry and indictment act as rituals of collective knowledge, enabling the isolation and disavowal of past wrongdoings and individuating responsibility, they enable the potential of liberalizing change, freeing the successor regime from the weight of the earlier state's evil legacies. The ritualized legal processes of appropriation and misappropriation, avowal and disavowal, and symbolic loss and gain all allow perceptions of transformation, and due in part to them, the society begins to move in a liberalizing direction.

Transitional practices suggest that criminal justice is, in some form, a ritual of liberalizing states, providing them with a public method of constructing their new norms. These processes allow them to draw a line, liberate a past, and let the society move forward. While punishment is conventionally considered to be largely retributive in its aim, in transitional situations its purposes become corrective, going beyond the individual perpetrator to the broader society. This function is clear in the case of systemic political offenses, for example, in the persistence of prosecutions of crimes against humanity—the archetypal offense addressed by transitional persecutory politics, which here use criminal law to mount a critical response to an earlier illiberal rule. Moreover, whereas punishment is ordinarily thought to divide society; the punishments exercised in transitional situations are so limited as to allow the possibility of a return to a liberal state. As such, criminal processes have affinities with other transitional responses.

## The Paradigmatic Transitional Response

The operative effects advanced by the limited criminal sanction—such as establishing, recording, and condemning past wrongdoing—display affinities with other legal acts and processes that are constructive of transition. The massive and *systemic* wrongdoing that is characteristic of modern repression demands recognition of the mix of individual and collective responsibility. There is an overlap of punitive and administrative institutions and processes; individualized processes of accountability give way to administrative investigations, commissions of inquiry, the compilation of public records, official pronouncements, and condemnations of past wrongs. These are often subsumed in state histories commissioned pursuant to a political mandate of reconciliation, as in South Africa. Whether or not state-sponsored forms of public inquiry and official truth-telling are desirable, and signify liberalization, is contingent on state legacies of repressive rule, but generalized uses of these independent historical inquiries can be seen in contemporary human-rights law.

The paradigmatic affinities discussed here bear on the recurrent question in transitional-justice debates: what is the right response to repressive rule, the response most appropriate to supporting a lasting democracy? The subtext of this question assumes a transitional ideal, and the notion that normative concerns somehow militate for a particular categorical response. But this is simply the wrong question. In dealing with a state's repressive past, there is no one right response. The question should be reframed. Among states, the approach taken to transitional justice is politically contingent, even at the same time that there appears to be a paradigmatic transitional response in the law. Transitional constitutionalism, criminal justice, and the rule of law share affinities in the contingent relation that these norms bear to prior rule, as well as in the work they do in the move to a more liberal political order.

## Transitional Constructivism

How is transition constructed? What is the role of law in political change? The paradigmatic form of the law that emerges in these times operates in an extraordinary fashion, and itself plays a constructive role in the transition. It both stabilizes and destabilizes, and, in this respect, its distinctive feature is its mediating function: It maintains a threshold level of formal continuity while also engendering a transformative discontinuity. The extent to which formal continuity is maintained depends on the modality of the transformation, while the content of the normative shift is a function of history, culture, and political tradition, as well as of the society's receptiveness to innovation.

Just what, exactly, do transitional legal practices have in common? Law constructs transitions through diverse processes, including legislation, adjudication, and administrative measures. Transitional operative acts include pronouncements of indictments and verdicts; the issuing of amnesties, reparations, and apologies; and, the promulgation of constitutions and reports. These practices share certain features: namely, they are ways to publicly construct new collective political understandings. Transitional processes, whether prosecution, lustration, or inquiry, share this critical dimension. They are actions taken to manifest change by publicly sharing new political knowledge. Law works at the margin here, as it performs the work both of separation from the prior regime and of integration with the successor regime. It has a liminal quality: it is law between regimes. The peculiar efficacy of these salient legal practices lies in their ability to effect functions of both separation and integration—all within continuous processes.

Transitional law often implies procedures that do not seem fair or compelling: trials lacking in regular punishment, reparations based on politically driven and arbitrary baselines, constitutions that do not necessarily last. What characterizes the transitional legal response is its limited form, embodied in the provisional constitution and purge, the limited sanction and reparation, the discrete history and official narrative. Transitional law is, above all, symbolic—a secular ritual of political passage.

The legal process has become the leading transitional response because of its ability to convey, publicly and authoritatively, the political differences that constitute the normative shift from an illiberal to a liberal regime. In its symbolic form, transitional jurisprudence reconstructs these political differences through changes in status, membership, and community. While the differences are necessarily contingent, they are recognized as legitimate, in light of the legacies with which a given successor society has to deal. Moreover, the language of law imbues the new order with legitimacy and authority.

In modern political transformations, legal practices enable successor societies to advance liberalizing political change. By mediating the normative hiatus and shift characterizing transition, the turn to law comprises important functional, conceptual, operative, and symbolic dimensions. Law epitomizes the rationalist liberal response to mass suffering and catastrophe; it expresses the notion that there is, after all, something to be done. Rather than resigning itself to historical repetition, the liberal society sees the hope of change in the air. Where successor societies engage in transitional justice debates, they signal the rational imagining of a more liberal political order.

In periods of political upheaval, legal rituals offer the leading alternative to the violent responses of retribution and vengeance. The transitional legal response is deliberate, measured, restrained, and restraining, enabling gradual, controlled change. As the questions of transitional justice are worked through, the society begins to perform the signs and rites of a functioning liberal order. Transitional law transcends the "merely" symbolic, to become the leading ritual of modern political passage. It is a ritual act that makes the shift between the predecessor and the successor regimes possible. In contemporary transitions characterized by a peaceful nature and an occurrence within the law, it is legal processes that perform the critical "undoings," the inversions of the predicates justifying the preceding regime. It is these public processes that produce the collective knowledge constitutive of the normative shift, simultaneously disavowing aspects of the predecessor ideology and affirming the ideological changes that constitute liberalizing transformation.

New democracies respond to legacies of injustice in different ways, but patterns across their various legal forms constitute a paradigm of transitional jurisprudence rooted in prior political injustice. The role of law is constructivist: Transitional jurisprudence emerges as a distinct, paradigmatic form of law responsive to, and constructive of, the extraordinary circumstances of periods of substantial political change. The conception of justice in transitional jurisprudence is partial, contextual, and situated between at least two legal and political orders. Legal norms are always multiple; the idea of justice, a compromise. Transitional jurisprudence centers on the paradigmatic use of the law in the normative construction of the new political regime.

## IV. The Construction of Liberal Narrative

The main contribution of transitional justice is to advance the construction of a collective liberalizing narrative. Its uses are to advance the transformative purpose of moving the international community, as well as individual states, toward liberalizing political change. Just how does transitional justice offer its narrative? What is the potential of law in constructing a story that lays the basis for political change? Let us begin with the trial.

### *The History of Law: The Uses of the Human Rights-Trial*

A primary role of transitional criminal justice is historical. Trials have longed played a crucial role in transitional history-making; criminal justice in these situations creates public, formal shared processes that link the past to the future, and the individual to the collective. Criminal trials are a historical, ceremonial form of constructed memory making, a way to work through controversy within a community. The purposes of even the ordinary criminal trial are not only to adjudicate individual responsibility, but also to establish the truth about an event that is in controversy; this is even more true of the role of the trial in settling the historical controversies that are characteristic of periods of transition. Since transitions follow regime change, and periods of heightened political and historical conflict, a primary purpose of successor trials is to advance a measure of historical justice.

What sorts of truths are established in such periods? I call them "transitional critical truths" namely, a shared political knowledge that is critical of the ideology of the predecessor regime. The collective historical record produced through the trial both delegitimizes the predecessor regime and also legitimizes the successor. Repressive leadership may be brought down by military or political collapse, but unless it is also publicly discredited, its ideology often endures. Leading historical trials, whether of the war criminals at Nuremberg, Argentina's military junta, or the Balkans' henchman, Slobodan Milošević, are now remembered not for their condemnation of individual wrongdoers but rather for their roles in creating lasting historical records of state tyranny.

Transitional criminal processes create authoritative accounts of evil legacies, allowing a collective history-making. The many representations that they involve— trial proceedings, written transcripts, public records, judgments—re-create and dramatize the repressive past. Radio and television reportage add to these possibilities (Consider The Hague today.). One might also add the Internet.

The contemporary, post–Cold War period has given rise to even more complicated and disaggregated understandings of responsibility, and to a problematizing of public and private. Consider the growing focus on the role of the multinationals in World War II, and the monetary settlements that attempt to legitimate the transforming global private regime.

The connection between legal proceedings and history adverts to the broader role of law in constructing the narrative of transition. I turn to explore that structure in the next part of this essay.

### Narratives of Transition

The narratives that are constructed in a transition—whether they develop out of trials, administrative proceedings, or historical commissions of inquiry—make a normative claim about the relationship of a state's past to its prospects for a more democratic future. As I will explain, the transitional narrative structure itself propounds the claim that particular knowledge is relevant to the possibility of personal and societal change. Narratives of transition offer an account of the relationship of political knowledge to the move away from dictatorship and toward a more liberal future.

Transitional narratives follow a distinct rhetorical form: Beginning in tragedy, they end upon a comic or romantic mode. In the classical understanding, tragedy implicates the catastrophic suffering of individuals, whose fate, due to their status, in turn implicates entire collectives. Some discovery or change away from ignorance ensues, but in tragedy, knowledge seems only to confirm a fate foretold. Contemporary stories of transitional justice similarly involve stories of affliction on a grand scale, but, while they begin in a tragic mode, in the transition they switch to a nontragic resolution. There is a turn to what might be characterized as a redemptive phase. Something happens in these accounts: the persons enmeshed in the story ultimately avert tragic fates, and somehow adjust and even thrive in a new reality. In the convention of the transitional narrative, unlike that of the tragedy, the revelation of knowledge actually makes a difference. The country's past suffering is somehow reversed, leading to a happy ending of peace and reconciliation.

The structure of the transitional narrative appears in both fictional and nonfictional accounts of periods of political transformation. National reports read as tragic accounts that end on a redemptive note. Suffering is somehow transformed into something good for the country; into a greater societal self-knowledge that is thought to enhance the prospect of an enduring democracy. After "Night and Fog" policies of "disappearance" were perpetrated throughout much of Latin America, for example, bureaucratic processes were deployed to set up investigatory commissions. Beginning with titles such as "Never Again," the truth reports produced by these commissions promise to deter future suffering. Thus the prologue to the report of the Argentine national commission on the disappeared declares that the military dictatorship "brought about the greatest and most savage tragedy" in the country's history, but history provides lessons: "Great catastrophes are always instructive." "The tragedy which began with the military dictatorship in March 1976, the most terrible our nation has ever suffered, will undoubtedly serve to help us understand that only democracy can save a people from horror on this scale."[1] Knowledge of past suffering plays a crucial role in the state's ability to make a liberating transition.

Confrontation with the past is considered necessary to liberalizing transformation. The report of the Chilean national commission on truth and reconciliation asserts that knowledge and the disclosure of past suffering are necessary to reestablishing the country's identity. The decree establishing the commission declares, that "the truth had to be brought to light, for only on such a foundation would it be possible to…create the necessary conditions for achieving true national reconciliation."[2] "Truth," then, is the necessary precondition for democracy. This is also the organizing thesis of the El Salvador truth commission, a storyline seen in the title of its report, "From Madness to Hope." The report tells a story of violent civil war followed by "truth and reconciliation." According to its introduction, the "creative consequences" of truth can "settle political and social differences by means of agreement instead of violent action." "Peace [is] to be built on [the] transparency of…knowledge." The truth is a "bright light" that "search[es] for lessons that would contribute to reconciliation and to abolishing such patterns of behavior in the new society."[3]

Even where the reporting is unofficial, the claim is similar: that the revelation of knowledge—in and of itself—offers a means to political transformation. The preface to the unofficial Uruguayan report *Nunca más* (Never again) casts writing in and of itself as a social triumph, claiming that transitional truthtellings will deter the possibility of future repression. It is the lack of "critical understanding which created a risk of having the disaster repeated…to rescue that history is to learn a lesson.…We should have the courage not to hide that experience in our collective subconscious but to recollect it. So that we do not fall again into the trap."[4]

In transitional history-telling, the story has to come out right. Yet these reports imply a number of poetic leaps. Was it the new truths that brought on liberalizing political change? Or was it the political change that enabled the restoration of democratic government, and then a reconsideration of the past? Or is it simply that, despite ongoing processes of political change, unless there is some kind of clarification of the concealments of the evil past, and some kind of ensuing self-understanding, the truth about that past will remain hidden, unavailable, external, foreign. In post-communist transitions characterized by struggles with past state archives, transitional accounts begin with stories of invasion and popular resistance; the foe is represented as the foreign outsider, before the story progresses to the ever more troubling discovery of collaboration that is closer to home and pervasive throughout the society. In the narratives of transition, whether out of a repressive totalitarian rule in the former Soviet bloc, or out of authoritarian military rule in Latin America, transitional stories all involve a "revealing" of supposedly secreted knowledge. What is pronounced is the tragic discovery.

What counts as liberalizing knowledge? These productions are neither original nor foundational; they are, however, contingent on state legacies of repressive rule. The critical function of the successor regime responds to the repressive practices of the prior regime. After military rule in Latin America, for example, where truth was a casualty of disappearance policies, the critical response is the "official story." After communist rule, on the other hand, the search for the "truth" was not a matter of historical production as such, for the "official story" had previously been deployed as an instrument of repressive control; instead, it was a matter of critical response to repressive state histories, to the securing of private access to state archives, to privatization of official histories, and to the introduction of competing historical accounts.

The link between the exposure of knowledge and the possibility of change means that the possibility of change is introduced through human action. The very notion of a knowledge that is objectified and exposed suggests not only that there was somehow a "logic" to the madness, but also that now there is something to be done. The message propounded is that, had the newly acquired knowledge existed earlier, events would have been different—and, conversely, that now that the truth is known, the course of future events will indeed be different. The liberal transition is distinguished by processes that illuminate the possibility of future choice. Transitional accounts hold the kernels of a liberal future foretold. The revelation of truth brings on the switch from the tragic past to the promise of a hopeful future. A catastrophe is somehow turned around, an awful fate averted. Transitional justice operates as this magical kind of switch: legal processes involve persons vested with transformative powers: judges, lawyers, commissioners, experts, witnesses with special access to privileged knowledge. Reckoning with the past enables the perception of a liberalizing shift.

Narratives of transition suggest that what is at stake in liberalizing transformation, is at minimum, a change of interpretation. The regimes of politics and of truth have a mutually constitutive role in this process: Societies begin to change politically when their citizens' understanding of the ambient situation changes. As Václav Havel has written, the change is from "living within a lie to living within the truth."[5] So it is that much of the literature of these periods involves stories of precisely this move, from "living within a lie" to the revelation of newly gained knowledge and self-understanding, effecting a reconstitution of personal identity and of relationships. These tales of deceit and betrayal, often stories of long-standing affairs, appear to be allegories of the relation between citizen and state, shedding light on the structure and the course of civic change.

What emerges clearly is that the pursuit of historical justice is not simply responsive to, or representative of, political change, but itself helps to construct the political transformation. Change in the political and legal regimes shapes and structures the historical regime. New truth regimes go hand in hand with new political regimes: indeed, they support the change. As transitional accounts connect a society's past with its future, they construct a normative relation. In this sense, narratives of transition are stories of progress, beginning with backward-looking reflection on the past, but always viewing it in light of the future. If the constructive fiction is that earlier awareness of the knowledge that has now been acquired might have averted the tragedy, a new society can be built on this claim. It is the change in political knowledge that allows the move from an evil past to a sense of national redemption.

Transitional narratives have a distinct structure. Their revelations of truth occur through switching mechanisms, critical junctures of individual and societal self-knowledge. There is a ritual disowning of previously secreted knowledge, a purging of the past, as well as an appropriation of a newly revealed truth, enabling a corrective return to the society's true nature. A new course is charted.

The practices of such periods suggest that the new histories are hardly foundational, but explicitly transitional. To be sure, historical narrative is always present in the life of the state, but in periods of political flux, the narrative's role is to construct perceptible transformation. Transitional histories are not "meta"-narratives but "mini"-narratives, always situated within the state's preexisting national story. They are not new beginnings, but they build upon preexisting political legacies. Indeed, the relevant truths are always implicated in the past political legacies of the state in question. They are not universal, essential, or metatruths; a marginal truth is all that is needed to draw a line on the prior regime. Critical responses negotiate the historical conflict that is apparent in contested accounts; as political regimes change, transitional histories offer a displacement of one interpretive account or truth regime for another, and, by doing so, preserve the state's narrative thread.

The importance of establishing a shared collective truth regarding repressive legacies from the past has become something of a trope in the discourse of political transition. The meaning of "truth" here is not universal, but rather socially contingent. Accordingly, the paradigmatic transitional legal processes rely on discrete changes in the public's salient political knowledge for their operative transformative action. Legal processes construct changes in the public justifications underlying political decision-making and behavior, changes that simultaneously disavow aspects of the predecessor ideology and afford justifications for the ideological changes constituting the liberalizing transformation. Legal processes can make these changes in the public rationale for the political order because they are predicated on authoritative representations of public knowledge. In this way, they contribute to the interpretive changes that create the perception of political and social transformation.

At the same time, transitional legal processes also vividly demonstrate the contingency in what knowledge will advance the construction of the normative shift. The normative force of these transitional constructions depends on their critical challenges to the policies, predicates, and rationalizations of the predecessor rule and ideology. Accordingly, establishing what the relevant "truths" are is an endeavor of disproportionate significance. In an example from this region, the Nanavaki commission accounts of the 1984 anti-Sikh riots, it is crucial whether a victim is identified as an "unarmed civilian" rather than as a "combatant." The critical truth turns on whether violence was "organized" and deliberate. Such findings of publicly shared political knowledge can topple a regime (at least on the normative level) by undermining a key ideological predicate of repressive national-security policies. These reinterpretations displace the predicates legitimizing the prior regime, and potentially offer newfound bases for the reinstatement of the rule of law.

Law offers a canonical language and the symbols and rituals of contemporary political transformation. Through trials and other public hearings and processes, legal rituals enable transitionally produced histories, social constructions of a democratic nature, with a broad reach. These rituals of collective history-making publicly construct the transition, dividing political time into a "before" and "after." Transitional responses perform the critical undoings that respond to prior repression—the releasing of justifications of the predecessor regime that is critical to political change. The practices of historical production associated with transition often publicly affirm what is already implicitly known in society, but also bring forward and enable a public letting go of the evil past.

Whether through trials or other practices, transitional narratives highlight the roles of knowledge, agency, and choice. Although the received wisdom on them is that their popularity in liberalizing states comes from their emphasis upon structural causation, they are actually complex, densely layered accounts that weave together and mediate individual and collective responsibilities. By introducing the potential of individual choice, the accounts perform transitional history's liberalizing function. By revealing "truths" about the past, they become narratives of progress, and by suggesting that events might have been different had this knowledge been previously known, they invoke the potential of individual action. Their message is one of avertable tragedy. Their expression of hope in individual choice and human action goes to the core of liberalism and human rights discourse.

Transitional narratives are also redemptive stories of return, of wholeness, of finding the way to political unity. They comprise a turn to the corrective and offer both state and public an alternative, successor identity centered on political unity. Emphasizing the possibility of bounded choice, of the reconciliation of the potential for individual agency with set political circumstances, they also stress the possibility of societal self-understanding and of averting tragic repetition associated with liberation. The message is that, despite past bad legacies, the contemporary liberal state offers redemptive political possibilities.

Transitional justice offers a way to reconstitute the collective across racial, ethnic, and religious lines, to ground it in a contingent political identity responsive to its particular legacies of fear and injustice. So it is that transitional justice has become an enduring feature of political liberalization. As liberal narrative, though, it should not become a fixed identity; despite its appeal, its entrenchment as a story of unity could undermine its potential for a revolutionary project. The entrenchment of policies of unity would stunt the development of party politics and a robust political culture. It would ultimately be illiberal. Transitional justice points instead to the significance of ongoing counter-narratives, and of nurturing transitional modality. These are the dynamic processes that characterize effective liberalization strategies and allow for ongoing political transformation.

## Notes

1. *Nunca más: The Report of the Argentine National Commission on the Disappeared* (New York: Farrar, Straus, Giroux, 1986), p. 6.

2. *Chilean National Commission on Truth and Reconciliation Report,* trans. Philip Berryman (Notre Dame, Ind.: Center for Civil and Human Rights, Notre Dame University, 1993).

3. *From Madness to Hope: The Twelve-Year War in El Salvador, Report of the Commission on the Truth for El Salvador* (United Nations Commission on the Truth for El Salvador, 1993), p. 11.

4. Servicia Paz y Justicia, *Uruguay Nunca más: Human Rights Violations, 1972-1985* (Philadelphia: Temple University Press, 1992), *trans.* Elizabeth Hampsten, pp. vii, x–xi.

5. Václav Havel et. al., *The Power of the Powerless: Citizens against the State in Central-Eastern Europe,* ed. John Keane (Armonk, N.Y.: M.E. Sharpe: 1985).

# 4 Conflict, Transition, and the Rule of Law

*The essay that forms this chapter was originally a contribution to a panel discussion on political violence at a symposium at Cornell Law School around 2005. I explore here what, if anything, transitional justice can contribute in situations of ongoing conflict, in particular the trials of political and military leaders in two fairly recent wars: the Balkans and Iraq. Whereas the Balkans trials were situated in the Hague at the U.N. Security Council–created Ad Hoc Tribunal, the trial of Saddam Hussain was conducted locally. These trials tell a complex and, to some extent, troubling story about the pitfalls and risks of deploying methods of transitional justice in the midst of conflict, rather than when a political transition has occurred and stabilized. These cases remind us that it is important to keep political considerations in mind when engaged in the evaluation of transitional justice in situations of conflict and post-conflict situations.*

# 7  The Law and Politics of Contemporary Transitional Justice

## Introduction

Slobodan Milošević, Saddam Hussein, Hissene Habre, Augusto Pinochet, Charles Taylor, Uhuru Kenyatta. There had never been more political leaders in the dock, or, under the shadow of its threat. Of what significance are these contemporary instances of transitional justice? This article will use the trials of Slobodan Milošević and Saddam Hussein as an occasion for revisiting and extending my ongoing project of tracing a genealogy of transitional justice.

In prior work, I have defined "transitional justice" as that conception of justice associated with periods of political change.[1] In an ongoing genealogy, I tie the legal developments in this area to distinct political phases of world history, a framework proposed for the study of the law and politics of transitional justice.[2] In this genealogy, the legal developments are tied to my sense of their varying political purposes. I also endeavor to analyze the extent to which there are trends in the legal changes. Last, the discussion of political context and aims ties the genealogy to thought relating to a history of responses to political conflict, yielding an intellectual genealogy of transitional justice.

Understanding the instant trials here discussed will necessitate an extension of our thinking regarding transitional justice, in an attempt to explore latter-day transitional justice. What follows are tentative conclusions about diverse circumstances. The criminal justice processes discussed here present conflicting consequences for the rule of law, further discussed *infra*, which well reflect the dilemmas of transitional justice written about more extensively in my book *Transitional Justice*.[3]

One set of questions addressed here relates to the goals of transitional justice and evaluates the shifts in genealogical phases in these terms. Transitional justice evokes many aspirations: rule of law, legitimacy, liberalization, nation-building, reconciliation, and conflict resolution. While the transitions literature appears to presume a goal of "transitions to democracy" as will be seen *infra*, the democratization goal is often in tension with other aspirations identified here, such as the new focus on conflict resolution and reconciliation.[4] This proposed genealogy seeks to help identify how these goals shift, and map their implications so as to clarify the distinctions between, and the differing implications of, these various aspirations.

The processes discussed here constitute instances of what I have characterized as a paradigm of global transitional justice: an increasing juridification among diverse legal systems, both international and national, and multiple paradigms of legitimacy in global order. Below, these transitional-justice responses are further elaborated along these lines. As will be seen, the two trial processes discussed here illustrate these alternative paradigms.

## Contemporary Transitional Justice: The Milošević and Hussein Trials

This Part discusses salient features of the Milošević and Hussein trials briefly and then proposes several points about what might characterize the contemporary phase in global transitional justice: the puzzle of the association of the marked increase in juridicization and an expansion of the reach of law in international affairs, while often in conditions of persistent conflict. These changes in conditions are reflected in the new developments in international humanitarian law, which now reaches beyond international conflict to intrastate incidents that occur even in peacetime, extending in particular to such extreme offenses as crimes against humanity. Even where internally based, legal responses to these developments can prevent the prospect of destabilizing policies.[5] Nevertheless, as will be discussed further on, contemporary legal responses do not necessarily express an unequivocal sense of a progressive rule of law.[6] Instead, as will be elaborated *infra*, one might best understand this by drawing on prior theories on transitional justice that shed light on law's relationship to its political context and the contextualized meaning of the rule of law in these political circumstances.[7]

Global transitional justice, as elaborated below, implies an expanded legalism, while at the same time reflecting its trends of juridicization and decentralization in terms of jurisdictional sites—local and transnational—as well as new legitimacies based on a paradigm shift from state-centered to human-centered discourses in foreign affairs. As discussed *infra*, a threshold humanitarian standard emerges. Below, contemporary processes of transitional justice are identified and discussed, with an eye to analysis and elaboration of these alternative paradigms.

### From Nuremberg to The Hague

With the trial of Milošević in The Hague, international war crimes trials returned to Europe for the first time since World War II in the genealogy of transitional justice. On its face, this development appears to present a return or cycling back to the post-war trials. Yet this may well be only a surface resemblance. To what extent do contemporary developments represent a sign of a true return to internationalism?

Revisiting the post-war trials from the present perspective sheds light on the meaning of internationalism in the genealogy of transitional justice. What becomes evident is that internationalism lacks a fixed meaning and that it is best understood within a hermeneutic, historical context. For example, seen from the present perspective, and infused by the inevitable comparison with the existing international criminal tribunals, Nuremberg, while reflecting an agreement of the four Allies, was ultimately not all that international.[8] Moreover, without a final judgment and confrontation against Hitler, Nuremberg lacked the ultimate symbol of a top political leader in the dock. Seen in a historical light, there is some overstatement in the extent to which the post-war trials laid the basis for contemporary transitional justice.

Accordingly, in some regard, one might say that it is the contemporary Hague trial of Slobodan Milošević that is the landmark case constituting the first prosecution of a political leader in an international proceeding. At the International Criminal Tribunal for the former Yugoslavia (ICTY), Milošević sits in the dock, charged with war crimes, crimes against humanity, and genocide. These offenses have been made subject to international jurisdiction, although some were committed domestically, reflecting radical developments in the construction of international criminal jurisdiction.[9]

To fully situate the contemporary ICTY's project necessitates reflection on its political context of post-conflict justice and, in particular, recognition of the full military and political context of the time, and its relation to the contemporary processes. Going back to its origins in the Balkans conflict, transitional justice's asserted goal was to restore peace. In the midst of the conflict, a U.N. Security Council–appointed commission of experts investigated atrocities that were committed in the region and concluded, *inter alia*, that there had been willful killing, organized massacres, torture, and rape. Moreover, the determination was made to set up a court that assertedly would help restore peace in the midst of political conflict.[10]

Of course, this account raises many questions, for, after all, in the absence of a clear military victory, what exactly is the role contemplated for international criminal justice? As shall become evident, in these conflictive circumstances, transitional justice is denoted by difficult dilemmas. In such conditions, even more than in ordinary transitional justice, there is an overly ambitious aim for the role of the law: justice-seeking in the absence of peace. At Nuremberg, building on the historical "just war" trials tradition, victors' justice was meted out over a defeated enemy in its vanquished country. At The Hague, however, this is simply not the case. The recourse to an international tribunal remains distant from the Balkan conflict, and justice was being meted out in the midst of political conflict. From the start, it was evident that, in the absence of full authority, there would be some compromise in the potential for the law to be effective, and a lack of full legitimacy. For example, the ICTY often lacks custody over the accused, as well as control over the evidence. Even after a decade, those most responsible for war crimes, such as Radovan Karadžić and General Ratko Mladić, remained at large.[11] Contrary to the mid-century post-war processes, in the contemporary setting, international justice bears a different relationship to political power. In the contemporary international tribunals, law bears a distinct relation to the exercise of military force and international intervention.

Therefore, a genealogical perspective necessitates thinking about these ICTY proceedings over a political time line. In this regard, one might consider the ICTY to have recently entered the latter stage of its proceedings. By 2008, it must wrap up all trials.[12] Indeed, at this point, one might distinguish between the strategy used at the ICTY's inception and the "exit strategy" of the present stage. Earlier, the pivotal issues concerning the international tribunal at The Hague centered on the parameters for the bases for the assumption of international jurisdiction. Whereas at the present stage, it is just the reverse: the relevant questions explicitly concern the jurisdiction's future devolution and what ought to be the normative relationship of the international legal regime to that of the relevant states. As will be seen, these questions about what ought to be the normative relation of the international to the national turn out to be endemic to Phase III, the phase of transitional justice that is associated with an emerging global rule of law.

## Transitional Justice in the Iraqi Occupation

While the political and military context associated with the Balkan conflict spurred the move toward international justice, in Iraq, even in similarly conflictive circumstances, there was a different move. Rather than recurring to an international forum, the trials in Iraq instead illustrate successor justice in the context of an ongoing military occupation.[13] While the initial attempts would later be abandoned in light of the security issues of the ongoing insurgency,[14] the Iraqi trials have given the appearance of continuing to be closely associated with a politics of occupation.

From the beginning in post-war Iraq, tragic mistakes were made, in what can now be seen as miscarriages of transitional justice.[15] The instant efforts at transitional criminal justice were preceded by attempts at deracinated constitutionalism: atomistic trials, radical purges, and compromised elections. In particular, there was a rush to de-baathification, resulting in the evisceration of existing institutions, such as the Iraqi parliament and army.[16] These purges needlessly sacrificed potential sources of legitimacy concerning, for example, ongoing constitutional reform at the time. In transitions, there is often a problem of how to deal with prior regime institutions, given the mix of individual and collective responsibilities associated with systemic persecution, and this dilemma poses a challenge to the parameters of transitional reforms of the police and military. The post-invasion rush to de-baathification, involving speedy purges of the military and the police, arguably sacrificed present security to the claims of justice, leaving the country with a real military and security vacuum. Yet, subsequently, this first response was revisited, and a new view emerged regarding the Iraqi army's capacity for democratic transformation.[17]

The failure of sweeping de-baathification spurred a partial turn away from the bureaucratic responses to the past regime to the individualized response characterizing criminal justice. This move to criminal justice opened up a vigorous debate over what authority ought be exercised over Saddam Hussein and, in particular, whether it ought to be national or international. While these questions reflect competing rule-of-law values, the waging of this debate at this time clearly reflects Phase III of transitional justice characterized by globalization.

The association of justice processes with the U.S. occupation raises issues as to the extent to which these trials can advance the purposes of the transition. The day of the purported withdrawal from Iraq also launched the first trial of Saddam Hussein.[18] At the time, the exhortation to justice had an air of Thermidor. With the former top leadership in custody, including Hussein, there was an imminent threat that heads would roll. Though this plan would be abandoned, given the then ongoing level of American control, the first trial would have been neither national nor international, but an "occupation tribunal," with consequences for legitimacy and the potential for contributing to the rule of law.[19] In any event, the selection of judges by what was widely viewed as a wing of the occupation, as well as the role of the United States in the 1980s, would seem to make the Iraqi case equally vulnerable to the claim of victor's justice.[20] Indeed, given the ongoing occupation status, the establishment of a state-trial policy would seem to be a symbol of Iraqi sovereignty. While such dilemmas are common to pre-transitional periods, contemporary Iraqi prosecutions pose an extraordinary and acute lack of security.[21]

Part II's discussion of the political context and mandates of both the ICTY and the Iraqi Special Tribunal (IST) becomes relevant to the argument elaborated in Part III regarding the character and form of transitional justice developments associated with this political moment. There are clear analogies with these trials that relate to the context of victor's justice and to the ambitious aims of democratization, peace, and reconciliation.

## Global Transitional Justice: Comparative Perspectives

This Part introduces what is termed here as Phase III "global transitional justice." Transitional justice in the Balkans and Iraq offers two instances of what this article characterizes as global transitional justice. This Part endeavors to situate these two trial processes in a political context in the immediate aftermath of conflict, and the pursuit of a related mix of aims both local and global, to post-conflict justice, to nation-building, and to the establishment of the rule of law. Despite their differences, consideration of this shared context enables comparative analysis.

Below, this chapter elaborates and analyzes issues concerning the diverse aims of contemporary transitional justice. The discussion is divided into four parts: first, transitional justice and normative regime change; second, issues posed by globalizing transitional justice; third, transitional justice for peace; and last, transitional justice's relation to the historical "just war" aims.

*Transitional Justice and Regime Change*

Transitional justice at present reflects a distinctive conception associated with the period of post–Cold War political change. Because of the political context of the current trials and their aim of justice-seeking amidst conditions of conflict, the onerous burden of creating a visible normative shift depends upon transitional justice. Where criminal justice is brought to bear from outside the state, one aim is to pre-transitional jump-start political transition processes on the ground.

Both trials discussed in this article aim to draw a line for the future. Yet, how can some sense of legitimacy be achieved in the transition? Where would it come from? Vivid construction of transition should be achieved by drawing a clear line distinguishing the past from the present. Can these contemporary trials express a clear message in this regard?

In current political conditions, any pursuit of justice goes to the very possibility of a global rule of law. This article pursues a genealogical structure of transitional justice and discusses current responses within a post–Cold War framework. What sort of rule of law do the current trials represent? To some extent, the message is incoherent because of the complexity and the scope of the sought-for normative change in terms of wartime justice, nation-building, and post-conflict justice. Implemented in the midst of conflict, these trials are aimed at jump-starting the political transition. In the absence of a more established matrix of rule of law, however, transitional justice here bears a heavy and complex burden. Indeed, the difficulties in the current administration of transitional justice reflect some of the dilemmas of justice-seeking processes in strained political conditions.

The overall normative aim of drawing a line of legitimacy between regimes is evident in the apparent interchangeability of transitional justice's various forms. For example, in Iraq, there was a debate about diverse modalities, whereby various transitional responses were proposed and abandoned in short order, reflecting the problem of sequencing in situations of diminished legitimacy. Which responses should come first? To what extent ought constitutions precede or follow elections? The persistence of these debates suggests a surface interchangeability in the modalities, concentrating on a largely symbolic modicum of transitional justice. It also suggests that there can be no fixed rule, and that the right modality will depend upon which institutions and processes can best advance legitimacy in the particular political and juridical conditions at stake.

From the start, the proposed sequence began with trials, followed by constitution-drafting and elections. Following political resistance, this proposal was abandoned, and a change of sequence ensued: elections preceding trials, and constitutionalism thereafter.[22] As with the constitutional project, the first impulse was to have early trials of Saddam Hussein and his henchmen. Postponement of the trials was welcome news because, at the time, given its lack of expertise in war crimes, the Iraqi judiciary could not handle such high-profile war crimes trials, and the United Nations would not bail them out.[23] Other good reasons existed to slow down the wheels of justice. Although the trials were postponed, the proposed timing reflected the purpose to link up the trials to the electoral transition. Criminal justice was aimed at promoting the political transition, that is, it was meant to underscore the illegitimacy of the prior regime and to advance political transformation.

Nevertheless, the question remains whether transitional justice can foster normative regime change in these political and juridical conditions. The ICTY offers a cautionary tale. By some measures, these international proceedings appear to have backfired by producing a nationalist backlash. The Hague tribunal's indictment hardly affected the political standing of Milošević, who was lured out of the country under false pretenses. By contrast, the political leader who openly cooperated with the tribunal, the late prime minister Zoran Đinđić, paid for it with his life. Recent Serbian elections turned into something of a referendum on Milošević.[24] Within this society, there continues to be extensive denial of the basic facts of the atrocities committed during the conflict.[25]

*Contemporary Transitional Justice and the Legalist Paradigm*

This Part discusses the contemporary understanding of legalism by evaluating the two trial processes discussed in this article as examples of alternative international and national legal models, and their potential contribution to the rule of law.

Post-war scholars, such as Judith Shklar, supported the international criminal tribunal at Nuremberg and the international law upon which it was predicated for their contribution to legalism.[26] In the post-war context, in light of the problems of Nazi law, the turn to international law made a contribution to the perception of the re-establishment of legality in Germany,[27] although scholars are divided on the extent to which the post-war trials ultimately contributed to the restoration of the rule of law.[28]

However, consider at this juncture whether international law is too facilely equated with legality. To what extent, ultimately, does it advance the rule of law domestically? In the post-war context, scholars were sober about the law's potential and characterized legality as a "continuum," a "matter of degree."[29] Therefore, political context is extremely important, and accordingly, one might expect that it is precisely in the associated post-war context that international law can make a contribution to the establishment of the rule of law. Were we to analyze the contemporary scene from the post-war perspective, therefore, the degree of legalism in the trials would be of relevance, as well as its potential impact on local politics, i.e., the relative contributions to the rule of law in these circumstances.

In this regard, the two processes discussed here, the ICTY at The Hague and the Baghdad tribunal, with their differences, reflect varying dimensions of legalism's potential, as well as its limits. Thus, for example, in the midst of the Balkan conflict, the turn to an international tribunal offered important elements of the rule of law.[30] The turn to international law offers continuity in the enforcement of equal protection and adherence to individual accountability under the law. There are other more particular values expressed in prosecutions of war crimes and crimes against humanity charges as discussed *infra*.

Nevertheless, the Milošević trial also demonstrates the limits of legalism. As the trial dragged on, the inevitable analogies to the Nuremberg trials wore thin.[31] While the Nazi Reich's top rung was convicted in a matter of months, those proceedings might well be considered to have occurred in conditions of diminished legalism. By contrast, at The Hague, one might conclude there to be an apparent surfeit of procedure and regulation.

Turning legalism on its head, Milošević took advantage of the process by insisting on representing himself, delaying the trial, and challenging the tribunal's jurisdiction and legitimacy.[32] The longer his self "defense" continued,[33] the more successful Milošević was in portraying himself as less a perpetrator than a "victim" of the international community and its legal processes. This strategy appears to have been effective in undermining the trial's effects in condemning perpetrators of the most heinous offenses at the top of the state power echelon.

From the start, the proposed trial of Saddam in the specially established IST reflected a lesser commitment to legalism.[34] To the extent that the IST exhibited procedural irregularities, negative consequences followed for the trial's capacity to lay the foundation for the rule of law in post-conflict Iraq. From the process's inception, there were a host of rule-of-law problems concerning such factors as the newly established court, its underlying charter, the appearance of discontinuity and selectivity, and arbitrariness in the law. Other issues go to due process, transparency, and the right to a fair defense. The first public glimpse of Hussein as an unrepresented defendant, however distorted, laid a basis for victimization. As in the Milošević trial, inadequate representation could hardly send a message of the re-establishment of rule of law in Iraq.[35] Issues of due process, the access necessary to a fair defense, and transparency persist.[36] The trial process was not open; rather, it reflects attempts to control the handover and related processes.

*Globalizing Justice: Transcending Old Dichotomies*

During the last century, the central point of reference in the conceptualization of the shape and role of international rule of law was constituted by the international-national dichotomy. At present, an evident remapping of public international law is afoot. A new paradigm has emerged the dimensions of which refer to expanded legalism, while at the same time they are also predicated upon fragmentation, proliferation, and multiplicity of jurisdictional sites—national, international, and transnational—and their attendant new legitimacies.

In the present post–Cold War context, there is an evident transformation in the significance of the expanded international criminal justice. Clearly, international criminal justice's aims and contributions are mixed, as justice-seeking in such new political circumstances inevitably implies diverse understandings of rule-of-law values. To begin, consider the extent to which international law at The Hague affords the rule-of-law values of fairness and neutrality, which one might juxtapose to other rule-of-law dimensions privileging local accountability. This breakdown in respect for rule-of-law values has historical resonance. For example, over much of its history, the United States has long emphasized popular sovereignty, local accountability, and, therefore, national over international law and its processes. Relatedly, at present, the United States (and most Iraqis) favors a nation-building model, where transitional justice is intended to serve local accountability and related purposes. By contrast, Europeans and the human rights community have tended to prefer multilateralism and to advocate U.N.-affiliated trials, such as those convened at The Hague to adjudicate atrocities in the Balkans and Rwanda, largely on the basis of privileging other rule-of-law values such as neutrality. Multiple rule-of-law rules serve the varying aims of transitional societies in global politics, while transitional conditions often exacerbate tension in adherence to these diverse rule-of-law values.

To some extent, the Milošević and Hussein proceedings reflect the varying dimensions of legality discussed above. One might even regard these two processes as mirror images of the international-national law dichotomy. Nevertheless, this chapter suggests that, to some degree, the dichotomy is overstated because what is frequently at stake in transition is a core rule-of-law dilemma which cuts across both the local and the international legal systems, though, in each instance, affecting different rule-of-law values.[37]

From its inception, transitional justice in Iraq raised profound dilemmas: To what extent could the trial of Saddam offer the sought-for restoration of the rule of law? What body, if any, had the legitimacy to sit in judgment? Should this have been an international adjudication presided over by a foreign judiciary, as in the cases of

Nuremberg, the ICTY, and Rwanda; or, alternatively, a "mixed" or "hybrid" tribunal, like those convened in Sierra Leone and East Timor?[38]

The choices were hardly clear-cut, with each jurisdictional scenario tied to a nexus that arguably fulfills different rule-of-law values. The international approach could have afforded a modicum of legal continuity through the International Criminal Court (ICC) and its charter, reflecting an apparent international penal code. This alternative legal system appeals to values of fairness and neutrality, while the mechanisms of national justice afford local accountability.[39] Accordingly, each jurisdiction advanced important but often competing rule-of-law values.

*From the International to the Global: From Primacy to Complementarity*

The contemporary phase of transitional justice characterized here as "global" is linked up to a changing relationship of the state to the international, in both its political and legal dimensions. New guiding principles apt for global politics, as this article contends, and as is elaborated below, are now overtaking the prevailing understanding of the relation of international to national justice, whereby it plays a sustained threshold role.

While there are differences among states regarding the internal status and weight of international law,[40] one might say that a hierarchic top-down understanding of jurisdiction well defines the twentieth century–view of the state within the international legal system. Yet, at Nuremberg, this assumption regarding the juridical relationship was not explicitly spelled out, because the exceptional political circumstances at the time did not present the usual status and relation of the state in the international realm but, rather, involved a conceded absence of national sovereignty. Although the Nuremberg tribunal did contemplate follow-up trials,[41] they would not occur in Germany until the state had recovered its political and juridical sovereignty. While this was the understanding at Nuremberg, the question of the international tribunal's jurisdiction—especially over violations committed against the state's own citizens—was the most controversial element that went to the heart of the post-war trials, particularly in the understanding of its legacy over time. For prudential reasons, the tribunal would end up limiting itself to those crimes against citizens that were associated with the waging of war, linking crimes against humanity up to more traditional, long-established war crimes.[42] This judicial self-limiting highlights the perceived vulnerabilities in the court's arrogation of authority over the state in the international realm. And, it would also illustrate the struggle to reconcile the universal aspirations of the law with the more particularist politics on the ground.

For about a half-century, the post-war trials discussed above would remain solitary precedents in international criminal adjudication. Indeed, the ad hoc tribunals of the last decade concerning the Balkans[43] and Rwanda articulate the unspoken assumptions at Nuremberg about international-national legal relations. These tribunals' constitutive instruments spell out that the relation of international and national law is clearly one of "primacy" in a hierarchical structure.[44]

Contemporary global legalism, however, redefines the status and relation of the international to national legal regimes in two major ways. First, in the contemporary moment, international criminal law is more pervasive, extending beyond the international realm and state borders, as well as circumstances of conflict. Second, while international law is more pervasive and has greater reach than before, it is also increasingly defined by its ongoing interstitiality. Interstitiality is here defined as the contemporary relation of the international to the national, as international criminal law operates not as an exceptional matter associated with extraordinary post-war sovereignty, but instead in a regular permanent way. These radically transformed circumstances for international criminal justice, both in scope and reach, beg the question of what is to be the relation of international to domestic law in the area of criminal justice. The transformed international system demands a guiding principle that is apt to address the ongoing relationship of the multiple legal regimes.

Such a principle exists, and this chapter articulates what, at present, may well be implied in the legal changes in the jurisdiction of the ICC, the first permanent international criminal judicial body. For the ICC is predicated upon an alternative jurisdictional principle to primacy, stated under the reconciling principle of "complementarity."[45] In the words of the Rome Statute, the ICC's jurisdiction is triggered if, and only if, the national legal system is "either unwilling or unable" to exercise jurisdiction. These conditions will need to be interpreted, but as prefatory to the ICC's substantive adjudicatory work, this evaluatory enterprise is already a substantial element of the work of the tribunal.[46] Indeed, according to the "complementarity" principle, when countries lack working legal systems for even minimal criminal justice, these international-law institutions and processes will lay a floor. Ultimately, this jurisdictional principle goes beyond the procedural to the substantive, to construct a global legal minimum which, insofar as it relates to the most heinous crimes, largely takes the form of a radical expansion of international humanitarian law.[47]

*Universality's Law*

Beyond the idea of global complementarity that was discussed above, other normative understandings have emerged in Phase III of transitional justice. While the above subpart elaborates how the traditional antinomies of the relationship of international to national law are transcended in, and by, the idea of complementarity, there are other mediating constructs in contemporary transitional justice, such as the concept of the law of humanity. The ascendance of this area of human-rights law reflects the changes in law's potential in present global politics.[48]

These normative understandings are raised in the instant processes of Milošević and Hussein in the relevant charges. In substance, the law of humanity implicates the most serious offenses, which transcend national borders and have come to be known as having "universal" jurisdiction. The concept of universality, as we will see, offers a basis for reconciling aspects of the local and the international in the contemporary global legal system.

For some time, crimes against humanity have captured the imagination in writings on transitional justice. Let us consider why. Judith Shklar conceived of the post-war trials' legitimacy as depending on the charge of crimes against humanity: "As far as the trial concerned itself with crimes against humanity it was both necessary and wise."[49] In the epilogue to her book *Eichmann in Jerusalem*, Hannah Arendt contends that the "offense against humanity" formed the basis of the post-war trials.[50] It was the mass murder of the German Jews that laid the foundations of the charge of crimes against "humanity." While these scholars wrote of trials involving both international and national processes, respectively, no matter: Crimes against humanity are the offense par excellence that defined the post-war trials not only as transcending an exercise in political justice, but also as a statement regarding the protection of humanity.

Take how crimes against humanity express the core rule-of-law norm that there is no escaping humanitarian law's protective force. The core legality values of equality and the general applicability of the law are expressed in two dimensions of the crime against humanity. First, the offense defines and condemns the persecution of "any" citizen group and therefore, is equally applicable to any citizen regardless of nationality, ethnicity, or religion.[51] Second, insofar as these charges may involve the abuse of power by political leaders, no one, even an acting leader, is immune from judgment. As such, the offense of the crime against humanity goes to the very basis of a core rule-of-law regime.

This rule-of-law message is also seen in the extent to which current human-rights law emphasizes crimes against humanity's universality. Prosecution of crimes against humanity appears to instantiate a universal norm because, by definition, such crimes offend the entire community of "humanity" and therefore are subject to universal jurisdiction. Moreover, because such offenses may be committed anywhere, under any circumstances, whether during war or in peacetime, they may be subject to transnational adjudications and prosecution by any state as a matter of universal concern.[52] Despite this idealistic view, however, there are always political constraints.

One might consider, both at The Hague and in Baghdad, the extent to which crimes against humanity lay the basis for the trials' ultimate claim to legitimacy.

Take the aims of the contemporary adjudications under the law of humanity and the application of universal jurisdiction in global transitional justice. One of contemporary transitional justice's goals is nation-building, and trials are commonly thought to assist in defining a community in the state consolidation process. However, where the crime adjudicated is defined as one against humanity, what is the relevant community? To what extent do such trials assist in nation-building? Some of these questions arose before, in the post-war successor trials.[53] Moreover, as prosecutions of leaders for acts committed against their own citizens, both trials discussed here challenge the traditional understandings of territoriality and sovereignty. Therefore, what aims do such trials accomplish? The association of these trials with present politics alludes to their potential role in spurring political regime-change in current global circumstances.

Despite their broad reach, there are ways that the charges of crimes against humanity may miss a critical point of the trials. Consider to what extent these offenses can capture the masterminds of repressive policies. After all, the instant proceedings differ from other historic successor trials. Milošević and Hussein are no Eichmanns. As their countries' top political leaders, they are far from mere cogs in the wheel, and their offenses form part and parcel of the promulgation of the ideological policies involving aggressive nationalism and ethnic persecution.

Moreover, insofar as the contemporary charges go beyond crimes against humanity to include war crimes, the trials risk politicization. Particularly, in the Milošević trial, prosecuting war crimes raises broader questions concerning the legality of the NATO intervention at the time of the indictment. Moreover, other issues raised by the reliance on the "joint enterprise" theory may well make it harder to hold Milošević individually responsible for genocide and crimes against humanity.[54]

Given the mix of aims served by transitional justice in this context, one might question whether and to what extent conducting crimes against humanity prosecutions in international fora can assist the advancement of nation-building.[55] In some ways, this raises the flip side of the national successor trials convened over recent decades. When they are conducted in pursuit of the aim of political transition, prosecutions of crimes against humanity express a core equality under the law norm and, therefore, can advance an important element of re-establishing the sense of a threshold rule of law.

While there was an assumption of the nexus of trials to democratization and nation-building that was central to the project of post-war trials at mid–twentieth century, at present, signs indicate that contemporary international trials could well be generating a nationalist backlash that post-war scholars would have found unimaginable.[56] As it also raises issues for the so-called "completion strategy," the backlash is likely deleterious for the trials' ultimate impact. When the tribunal closes its doors, where should its unfinished, remaining cases go? When Chief Prosecutor Del Ponte called for "new partnerships for justice," what realistically were the choices? In this latter stage, can the ICTY's indictments be turned over to the national courts? Will the region's domestic judiciaries step up to the plate and extricate themselves from the surrounding fractious politics?

So far, the picture is not promising.[57] The very few trials held in the region reflect pervasive ethnic bias. In all of Republica Srpska, to date, there has only been one war crimes prosecution involving a Bosnian Serb.[58] The local judiciary seems so far to be unable to run fair trials without assistance. Were international assistance to be given, it could proceed along the distinct relation of the international to the national that characterizes Phase III of global transitional justice. Along the lines of the "complementarity" continuum, ultimately international law may well have a lesser role than a full tribunal, but would nevertheless contribute a measure of legality by integrating the international into the local, either institutionally or, alternatively, through adding select personnel or embedding itself in local law. Yet, the legitimacy of this sort of legal nexus would depend on the recognition by the locals of the potential of such institutions and processes to advance the rule of law.

Contemporary political leaders' trials may well offer lessons on a number of issues, ranging from the problem of proof, to the way that the substance of the charges risk the trial's politicization. Accordingly, the focus of the Iraqi trials' subject matter jurisdiction needs to be upon crimes against humanity, that is, on what Hussein did to his own citizens, because this goes to the heart of the illegitimacy of the prior regime and, therefore, at least in part to the legitimacy of the occupation and the establishment of a successor regime. Even limiting jurisdiction to the relatively undisputed crimes against humanity charges, especially those concerning the Kurdish minority, while it would serve the purpose of inclusion at this delicate moment in the country's political transition, is likely to raise broader issues in the region.[59] In his defense, perhaps absorbing the lessons of the Milošević trial, Saddam may well challenge the United States with "tu quoque" defenses on the basis of its recent invasion, as well as its broader historic role in the region.[60] This could well risk the trial's potential contribution to establishing the legitimacy of the successor regime. It is clear that the many trade-offs raised by the convening of the trial of Saddam Hussein at this stage of the transition pose profound challenges to the trial's potential for contributing to the country's liberalization and establishing the rule of law.

Consider other aims of prosecuting crimes against humanity and related human rights violations in present global political circumstances. Beyond their role in the transition, they serve not only as a basis to do justice with respect to crimes committed in relation to the war, but also as a form of post-conflict justice, to justify the initiation of war and the basis for military intervention. This conflictive and potentially contradictory dimension of present transitional punishment processes is taken up in the next part.

## Justice at War and for Peace

The trial processes discussed here share a close association with, and relation to, conditions of conflict that raise distinct aims and purposes that are inextricably intermingled with relevant political circumstances. In this regard, these trials' transitional goals transcended their individual parameters and differences. Both trials involve globalized conditions of conflict and distinct circumstances of justice that also shape the trials' purposes. Both trials operated not solely, or even primarily, for retribution but, rather, to effect change, to end conflict and to bring about reconciliation. Yet, to what extent can war-crimes trials help bring about peace and reconciliation? In circumstances of ongoing conflict, can the pursuit and even imposition of justice advance the aims of deterrence, peace, and reconciliation?[61]

Pursuit of a genealogical approach here necessitates inquiry into the form of justice associated with present political conditions, which illustrates the normalization of Phase III transitional justice. Both the Milošević and Hussein trials exemplify instances of trials in the midst of ongoing conflict and trials that were assertedly convened to advance conciliatory purposes. In this regard, both the ICTY and Baghdad reflect an extraordinary and difficult context of exercises of law, in the midst of conflict, for justice and peace.[62] Perhaps, not surprisingly, the trials' aims are often contradictory and involve difficult trade-offs, which makes the message of these trials often ambivalent.

While modeled after Nuremberg, the Hague tribunal was established in distinctive political circumstances. While the post–World War II trials were seen by many as a form of victors' justice, the ICTY, convened in the midst of a bloody conflict, lacked an analogous authority. Its mandate was not merely to shape the meaning of a prevailing peace but, instead, to hold individuals to account for their acts, in an effort to establish and promote peacemaking and reconciliation.

Consider the potential nexus between international criminal justice and peace. The question became to what extent could justice delivered in a courtroom in The Hague, isolated from the conflict on the ground, nevertheless contribute to peace in the region? While the ICTY's central mission was to transform the conflict in the Balkans to one of individual crimes answerable to the rule of law so as to achieve peace and reconciliation in the region, its efforts to accomplish this mission underscored the rule of law's dependence on a supportive matrix that is generally dependent on the vitality of both the international and the national legal systems.

The ICTY's double mission may well have compounded its difficulties as well as obscured the public perception of its success. Since the tribunal was created not merely to dispense justice, but also to achieve reconciliation in the region, these twin aims have become the measure of the effectiveness of the tribunal. Yet, how is the accomplishment of international criminal justice to advance regional peace? While victor's justice sums up a cognizable relationship of law to power that has been formed over centuries of human experience, the transitional institutions in The Hague and Iraq lack the legitimacy that is generally associated with a humanitarian intervention.

From its beginning, the ICTY was vulnerable, owing to the many differences between The Hague and Nuremberg. Unlike Nuremberg, The Hague was convened not after, but during, the conflict, with distinct consequences. Created as a peace-keeping measure by the international community during the conflict, the ICTY lacks the clear authority of victor's justice. As such, the tribunal has lacked full control over the judicial process, whether over the relevant evidence or over the accused, frequently turning to the international community for assistance.

Moreover, since it was established during the conflict, in important ways, the ICTY's aims have been more ambitious than those at Nuremberg. As in the post-war trials, justice was aimed at restoring the rule of law in the region. Yet, having been launched under the Security Council's "Chapter 7" peacemaking powers, the international criminal tribunal's purpose was nothing less than to "bring on peace."[63] If, by this, the aim was deterrence of future violence, the tribunal's success seems tenuous in light of the ongoing massacres.[64]

The ICTY's other purposes transcend the mere cessation of hostilities and involve the aim of societal reconciliation. From its inception, the ICTY pursued an ethno-conscious prosecutorial policy, assertedly to foster reconciliation in the region.[65] It was hoped that the condemnation of ethnic persecution, together with individual accountability, would transcend identity politics and advance a shift toward a more liberal order.

Despite this lofty goal, however, the project of reconciliation remains largely aspirational. Given that the ICTY was established by the Security Council as a "peacemaking" measure,[66] the coincidence of the Milošević indictment with the NATO bombing posed a countervailing symbol of collective attack. When the tribunal declared its intention to indict Bosnian Serb leaders Radovan Karadžić and General Ratko Mladić, these indictments appeared to endanger the delicate balance of peace in the region.

Regrettably, there continues to be massive resistance in the region, even resistance to the mere recognition of past wrongdoings. More than a decade since the

1995 massacre at Srebrenica, the fact of past atrocities has yet to be incorporated in the nation's history. Debate continues to rage over responsibility for war crimes, and many cling to their own sense of suffering and historical exceptionalism. Prime Minister Kostunica's ill-fated attempt in 2001 to set up a truth commission, doomed from the start by allegations of bias, was disbanded a year later without producing a report.[67] The ICTY has exacerbated divisions over the region's relationship to the West, the European Union, and the international community.

Last, in what this chapter characterizes as the ICTY's second stage, the challenge is shifting from the international assumption of jurisdiction associated with an apparent nationalist backlash, discussed *supra* to its relegation and to the devolution of power back to national courts.[68] Moreover, in this latter stage, insofar as there is a perception of either failure or diminished expectations of the ICTY, it has given way to the new international institutions such as the ICC and, thus, a shift to the new generation of tribunals that endeavor to mediate the old national-international dichotomies through the creation of hybrid legal institutions, processes, and jurisdictional principles.[69]

### Can Justice Buy Peace in Iraq?

Turning to Iraq, consider the asserted aims of the trials of Hussein and his henchmen. In the midst of extraordinary insecurity associated with the ongoing conflict raging with the insurgency, to what extent can justice buy peace?[70] Here, some might argue that there is a precedent in the ICTY, convened during the conflict in the Balkans precisely for the purposes of reconciliation and peacemaking. Still, despite the precedent, it remains a tall order for a court to make peace, particularly when, unlike the ICTY, the court was established on the site of ongoing conflict. Indeed, ordinarily the pursuit of justice is thought to be plausibly in tension with peacemaking, which is often understood to involve compromise and closure.

There is a vivid tension in transitional justice's goals in this post-conflict context, for the trial's association with the occupation hints at the goals of not only legitimating the military intervention in Iraq, but also supporting the story of regime change. This mix of purposes means there will be considerable tension over transitional justice from the start and, therefore, raises acute dilemmas over the questions of the appropriate judiciary and processes. Indeed, the first postponement of the trials arguably reflected a shift in goals and a move away from justification of the intervention toward transitional work, such as the delegitimation of the prior regime and legitimation of the present successor regime. If the goal was to restore legitimacy for Iraq, then postponing trials until there was an apt local judiciary in more secure conditions would have been better than risking sending a wrong message about the rule of law in this post-war context.

*Post–Cold War, Post-Conflict Justice*

In its historical post-war context, the main purpose at Nuremberg may well have been the justification of the Allied intervention.[71] Considering the latest developments, however, the contemporary trials raise the question of to what extent there is an assumed linkage between contemporary transitional justice and the legitimacy of war and its initiation currently characterized as "humanitarian intervention."[72]

Perhaps, not surprisingly, with the lifting of the Cold War political impasse, there has been a conspicuous return to various forms of transitional justice, particularly its international variants. Relatedly, moreover, there is a heightened potential for military intervention. At present, forms of transitional justice are being used as bases for the justifications for humanitarian intervention.

Accordingly, the trials of Milošević and Saddam were not merely aimed at restoring peace in their respective regions. There is a vivid, more complex role to these trials that goes to the broader problem of legitimacy and law's relationship to the use of force. Insofar as the trials characterize the implicated offenses as violations of international humanitarian law, to some degree they will be laying the bases for "humanitarian intervention." While these bases clearly existed in Kosovo and Bosnia, the lack of authority pursuant to convened international proceedings regarding Kosovo nevertheless muddied the waters early on insofar as recognizing bases for international legality. Thus, the ambivalent status of the ICTY trials derives from multiple angles: its initial wartime context, its distance from the implicated region, as well as its initiation of the ongoing paradigm shift in international justice. While the shift in the uses of humanitarian law outside of traditional war-crimes trials may well aim at advancing political change, so far, there remains an evident lack of political support for the dimension of humanitarian intervention.[73]

Yet, what is at stake is also a symbol of another internationalist project, raising squarely the profound question of the legitimacy of the imposition of democracy and the rule of law. While analogies are often made to post-war Germany and Japan, these occupations and their trials are distinguishable. Iraq is also distinguishable from the Balkans and Afghanistan because the illegality of the invasion puts additional pressure on post-conflict justice.[74]

The question remains how to achieve some sense of legitimacy in the transition, and from where it ought to derive. What is important here, from a genealogical perspective, is that the transition in Iraq ought not be facilely analogized to the post–World War II period, nor generalized to elsewhere in the Middle East. Moreover, given what we now know about the time line of transitions, it is definitely too soon to call the question.[75]

Even in the concededly enhanced climate for international human rights law, its enforcement still remains ad hoc, reflecting the risk of law's politicization. Thus, adjudicating humanitarian law violations constituted a basis to support the intervention in Kosovo. Similarly, the project of the prosecution of crimes against humanity will likely be used to lay the basis for justifying the military intervention in Iraq. The contemporary relation that international humanitarian law bears to politics, and to the legitimation of the use of force, highlights the profound tensions and contradictions in the present global paradigm shift.

## Conclusion

This chapter set out to review contemporary developments in transitional justice from a genealogical perspective. More particularly, it sought to situate the contemporary trials of Milošević and Hussein within the structure of the arc of transitional justice that began in the mid–twentieth century and culminates in a framing characterized by post–Cold War global politics.

To that end, this chapter discussed the distinct political circumstances of the trials of political leaders Slobodan Milošević and Saddam Hussein, addressing these processes' aims and purposes, while highlighting areas of commonality and difference. In its remaining parts, this chapter identified numerous aims of transitional justice and mapped them out onto a genealogy.

In terms of the relevant aims and purposes of transitional justice discussed here, this chapter compared both processes and discussed the potential for the role of criminal justice in spurring normative regime change. In particular, it analyzed the current emphasis on crimes against humanity as the subject matter that best expresses violations of human rights that go the heart of state repression and abrogation of the rule of law. These developments are seen in tandem with the effects of political and legal globalization identified in the modern developments in centralization and decentralization of sovereignty and jurisdiction. These ramifications are evident in the current treatment of crimes against humanity, and the related efforts toward expansion of the principle of universality.

Last, this article discussed the relationship of transitional justice to conflict, suggesting that this relationship has been altered and jeopardized by the complex expanded role of the contemporary international humanitarian law regime. The instant trials reflect the potential for conflicting aims in transitional and post-conflict justice. As the trend toward juridicization continues apace, contemporary adjudications of international humanitarian rights violations serve as both a basis of, and a constraint upon, humanitarian intervention. From a genealogical perspective, the current trials of Milošević and Hussein appear more and more within a paradigm of post-conflict justice.

## Notes

1. RUTI TEITEL, TRANSITIONAL JUSTICE 3 (2000).
2. Ruti Teitel, *Transitional Justice Genealogy*, 16 HARV. HUM. RTS. J. 69, 69 (2003).
3. TEITEL, *supra* note 1.
4. *See generally* HUMAN RIGHTS IN TRANSITION: GETTYSBURG TO BOSNIA (Carla Hesse & Robert Post ed., 1999) (discussing reconciliation in Balkans); JAMES L. GIBSON, OVERCOMING APARTHEID: CAN TRUTH RECONCILE A DIVIDED NATION? (2004) (discussing reconciliation in South Africa).
5. *See infra* text accompanying notes 44–60.
6. *See infra* text accompanying notes 22–38.
7. *See* Teitel, *supra* note 2, at 74.
8. Compare the Nuremberg Charter with other contemporary charters, such as those of the ICTY and other creatures of the U.N. bodies, either the Security Council, in the case of ad hoc tribunals, or the General Assembly, in the case of the International Criminal Court. *See* Charter of the International Military Tribunal, Aug. 8, 1945, 82 U.N.T.S. 280 [hereinafter the Nuremberg Charter]; Statute of the International Criminal Tribunal for the former Yugoslavia, May 25, 1993, 32 I.L.M. 1192, *available at* http://www.un. org/icty/basic/statut/statute.htm [hereinafter the ICTY Statute]; Rome Statute of the International Criminal Court, July 17, 1998, 2187 U.N.T.S. 90, *available at* http://www.un. org/law/icc/statute/romefra.htm [hereinafter the Rome Statute].
9. Milošević first appeared before the ICTY on July 3, 2001. Prosecutor v. Milošević, Case No. IT-02-54, Initial Appearance (July 3, 2001).
10. *See* Report of the Security Council Mission Established Pursuant to Resolution 819 (1993), U.N. SCOR, 48th Sess., U.N. Doc. S/25700 (Apr. 30, 1993).
11. *See* Press Release, Human Rights Watch, Bosnia: Arrest of Srebrenica Indictee Hailed, Karadžić, Mladić Still At Large (Apr. 17, 2001), *available at* http://hrw.org/english/docs/2001/04/17/bosher171.htm. [Since the initial publication of this essay, both Radovan Karadžić and Ratko Mladić have been indicted on charges of genocide and crimes against humanity and are presently on trial in two separate criminal proceedings before the ICTY.]
12. *See* Press Release, U.S. Dept. of State, Minikes: US Supports Completion Strategy for War Crimes Tribunals, Says ICTY Plays Important Role in Moving Balkans Towards Euro-Atlantic Integration (Nov. 5, 2003), http://usinfo.state.gov/dhr/Archive/2003/Nov/06-767701.html.
13. Though there was a substantive debate over what ought to be the site of the trial, *see infra* text accompanying note 70.
14. *See* Michael P. Scharf, *Can This Man Get a Fair Trial?*, WASH. POST, Dec. 19, 2004, at B1.
15. *See generally* LARRY DIAMOND, SQUANDERED VICTORY: THE AMERICAN OCCUPATION AND THE BUNGLED EFFORT TO BRING DEMOCRACY TO IRAQ (2005).
16. *See* Peter Slevin & Rajiv Chandrasekaran, *Iraq's Baath Party Is Abolished; Franks Declares End of Hussein's Apparatus as Some Members Retake Posts*, WASH. POST, May 12, 2003, at A10 (noting that de-baathification was a goal of U.S. authorities during the occupation period).

17. *See* Bradley Graham & Peter Baker, *Deadline for Troop Withdrawal Ruled Out*, WASH. POST, Jan. 30, 2005, at A1.

18. *See* Peter Landesman, *Who v. Saddam?*, N.Y. TIMES MAG., July 11, 2004, at 34.

19. *See* Ken Roth, *War in Iraq: Not a Humanitarian Intervention, in* HUMAN RIGHTS WATCH WORLD REPORT 2004, at 13, *available at* http://hrw.org/wr2k4/download/wr 2k4.pdf.

20. *See* John F. Burns, *Hussein Tribunal Shaken by Chalabi's Bid to Replace Staff*, N.Y. TIMES, July 20, 2005, at A9.

21. Roth, *supra* note 19.

22. *See* Ruti Teitel, *Operation Iraqi Freedom: Just or Unjust War? Humanitarian Action, or Simply Geopolitics?*, FINDLAW, Apr. 8, 2003, http://writ.news.findlaw.com/commentary/20030408teitel.html; *Iraq Self-Rule*, ONLINE NEWSHOUR, Nov. 13, 2003, http://www.pbs.org/newshour/bb/middle_east/july-dec03/iraq_11-13.html.

23. *See* Warren Hoge, *U.S. and U.N. Are Once Again the Odd Couple Over Iraq*, N.Y. TIMES, Nov. 14, 2004, at A15.

24. *See* Bogdan Ivanisevic, *Softly-Softly Approach on War Crimes Doesn't Help Democracy in Serbia*, HUMAN RIGHTS WATCH COMMENTARY, http://hrw.org/english/docs/2004/06/25/serbia8966.htm (last visited July 30, 2005).

25. *See* Nicholas Wood, *Video of Serbs in Srebrenica Massacre Leads to Arrests*, N.Y. TIMES, June 3, 2005, at A3.

26. *See generally* JUDITH N. SHKLAR, LEGALISM: LAW, MORALS, AND POLITICAL TRIALS (1964).

27. *Id.* at 156. For Hannah Arendt, the international component was important for its symbolism.

28. *See* JEFFREY OLICK, IN THE HOUSE OF THE HANGMAN: THE AGONIES OF GERMAN DEFEAT, 1943–1949 (2005).

29. SHKLAR, *supra* note 26.

30. For discussion of international law's potential for contribution to rule-of-law values, see TEITEL, *supra* note 1, at 20–21.

31. At the time of this writing, the proceedings are into their fourth year.

32. Ian Traynor, *Milošević Trial Falters After Judge Retires*, THE GUARDIAN (London), Feb. 24, 2004, at 17.

33. His defense also relied on frequent claims to illness, also building the victim role. See *Id.*

34. *See* Statute of the Iraqi Special Tribunal, Dec. 10, 2003, 43 I.L.M. 231, *available at* http://iraq-ist.org/en/about/statute.htm [hereinafter The IST Statute].

35. William Langewiesche, *Ziad for the Defense*, 295 THE ATLANTIC MONTHLY 65 (2005), *available at* http://www.theatlantic.com/doc/prem/200506/langewiesche.

36. *See* Anthony Dworkin, *Saddam Hussein and Iraq's War Crimes Tribunal*, CRIMES OF WAR PROJECT, Dec. 21, 2003, http://www.crimesofwar.org/onnews/news-saddam1.html.

37. *Id.* at 8–9.

38. For instances of hybrid trials and discussion of their advantages in advancing transitional rule of law, see Statute of the Special Court for Sierra Leone, *available at* http://www.icrc.org/ihl/INTRO/605?OpenDocument; *see also* Jack Snyder & Leslie Vinjamuri, *Trials and Errors: Principle and Pragmatism in Strategies of International Justice*, 28 INT'L SEC. 5, 20–30 (2003).

39. For discussion of the potential of diverse judicial legal systems for their connection to the advancement of the establishment of the rule of law, see Paul Kahn, *Independence and*

*Responsibility in the Judicial Role, in* Transition to Democracy in Latin America: The Role of the Judiciary 73–87 (Irwin P. Stotzky ed., 1993).

40. On monist and dualist systems, see J.H.H. Weiler, *The Transformation of Europe*, 100 Yale L. J. 2403, 2413–15 (1991); *see also* Curtis A. Bradley, *Breard, Our Dualist Constitution, and the Internationalist Conception*, 51 Stan. L. Rev. 529, 530–31 (1999).

41. For a bibliography of war crimes trials, see War Crimes, War Criminals, and War Crimes Trials: An Annotated Bibliography and Source Book (Norman E. Tuterow ed., 1986).

42. *See* Telford Taylor, The Anatomy of the Nuremberg Trials: A Personal Memoir 583 (1992).

43. The arrest, surrender and trial of Slobodan Milsoevic will remain a defining moment in the evolution of global international justice. The four-year trial, which began in February 2002, came to an abrupt end after Milošević's death in March 2006. Although Milošević's death deprived the ICTY of the opportunity to render a verdict, the legacy of this trial has helped to shape future trial proceedings. *See* Hum. Rts. Watch, Weighing the Evidence: Lessons from the Slobodan Milošević Trial (2006), http://www.hrw.org/node/11081/section/2.

44. *See, e.g.*, ICTY Statute, *supra* note 8, art. 9.

45. Rome Statute, *supra* note 8, art. I.

46. *See id.* pt. 2 ("Jurisdiction, Admissibility and Applicable Law").

47. *Id.* art. I.

48. Ruti Teitel, *Humanity's Law: Rule of Law for the New Global Politics*, 35 Cornell Int'l L.J. 355, 370–73 (2002).

49. Shklar, *supra* note 26, at 155.

50. Hannah Arendt, Eichmann in Jerusalem: A Report on the Banality of Evil 258 (1994).

51. For the first positive definition of crimes against humanity, see Nuremberg Charter, *supra* note 8, art. 6(c); ICTY Statute, *supra* note 8, art. 5; Rome Statute, *supra* note 8, art. 7.

52. *See* David Luban, *A Theory of Crimes Against Humanity*, 29 Yale J. Int'l L. 85, 124–31 (2004) (contending for the nexus between the offense against humanity and universal jurisdiction); *see also* Stefaan Smis & Kim Van der Borght, *Belgium: Act Concerning the Punishment of Grave Breaches of International Humanitarian Law*, 38 Int'l Leg. Mat. 918 (1999).

53. *See* Arendt, *supra* note 50, at 269 (arguing for an international tribunal to adjudicate crimes against humanity).

54. *See* Rome Statute, *supra* note 8.

55. For a critique of the view that punishment in the ICTR will advance transitional aims, see generally Jose Alvarez, *Crimes of States/Crimes of Hate: Lessons from Rwanda*, 24 Yale J. Int'l Law 365 (1999).

56. Shklar, *supra* note 26, at 169.

57. It is important to note that this situation has evolved since original publication.

58. Human Rights Watch, *Justice at Risk: War Crimes Trials in Croatia, Bosnia and Herzegovina, and Serbia and Montenegro*, 16 Human Rights Watch Report No. 7(D), 9 (2004), *available at* http://hrw.org/reports/2004/icty1004/icty1004.pdf.

59. *See* Human Rights Watch, Whatever Happened to the Iraqi Kurds? (1991), http://www.hrw.org/reports/1991/IRAQ913.htm.

60. *Tu quoque*, or the "dirty hands" strategy, has been used regularly by the defense in post-conflict trials to characterize the trials as politically motivated. Among others, Jacque Verges used this strategy against France in the trial of Nazi Chief in Lyons Klaus Barbie. *See* Richard Bernstein, *Spirits Haunting a Belated Courtroom Reckoning*, N.Y. TIMES, May 18, 1987, at A4; and Guyora Binder, *Representing Nazism: Advocacy and Identity at the Trial of Klaus Barbie*, 98 YALE L.J. 1321, 1357–58 (1989).

61. More and more, transitional criminal justice is said to be not in tension with reconciliation aims but, instead, itself a means toward reconciliation. *See* KADER ASMAL, LOUISE ASMAL & RONALD SURESH ROBERTS, RECONCILIATION THROUGH TRUTH: A RECKONING OF APARTHEID'S CRIMINAL GOVERNANCE (1996). For critical analysis, see Ruti Teitel, *Bringing the Messiah Through the Law, in* HUMAN RIGHTS IN POLITICAL TRANSITIONS: GETTYSBURG TO BOSNIA, *supra* note 4, at 177; Fionnuala Ni Aolain & Colm Campbell, *The Paradox of Transition in Conflicted Democracies*, 27 HUM. RTS. Q. 172 (2005).

62. The ICTY was established during the Balkans conflict but was geographically detached from the site of conflict, while Nuremberg, a post-conflict creation, was established in the state of the site of conflict. Finally, the IST began functioning in a situation of great insecurity, created on site in the midst of continuing insurgency. *See* David Scheffer, *Saddam Trial Is a Critical Test for Iraq's Future*, FIN. TIMES, Aug. 12, 2005, at 17.

63. *See* U.N. Charter ch. VII; S.C. Res. 808, U.N. Doc. S/RES/808 (Feb. 22, 1993).

64. An example is the Srebrenica massacre occurring at this time. For discussion, see Teitel, *supra* note 4.

65. *See* Richard Goldstone, *Assessing the Work of the United Nations War Crimes Tribunal*, 33 STAN. J. INT'L L. 1, 7 (1997) (stressing the importance of prosecuting war criminals).

66. U.N. Charter ch. VII.

67. *See* Laura Secor, *Belgrade Spring*, BOSTON GLOBE, June 22, 2003, at D1.

68. Regarding the backlash, see Snyder & Vinjamuri, *supra* note 38, at 21. On the backlash in Croatia, see Victor Peskin & Mieczylslaw Boduszynski, *International Justice and Domestic Politics: Post-Tudjman Croatia and the International Criminal Tribunal for the former Yugoslavia*, 55 EUR.-ASIA STUD. 1117 (2003).

69. *See* Project on International Courts and Tribunals, Hybrid Courts, http://www. pict-pcti. org/courts/hybrid.html (last visited Oct. 11, 2005).

70. *See* Robert F. Worth, *The Conflict in Iraq: Insurgency, 23 Are Killed in a Series of Attacks Across Iraq*, N.Y. TIMES, Mar. 26, 2005, at A5 (reporting continuing attacks and casualties in Iraq).

71. *See* TAYLOR, *supra* note 42, at 575–81 (discussing the primacy of the charge of "aggression" in the Nuremberg Charter).

72. *See* Robert Meister, *Human Rights and the Politics of Victimhood*, 16 ETHICS & INT'L AFF. 91 (2002); SIMON CHESTERMAN, JUST WAR OR JUST PEACE?: HUMANITARIAN INTERVENTION AND INTERNATIONAL LAW 35–44 (2003).

73. However, the process of millennial U.N. reform addresses this proposed change to some extent. *See* The Secretary General, *In Larger Freedom: Towards Development, Security and Human Rights For All*, delivered to the General Assembly, U.N. Doc. A/59/2005 (Mar. 21, 2005).

74. *See* Jose Alvarez, *Hegemonic International Law Revisited*, 97 AM. J. INT'L L. 873 (2003).

75. In my book, I proposed that this was the "paradox of the passage of time" of how our ordinary intuitions are not borne out. TEITEL, *supra* note 1, at 62. My observation has been proven more and more true with the many subsequent trials in Latin America and elsewhere. See Larry Rohter, *After Decades, Nations Focus on Rights Abuses*, N.Y. TIMES, Sept. 1, 2005, at A4.

*This chapter was originally a contribution to a symposium celebrating the 25th anniversary of Michael Walzer's* Just and Unjust Wars, *held at NYU Law School the year Walzer was in residence at NYU as a Strauss and Tikvah fellow. I have long found Walzer's writing illuminating on the moral dilemmas surrounding political violence. Taking Michael Walzer's and Larry May's reflections on* jus post bellum *as a point of departure, I explore here some of the limits of what might be called the inherited notion of* jus post bellum. *I then articulate a broader perspective for* jus post bellum, *influenced by thinking on transitional justice. I argue that, given the nature of modern warfare and the evident shift to wars of humanitarian intervention, the contemporary understanding is no longer limited to restorative ex post justice, but should also include forward-looking aims, and for this purpose the discourse of transitional justice is better-suited.*

# 8 Rethinking *Jus Post Bellum* in an Age of Global Transitional Justice

## ENGAGING WITH MICHAEL WALZER AND LARRY MAY

LARRY MAY INVOKES Michael Walzer's *Just and Unjust Wars: A Moral Argument* to articulate a conception of justice at the end of war that is appropriate to our situation. Taking Walzer's and May's observations on these issues as a point of departure, I will here explore some of the limits of what might be called the inherited notion of *jus post bellum*. I will then articulate a broader perspective for *jus post bellum*,

influenced by thinking on transitional justice. This perspective, like transitional justice itself, is both backward- and forward-looking. By contrast, the inherited notion
of *jus post bellum* tends to view conflict as the interruption of a putatively just or
stable status quo ante, which is to be restored to the fullest extent possible.[1] Given
the nature of modern warfare and the evident shift to wars of liberal intervention,
the contemporary understanding is no longer limited to restorative ex post justice,
but must also include forward-looking aims, and for this purpose the discourse of
transitional justice is better- suited.

Wars are being waged within a highly developed set of constraints under human
rights and international humanitarian law, as well as expectations of democratization. There is thus an extraordinarily high demand for *post bellum* justice, while the
guiding principles and values for such remain controversial.

May observes that, in relation to the larger law of war, the issue of *jus post bellum*
is undertheorized. He notes that "Walzer seems to subsume *jus post bellum* considerations under *jus ad bellum*."[2] Of course, this is, in and of itself, a significant normative statement about the meaning of *jus post bellum*: i.e., that there are limited
post-war norms and, moreover, that these norms are most crucially connected to
the principles which guide the initiation of war. Accordingly, the focus in the *post
bellum* phase here is in response to aggressive war. The just aftermath is one that
imposes constraints following such wars.

May draws from Walzer's articulation of the just-war tradition the guiding principle that there ought to be a thoroughgoing proportionality regarding *jus post bellum*.
Moreover, he reasons that such a calculus might well lead to "contingent pacifism."[3]
The application of the principle of proportionality, he argues, should move us in the
direction of trying to avoid war altogether—a utopian direction.

On the 35th anniversary of Michael Walzer's *Just and Unjust Wars*, there is a
growing appreciation of the potential importance of the area of the law of war
that is known as *jus post bellum*. Yet the relationship of law to conflict today is a
complex one, and contemporary circumstances hardly reflect May's utopianism.
Rather, one might perhaps see the current legal panorama as constituting a new
view of peace—in the just-war analysis—namely, one that moves away from that
associated with inter-state conflict toward a calculus that reconceives a just peace
in terms of *human* security, with implications for a transformed understanding of the meaning and role of justice during such periods. I have discussed this
framework at greater length elsewhere.[4] Below, I outline some of the changes in
*post bellum* expectations and the ways in which these are best captured by a more
comprehensive concept and vocabulary associated with these periods of political
flux: transitional justice.

## Just and Unjust Wars, Half-a-Century On

To begin, post-conflict justice is, as Walzer himself would admit, hardly a central theme in *Just and Unjust Wars*. Insofar as he addresses *jus post bellum* at all, it is through the problem of "settlements," as well as the question of responsibility, where he brings to bear other strands of the just-war tradition, particularly those norms concerning the justification of war at the outset (*jus ad bellum*). As Walzer subsequently observed in his most recent book, *Arguing about War*, written after the war in Iraq, *jus post bellum* was not a central concern until after World War II, nor even more recently, with decolonization and later transitions.

What is owed to the people of Iraq, or to other peoples who are the "beneficiaries" of wars of supposed liberation?[5] This is the burning question of the last decade in Iraq, Afghanistan, and most recently Libya. Where a war is justified on humanitarian grounds, i.e., a *just* war, what are the implications of this justice in the *ad bellum* for *jus post bellum*? One might well pose the question: What is the relationship of *jus post bellum* to *jus ad bellum*? On the other hand, might the injustice of a war's beginning imply greater post-war duties? Or does the logic work the other way around? In the event that a war is initiated for humanitarian reasons, might that well imply added duties, whether during or after the conflict?[6] Just how does post-war justice relate to the broader questions concerning the meaning and direction of the justice of war? To what extent does the contemporary iteration of the just-war tradition, its principles and values, help to guide us in answering the question of what must be done following a conflict? In his post-Iraq book, which elaborates upon the just-war tradition in light of more recent wars, Walzer poses the problem of "aftermaths," in particular those following an unjust war. In his words, "[j]ust how is postwar justice related to the just war tradition," i.e., the justice of the war itself and the conduct of its battles?[7]

## Getting Beyond the Restoration of the Status Quo Ante

With the end of the Cold War, we have seen a return to wars of intervention, with implications for the scope and character of *jus post bellum*. There is a need to rethink the earlier classical approach to post-war justice as being fundamentally restorative. Posing the question today of what values and related principles regarding rights and duties should apply *post bellum* inevitably constitutes a departure from a focus on restoration (which takes, implicitly or explicitly, the pre-war status quo as a decisive normative benchmark). Historically, this area was dominated by a preoccupation with unjust wars and the settlements that followed them, focusing on restraining or regulating the punishment of the aggressor for disrupting the status quo ante.

In this context, victors were free to punish, within determined constraints—limits on collective punishment, spoils of war, plunder, return of prisoners of war, occupied territory, etc. This was often complemented by amnesties and reparation schemes that were animated by restorative objectives. The post–World War I settlement at Versailles was widely regarded as an instance of failed justice and, even worse, as having the effect of promoting the return of war.[8]

For Walzer, even enemy nations that are guilty of aggression have a right to their continued existence.[9] Building on Walzer,[10] May offers proportionality as a "meta-norm."[11] One could conceive this view of *post bellum* in historical or retrospective terms—where what is at stake is responsibility in a backward-looking way, as guided by the justice of the war's purpose itself and the goal of returning to the *pre bellum* or status quo ante.

Now, however, we can see that we are moving away from this traditional approach to *jus post bellum* in a number of ways: First, there is a move away from the dominant concern of *jus post bellum* conceived as a backward-looking enterprise, and as restraint, and toward a broader framework involving a host of duties that relate not just to the past, but also to an often-protracted present, as well as forward-looking goals for a peaceful future. The aegis or subject of *post bellum* norms has become greatly expanded.

Many questions today concerning what obligations attend aftermaths are being raised in the context of transition, sometimes following conflict, but just as often not. For a number of reasons, this view increasingly overlaps with conflict. At a time of persistent smaller conflicts, i.e., of pervasive violence, often of ongoing internal conflicts where there is no clear end,[12] and which are not even clearly about state-building or democratization, this inquiry leads to a questioning of the meaning of "*post bellum*" in *jus post bellum*. As May concedes, the parameters of *post bellum* have become murky.[13]

Along similar lines, there has been a shift in our understanding of responsibility away from the view that holds the state-centric view as the singularly relevant subject of *jus post bellum,* as the older view of restoration assumed the state to be the relevant object of restoration. At the same time, there has been a move away from collective sanctions being levied upon a state or its people. Individualized punishment is clearly on the rise, most dramatically through international criminal justice.[14]

## Toward an Alternative Paradigm: What Normative Framework Should Apply?

In the current context, justice considerations enter the picture from the outset; consider, for example that humanitarian considerations have been invoked as a justification for war itself. In today's wars of liberation, internal ethnic conflicts are often involved; the issue is as much or more to do with settling scores with fellow citizens as it is about punishing a foreign aggressor. Clearly, this situation brings transitional justice to the fore.

Insofar as the new wars are often conflicts that are animated by the values of liberalization, freedom, and so on, we can see ways in which the aegis of *jus post bellum* overlaps with the aims of transitional justice. Justice is not conceived as strictly punishment-oriented, as assumed in the legalist paradigm. Nor is it confined to restitution and the restorative dimension that was implied by the earlier understanding of post-war justice. Indeed, it could well take in the full context and modalities of transition and transformation. The issue is being reconceived now in terms of justice as security. Within the evolving framework, there is a concern focused on identifying responsibility beyond the state, and to private actors as well. There are duties that follow even when a war is just.

Thus, "*post bellum*" seems too limited or inappropriate today because of the unstable or undetermined boundaries between conflict and post-conflict situations.[15] Transitional justice is arguably more capacious a concept, because it allows for purposes beyond those associated with a war's beginning, such as transformation: purposes going beyond retributive or restorative justice.

Rethinking the regulation of conflict in contemporary circumstances entails the challenge of integrating and recalibrating the norms that were traditionally shaped by their strict association or correlation with a defined point in the course of the conflict—*ad bellum, in bello, post bellum*. Today, however, we see that international humanitarian law or *jus in bello* applies during armed conflict and beyond. At least one tribunal has declared that it extends beyond this point.[16] While *jus ad bellum* was generally understood to relate to the beginning of conflict, and therefore to guide questions of the legitimacy of the use of force in international law, today we can see that the traditional inquiry regarding aggression has given way to a broader inquiry regarding the treatment of civilians, human security, etc. Moreover, the question of *jus ad bellum*—whether a war is unjust or just—evidently has ramifications for the duties of justice in the aftermath.

With the complexity of the new phenomena, we observe that multiple legal orders are applicable in guiding the law of war, including *post bellum* and *in bello*, i.e., international humanitarian law, as well as occupation law and human-rights law. This implies specific requirements associated with each of these areas, for instance, *jus in bello*, or the norms regarding the treatment of prisoners and other noncombatants set out in the Geneva Conventions. Occupation law, too, is generally the guiding principle for the protection of the status quo in occupied territories.[17] Last, human-rights law, while generally associated with the guarantees that a state gives its citizens in peacetime, also now applies in situations of conflict, along with the law of war.[18] Other specific guarantees, in certain situations, may be in tension with one another.[19] To what extent are there broader guiding values?

For Walzer, "[d]emocratic political theory…provides the central principles of the account."[20] Yet one is inclined to suggest that the values ultimately underpinning Walzer's proposal are broader, namely those of human protection and security. He thus elaborates, "What determines the overall justice of a military occupation is less its planning or its length than its political direction and the distribution of the benefits it provides."[21] The question then becomes: To what extent are people's lives improved? Consider, in this regard, the significance of various measures such as de-baathification (in Iraq), and the equal treatment of various groups, which involve commitments beyond pure or simple democracy.

I employed the term "transitional justice" in 1991 to represent a move away from the discourse that associated such phenomena purely with the law of conflict.[22] The idea was that the aims of such processes were in part forward-looking—involving democratization—and not backward-looking and associated with war. Moreover, the use of the term "transitional justice" also addressed the central issue of the time: the extent to which the relevant democratization processes seemed less revolutionary and more gradual, more *transitional* than in the past, often taking decades, for example in post-Dirty War Latin America. We now have a rich set of illustrations from the post-Soviet bloc, Asia, and the Middle East.

## The Peace Versus Justice Debate

By contrast, it is in the dynamic contemporary context that questions regarding conflict-related justice are being confronted today; namely, questions arising from situations in which conflict has not completely ceased and where there are multiple actors and aims. Let us return now to May's proposal that the *post bellum* context be guided by the principle of proportionality.[23] What does it mean to apply the principle of proportionality in *jus post bellum*? Today, this question has gained traction. Applying the proportionality principle requires thinking through the likely effects of *jus post bellum* strategies in periods of substantial flux. What is the likely impact of criminal justice on the consolidation of human-rights protection in a given society? The first rule is that it should do no harm: "[w]hatever is required by the application of other *jus post bellum* principles must not impose more harm on the peoples of the world than is alleviated by the application of these principles."[24]

The respective roles of trials and amnesties in the transition from war to peace have been examined by political scientists within an instrumentalist framework that understands proportionality in terms of trade-offs. For Jack Snyder and Leslie Vinjamuri,[25] the inquiry regarding proportionality is essentially about the extent to which justice advances or undermines peace, where the critical variable or objective is peace, marshalling for the primacy of peace considerations over justice.[26] Some analysts are simply skeptical about criminal trials, and see them as threatening the objective of peace, while Leigh Payne, based on an empirical study of transitional-justice outcomes in a wide range of situations, views a mix or balance of trials, truth commissions, and amnesties as more likely to produce outcomes that are supportive of the rule of law and of peaceful democratic transition.[27]

## Jus Post Bellum as Transitional Justice

The increasingly pervasive involvement of courts and tribunals in matters of post-conflict justice demands a conception of proportionality that is not simply political but also jurisprudential. This conception is far from being limited to criminal trials. One also thinks of Alien Torts Claims actions in the United States, and the roles of the Inter-American Court of Human Rights and the European Court of Human Rights in post-conflict accountability. Justice has gone from a prerogative of the victor, which needs restraining, to a shared international obligation. This development, in and of itself, informs the meaning of the new proportionality.

The constitutive instruments of the ad hoc criminal tribunals and the International Criminal Court reflect this change. Their preambles assert that their purpose includes guarding the peace. Meanwhile, they also function in a more traditional way, offering constraints on victors' justice—because the many rules as to the scope and jurisdiction of tribunals and offenses are fixed—thereby defining the very parameters of the offense. Through these tribunals, we have moved away from traditional post-war judgments which were expressly disconnected from the end of war, and away from the focus on the accountability of any one state, i.e., the victor. This was made very clear by the International Criminal Tribunal for the former Yugoslavia, as it was established during wartime and contemplated the prosecution of actors on all sides of the conflict, with even-handedness with respect to nationality and ethnicity.[28] This move depoliticizes and entrenches a timeless approach to *jus post bellum.* The response is punitive, but the punishment is individualized, not collective. This is the fundamental challenge of *jus post bellum* as criminal justice: How can individualized punishment address the systematic wrongs of war that is waged between collectivities?

Increasingly, the normative regime pertaining to war is also peace-related. It has become heavily regulated by a new area of law—international criminal law—and institutionalized via the new tribunals. The ad hoc criminal tribunals, beginning with the ICTY, were instituted to "maintain or restore international peace and security,"[29] i.e., to manage war. The tribunals were intended to operate—and did operate—during the course of the conflict, but with a view to facilitating its end. Here, the controversy is not about victor's justice, but rather about justice being imposed by the "international community" upon the region. The approach of the tribunals, reflected in the purposes stated in their constitutive instruments, suggests that there are no tragic choices or trade-offs between peace and justice, but only positive synergies. There is thus clearly a tension between this legal project of international criminal accountability and the perspective of pragmatic peace-building in the work of the political scientists discussed above.

## Conclusion

There is a new relationship between the three strands of the law of war. The justification for war, especially where humanitarian justice considerations are prominent, sets the stage for higher expectations of humanitarianism, both in relation to how war is waged and in the responsibilities of the victors post-conflict. If one understands humanitarianism in terms of the demand or aspiration for human security, then there is indeed a potential to evolve a notion of proportionality that navigates, so to speak, between the legalist and pragmatist perspectives. Going to war for the purposes of countering or preventing violations of humanitarian norms is normatively incoherent from both of these perspectives if the ultimate result is a reduction, rather than an increase, in human security, either because of the inherent impossibility of achieving the humanitarian goals through methods that themselves are adequately respectful of humanitarian norms, or because of the exorbitant costs of establishing human security in the post-conflict environment (for instance, in Iraq). This notion of proportionality demands a consonance of purposes, means, and consequences that straddles *jus ad bellum, jus in bello,* and *jus post bellum.*

With renewed demands for military intervention, interest in *post bellum* justice has never been greater. Given the human-rights revolution, interventions are not only justified on human-security grounds, but also waged in the context of new constraints, of human rights and international humanitarian law, as well as expectations of democratization. This goes some way to explaining the extraordinarily high demands for *post bellum* justice, which has now transcended its earlier limits to cover a larger period associated with conflict, and to address the security, not just of states, but of persons and peoples.

## Notes

1. See M. Walzer, *Just and Unjust Wars: A Moral Argument with Historical Illustrations* (4th edn, 2006); and Bass, '*Jus Post Bellum*', 32 *Philosophy & Public Affairs* (2004) 384.
2. May, '*Jus Post Bellum* Proportionality and the Fog of War', in this issue, at 315.
3. L. May, *After War Ends: A Philosophical Perspective* (2012), at 219 ff.
4. See R. Teitel, *Humanity's Law* (2011).
5. See N. Feldman, *What We Owe Iraq: War and the Ethics of Nation Building* (2004).
6. See Teitel, 'The Wages of Just War', 39 *Cornell Int'l LJ* (2006) 689.
7. M. Walzer, *Arguing About War* (2004), at 164.
8. N. Ferguson, *The Pity of War: Explaining World War I* (1995).
9. See Walzer, *supra* note 1, at 123.
10. See Walzer, *supra* note 1, at 119–20.
11. See May, *supra* note 3, at 6.
12. On the new wars, see M. Kaldor, *New and Old Wars: Organized Violence in a Global Era* (2nd edn, 2007).
13. See May, *supra* note 3, at 2–3.
14. See *Prosecutor v. Tadić*, Case No. IT-94-1-T, Opinion and Judgment (ICTY, 7 May 1997). The recent ICJ rulings in *Bosnia v. Serbia* and *Jurisdictional Immunities of the State (Germany v. Italy, Greece intervening)* Judgment, 3 Feb. 2012, available at: www.icj-cij.org/docket/files/143/16883.pdf can be viewed as setting or reinforcing limits to post-war collective guilt or responsibility.
15. See U.N. Development Programme, *World Development Report 2011: Conflict, Security, and Development*, at 2–8 (discussing the 'challenge of repeated cycles of violence'). See I. Rangelov and M. Theros, *Field Notes from Afghanistan: Perceptions of Insecurity and Conflict Dynamics*, LSE Global Governance, Working Paper No. WP 01/2010, Apr. 2010.
16. See *Prosecutor v. Tadić*, Case No. IT-94-1-I, Decision on Defence Motion for Interlocutory Appeal on Jurisdiction, at para. 69 (ICTY, 2 Oct. 1995).
17. See Ben-Naftali, Gross, and Michaeli, 'Illegal Occupation: Framing the Occupied Palestinian Territory', 23 Berkeley J. Int'l L. (2005) 551.
18. See App. No. 57950/00, *Isayeva v. Russia*, 41 ECHR (2005) 38.
19. *Ibid.* (discussing the tensions involved in applying human-rights law in occupied territories).
20. See Walzer, *supra* note 7, at 164.
21. *Ibid.*, at 165.
22. See David Luban, Review of Jon Elster, "Closing the Books: Transitional Justice in Historical Perspective", 116 *Ethics* (2006) 409; and R. Teitel, *Transitional Justice* (2000).
23. May, *supra* note 2, at 324–25.

24. See May, *supra* note 3, at 14.

25. See Snyder and Vinjamuri, "Trials and Errors: Principle and Pragmatism in Strategies of International Justice", 28 *International Security* (2003).

26. *Ibid.*

27. T.D. Olsen, L.A. Payne and A.G. Reiter, *Transitional Justice in Balance: Comparing Processes, Weighing Efficacy* (2010).

28. See ICTY, Office of the Prosecutor, press release, 25 July 1995, at 3; see also 'Statement by Justice Richard Goldstone', 24 Apr. 1995.

29. See Statute of the ICTY.

*To what extent does transitional justice offer an extraordinary jurisprudence of change when it comes to the established rule of law? Where should the conceptualization of this phenomenon situate itself vis-a-vis the ordinary rule of law?*

*Beginning with debates stemming from the Eastern European transitions, this chapter explores these questions. I recall the beginnings of thinking regarding this topic, and it challenges the view of transitional justice as exceptional.*

*Indeed, one recurring question goes to the ways in which the conceptualization of transitional justice might reframe the view of change generally. This is especially true when it comes to critical legal theory.*

*What can the study of transitional justice contribute to our understanding of the rule of law? Nowadays, one can see—with the passage of time and the entrenchment and ratification of many transitional-justice processes—that there is likewise a normalization and the potential closing of the legality gap. This has become even more true today, when there is more law of transitional justice, and more legalization of it.*

# 9    Transitional Rule of Law

## Introduction

Societies throughout much of the world—Latin America, Eastern Europe, the former Soviet Union, Africa—have been engaged in transition: postcolonial changes, and the overthrowing of military dictatorships and totalitarian regimes, for greater freedom and democracy. In these times of massive political movement from illiberal rule, one burning question recurs: How should societies deal with their evil pasts?

What, if any, is the relation between a state's response to its repressive past, and its prospects for creating a liberal order?

For several decades now, the point of departure in the transitional-justice debate is the notion that the move toward a more liberal democratic political system implies a universal norm. Indeed, this methodological question is the subject of a paper by one of the editors of this book.[1] Yet, I suggest that this way of framing the debate is too stark. Instead, my remarks propose an alternative way of thinking about the relation of law to political transformation. Exploring an array of experiences describes a distinctive conception of justice and rule of law in the context of political transformation.

The problem of transitional justice arises within the distinctive context of transition—a shift in political orders, and more precisely, of change in a liberalizing direction. Understanding the problem of justice in the transitional context requires entering a distinctive discourse that is organized in terms of the profound dilemmas that are characteristic of these extraordinary periods. One can see the basic dilemma that arises from justice seeking in the context of political transformation: Law is caught between the past and the future, between the backward-looking and the forward-looking, between the retrospective and the prospective. Transitional justice, therefore, is that justice that is associated with these political circumstances. Transitions imply paradigm shifts in the conception of justice; therefore, law's role appears deeply paradoxical. In ordinary times, we expect law to provide order and stability, but in extraordinary periods of political upheaval, law has to maintain order, even as it enables transformation. Accordingly, in transition, the ordinary intuitions and predicates about law simply do not apply. What this means is further elaborated in the chapter. It does not mean that ideals of rule of law are irrelevant to transitions, but rather that they are inapplicable to these exceptional circumstances without our making a variety of adjustments, both to the context of transition, and to the particulars of that state's political conditions. In dynamic periods of political flux, legal responses generate a sui generis paradigm of transformative law.

What emerges is a conception of justice that is contextualized and partial: It is constituted by, and constitutive of, the transition. The very notion of what is just is contingent, and informed by prior injustice. As a state undergoes political change, legacies of injustice have a bearing on what is deemed transformative.

Indeed, at some level, one might say that the legal responses create transition: In transition, the rule of law is historically and politically contingent, elaborated in response to past political repression that had often been condoned. While the rule of law ordinarily implies prospectivity in the law, transitional rule of law is both backward- and forward-looking, as it disclaims illiberal past values, and reclaims liberal norms.

## Punishment or Impunity

In the prevailing view of transitional justice, the core debate, as it takes as its point of departure ordinary times, frames the relevant question as whether or not to punish the predecessor regime. This is the so-called "punishment or impunity" debate. Punishment often dominates our understandings of transitional justice, and of the rule of law. In the public imagination, transitional justice is generally linked with the trials of ancien regimes. The contemporary wave of transitions from military rule, throughout Latin America and Africa, as well as from communist rule in Central Europe and the former Soviet bloc, has revived the debate over whether to punish. While trials are thought to enable drawing a bright line demarcating the normative shift from illegitimate to legitimate rule, the exercise of the state's punishment power in the circumstances of radical political change raises profound dilemmas. Transitional trials are few and far between, particularly in the contemporary period. The low incidence of successor trials reveals the real dilemmas in dealing with systemic wrongdoing by way of the criminal law. In the transitional context, conventional understandings of individual responsibility are frequently inapplicable, and have spurred the emergence of new legal forms: partial sanctions that fall outside conventional legal categories.

This harshest form of law is emblematic of accountability and the rule of law; yet, its representation far transcends its actual exercise.

## Transitional Rule of Law and the Limited Criminal Sanction

Despite the call for justice in the abstract, transitional practices over the last half-century reveal the recurring problems of justice as a result of the norm shift characterizing transition. These compromised conditions of justice mean that there are real limits on the exercise of the punishment power in periods of political transition. These real rule-of-law dilemmas help explain why, despite the dramatic expansion in criminal liability in the abstract, enforcement lags far behind. Indeed, transitional practices reveal a pattern of criminal investigations and prosecutions, often followed by little or no penalty. While ordinarily punishment is conceptualized as a unitary practice that includes both the establishment of, and the penalizing of wrongdoing, in the transitional criminal sanction, the elements of investigation and condemnation have become somewhat detached from one another. It is this partial criminal process that are conscribed as the "limited sanction" that distinguishes criminal justice in transition.

The "limited criminal sanction," as was taken up in earlier chapters, constitutes compromised prosecution processes that do not necessarily culminate in full punishment, and that imply differentiation of the phases of establishing responsibility, and ascribing a penalty. Depending on just how limited the process may be, investigations may or may not lead to indictments, adjudications, and convictions. Convictions are often followed by little or no punishment. In transition, the criminal sanction may be limited to an investigation establishing wrongdoing.

The limits of the transitional criminal sanction are well-illustrated throughout history: in the post–World War I and World War II cases, in the postmilitary trials of Southern Europe, as well as by the contemporary successor criminal proceedings in Latin America and Africa, and in the wave of political change in Central Europe following the Soviet collapse. Though the story is often repressed, post–World War II successor justice illustrates the limited criminal sanction. In the midst of the Allied Control Council No. 10 follow-up trials, the International Military Tribunal began the reversal of the Allied punishment policy. Between 1946 and 1958, a process of reviews and clemency culminated in the mass commutation of sentences for war criminals. In Germany's national trials, a similar sequence unfolded. Out of the more than one thousand cases tried between 1955 and 1969, fewer than one hundred of those convicted received life sentences, and fewer than three hundred received limited terms. Years later, in Southern Europe, a similar sequence unfolded. Greece's trials of its military police culminated largely in suspended or commutable sentences. A similar pattern appeared in the transitions out of military rule in Latin America. In the 1980s, soon after the Argentine junta trials, began the limits on the follow-up trials. Ultimately, pardons would be extended to everyone convicted of atrocities, even the junta leaders. Amnesties became the norm throughout much of the continent: Chile, Nicaragua, and El Salvador.

The story repeats itself in Central and Eastern Europe after the communist collapse. Ten years after the revolution and the real story is the transitional limited criminal sanction. In unified Germany's "border guards" trials, suspension of sentences is the norm. This was also true of the few prosecutions in the Czech Republic, Romania, Bulgaria, and Albania.

Sometimes, the limiting of the criminal sanction is used strategically, as an incentive to achieve other political goals, such as cooperation in investigations or other political projects; in Chile, a law exempting its military from prosecution was conditioned on officers' cooperation in criminal investigations. In post-apartheid South Africa, penalties were dropped upfront and on the condition of full disclosure, with the amnestying of crimes deemed "political" in the Truth and Reconciliation Commission. This left a window open for investigations into past wrongs, a practice that could also be understood as a limited prosecutorial process.

Other contemporary legal responses, such as the ad hoc International Criminal Tribunal established to adjudicate genocide and war crimes of the former Yugoslavia, reflect similar developments. The common problem of securing custody over the accused, as well as the lack of control over the evidence, as well as the many other constraints relating to war crimes prosecutions—together mean that the International Tribunal has often had little choice but to investigate and indict—but to go no further.

One can understand the "limited criminal sanction" as the pragmatic resolution of the core rule-of-law dilemma of transition: namely, the problem of attempting to identify individual responsibility for systemic wrongs perpetrated under repressive rule. The basic transitional problem is whether there is any theory of responsibility that can span the move from a repressive, to a more liberal, regime. The emergence of the limited sanction suggests a more fluid way to think about what punishment does: namely, clarify and condemn wrongdoing, without a necessary attribution of individual blame and penalty. The transitional sanction prompts rethinking the theory of punishment. Specifically, it asks us to think about punishment's justification as more closely connected to discrete stages of the criminal process. It points to an alternative sense of the retributivist idea. Though this sanction is characterized by its limited character, transitional practices suggest that core retributive purposes of the recognition and the condemnation of past wrongdoing are vindicable by diminished—even symbolic—punishment. The sheer recognition and condemnation of past wrongdoing has transformative dimensions. Where wrongdoing is publicly established, it liberates the collective in a measured process of transformation. Mere exposure of wrongs can stigmatize and disqualify affected persons from entire realms of the public sphere. In extraordinary circumstances of radical political change, some of the purposes that are ordinarily advanced by the full criminal process are advanced in the sanction's more limited form.

Practices in such periods suggest the transitional limited sanction is that mediating form. The absence of traditional plenary punishment in periods of political transition suggests that more complex understandings of criminal responsibility emerge in the application of the principle of individual responsibility in the distinct context of criminal justice associated with systemic crimes in shifts out of repressive rule. Rule of law within a liberalizing state is commonly equated with individual accountability, an individual responsibility central to law in the liberal state. Yet, this perspective on punishment does not account well for its role in times of radical political flux, where the transitional criminal form is informed by values related to the distinctive project of political change. Ordinarily, criminal justice is theorized in starkly dichotomous terms, as animated by either a backward-looking concern with retribution, or a forward-looking, utilitarian concern with deterrence, considered internal to the justice system. In transition, however, punishment is informed by a mix of retrospective and prospective purposes, raising questions such as whether to punish, or to confer amnesty, to exercise or restrain from exercising criminal justice is rationalized in overtly political terms. Values such as mercy and reconciliation, commonly treated as external to criminal justice, are an explicit part of the transitional deliberation. The explicit politicization of criminal law in these periods challenges ideal understandings of justice, and yet turns out to be a persistent feature of jurisprudence in the transitional context.

The extraordinary transitional form of punishment that I term the "limited" criminal sanction is directed less at penalizing perpetrators than it is at advancing the political transformation's normative shift. The limited sanction is well-illustrated historically, not only in post-war policy, but also in the course of punishment following more recent cases of regime change, during which the sanction performs important operative acts—formal public inquiry into and clarification of the past, and the indictment of past wrongdoing, thereby advancing the normative shift that is central to liberalizing transition. Even in its limited forms, the sanction is a symbol of the rule of law that enables the expression of a critical normative message.

What distinguishes transitional criminal measures is their use to construct normative change. This is plainly seen in the way transitional responses' focus varies from country to country to "undo" rationalized past political violence, through procedures of inquiry and indictment, rituals of collective knowledge that enable the isolation and disavowal of past wrongdoings. Where the prior regime was sustained by persecutory policy rationalized within a legal system, this policy rationale is addressed by the transitional critical legal response. Critical responses to past persecution express the message that the policy is man-made, and, therefore, reformable. The transitional criminal sanction, by isolating knowledge of past wrongdoing and individuating responsibility, enables the potential of liberalizing change, in this way liberating the successor regime from the weight of states' evil legacies. Through ritualized legal processes of appropriation and misappropriation, of avowal and disavowal, of symbolic loss and gain, allowing the perceptions of transformation, societies begin to move in a liberalizing direction.

Criminal justice in some form, transitional practices suggest, is a ritual of liberalizing states, as it is these practices that publicly construct rule-of-law norms. Through these processes, a line is drawn, liberating a past that allows the society to move forward. While punishment is often considered largely retributive in its aim, in transition, punishment's purposes become largely transformative or forward-looking, going beyond the individual perpetrator to the broader society. This function is seen in the primacy of systemic political offenses, for example, in the persistence of prosecutions of crimes against humanity—the archetypal offense of persecutory politics, constituting a critical response to illiberal rule through the criminal law. Moreover, whereas ordinarily punishment is thought to divide society, in transition, wherever punishment is exercised, it is done in a limited fashion, to allow the possibility of the return to a liberal state. As such, criminal processes have affinities with other transitional exercises of the rule of law.

## The Paradigmatic Transitional Rule-of-Law Response

The operative effects advanced by the limited criminal sanction, such as establishing, recording, and condemning past wrongdoing, display affinities with other legal acts and processes that are constructive of transition. The massive and *systemic* wrongdoing that is characteristic of modern repression implies a recognition of a mix of individual and collective responsibility. There is a pronounced overlap of punitive and administrative institutions and processes. Individualized processes of accountability give way to administrative investigations and commissions of inquiry, the compilation of public records, official pronouncements, and condemnation of past wrongs. These are often subsumed in state histories that are commissioned pursuant to a political mandate for reconciliation. However, whether bureaucratic forms of public inquiry and official truthtellings are desirable, and will signify liberalization, is contingent on the nature of the state legacies of repressive rule. To illustrate, one might compare, in this regard, postmilitary Latin America with the post-communist bloc on the social meaning of state history and accountability. As I elaborate further on, the diversity in their historical responses reflects their disparate histories of repression.

The paradigmatic affinities discussed here bear on the recurrent question in transitional justice debates concerning what is the right response to repressive rule, toward supporting a lasting democracy. The subtext of this question assumes a transitional ideal, and that normative concerns somehow militate for a particular categorical response. However, this is simply the wrong question: There is no one right response to the questions of how to deal with a state's repressive past, and how to liberalize for the future. This question should be reframed. Among states, the approach that is taken to transitional justice is politically contingent. Nevertheless, it is worth distinguishing between states undergoing juridical transitions, where there is an established rule-of-law tradition, and those where there is not. At the same time, there appears to be a paradigmatic transitional response in the law. Transitional constitutionalism, criminal justice, and the rule of law share affinities in the contingent relation that these norms bear to prior rule, as well as in their operative work in the move to a more liberal political order.

## Transitional Constructivism

I will now turn to the constructive role of law in transition. How is transition constructed? What is law's role in political change? The paradigmatic form of the law that emerges in these times operates in an extraordinary fashion, and itself plays a constructive role in the transition. It both stabilizes and destabilizes. In these circumstances, law's distinctive feature is its mediating function, as it maintains a threshold level of formal continuity, while enabling transformative discontinuity. The extent to which formal continuity will be maintained depends on the modality of transformation, while the content of the normative shift will be a function of history, legal culture, and political tradition, as well as the society's receptiveness to innovation.[2] What this also implies, of course, is that states with more established rule-of-law traditions will have an easier time re-establishing order.

Just what do transitional legal practices have in common? Law constructs transitions through diverse processes, including legislation, adjudication, and administrative measures. Transitional operative acts include pronouncements of indictments and verdicts; the issuing of amnesties, reparations, and apologies; and the promulgation of constitutions and reports. These transitional practices share features; namely, they are ways to publicly construct new collective political understandings. Transitional processes, whether taking the forms of prosecution, lustration, or inquiry, share this critical dimension. These are all transitional actions taken to manifest change by publicly sharing new political knowledge. Law here works on the margin, as it performs the work of effecting a separation from the prior regime, and ensuring integration with the successor regime. Transitional law has a liminal quality, in that it is law between regimes. The peculiar efficacy of these salient transitional legal practices is their ability to effect both separation and integration functions—all within continuous processes.

Transitional rule of law often implies procedures that do not seem fair or compelling: trials lacking in regular punishment, reparations based on politically driven and arbitrary baselines, constitutions that do not necessarily last. What characterizes the transitional legal response is its limited form, embodied in the provisional constitution and purge, the limited sanction and reparation, the discrete history and official narrative. Transitional rule of law is, above all, limited and symbolic—a secular ritual of political passage.

The legal process has become the leading transitional response due to its ability to convey publicly and authoritatively the political changes that constitute the normative shift between regimes. What is constructed through these processes is the relevant political difference between illiberal and liberal regimes. In its symbolic form, transitional jurisprudence reconstructs the relevant political differences through changes in status, membership, and community. While the relevant critical difference is necessarily contingent, it is recognized as legitimate, in light of a given successor society's past legacies. Moreover, the language of law imbues the new order with legitimacy and authority.

In modern political transformation, legal practices enable successor societies to make liberalizing political change. By mediating the normative hiatus and shift characterizing transition, the turn to law comprises important functional, conceptual, operative, and symbolic dimensions. Law epitomizes the liberal rationalist response to mass suffering and catastrophe; it expresses the notion that there is, after all, something to be done. Rather than resignation to historical repetition, in the liberal society committed to rule of law, the hope of change is put in the air. By their engagement in transitional justice debates, successor societies signal the rational imagining of a more liberal political order.

Legal rituals offer the leading alternative to the violent responses of retribution and vengeance in periods of political upheaval. The transitional legal response is deliberate, measured, restrained, *and* restraining; in their transitional form, ritualized legal processes enable gradual, controlled change. As the question of transitional justice is worked through, the society begins to perform the signs and rites of a functioning liberal order. One can see that transitional law transcends the "merely" symbolic to become a leading ritual of modern political passage. Ritual acts enable the shift between two orders: those of the predecessor and successor regimes. In contemporary transitions, characterized by their peaceful nature and occurrence within the law, legal processes perform the critical "undoings," the inversions of the predicates justifying the prevailing regime, through public processes that produce the collective knowledge that is constitutive of the normative shift. Legal processes simultaneously disavow aspects of the predecessor ideology, and affirm the ideological changes constituting liberalizing transformation.

These are various ways in which the new democracies respond to legacies of injustice. Patterns across legal forms constitute a paradigm of "transitional jurisprudence," rooted in prior political injustice. Law's role is constructivist: Transitional jurisprudence emerges as a distinct paradigmatic form of law responsive to, and constructive of, the extraordinary circumstances of periods of substantial political change. In transitional jurisprudence, the conception of justice is partial, contextual, and situated between at least two legal and political orders. Legal norms are multiple; the idea of justice, pragmatic. Transitional jurisprudence centers on the law's paradigmatic use in the normative construction of the new political regime.

## Transitional Rule of Law as Liberal Narrative

Transitional justice's main contribution is to advance the construction of a collective liberal narrative. Its uses are to advance the transformative purpose of moving the international community, as well as individual states that are in transition, toward greater liberalizing political change. Consider law's potential in constructing a story that lays the basis for political change. Let us begin with the trial, though we should observe that the transformative dimension is also advanced in other legal responses.

### Law's History

One of transitional criminal justice's primary roles is historical. Trials have long played the arch role in transitional history-making. Criminal justice creates public, formal shared processes that link up the past to the future, and the individual to the collective. Criminal trials are the historical, ceremonial form of shared construction of memory a way to work through a community's events that are in controversy. Even the ordinary criminal trial's purposes are not only to adjudicate individual responsibility, but also to establish the truth about an event that is in controversy in a society; this is even more true of the trial's role in settling historical controversies that are characteristic of periods of transition. Transitions follow regime change, and periods of heightened political and historical conflict; therefore, a primary purpose of successor trials is to advance a measure of historical justice.

What sort of "truths" are established in such periods? They are "transitional critical truths," namely, shared political knowledge that is critical of the ideology of the prior regime. Through the trial, the collective historical record that is produced both delegitimizes the predecessor regime and legitimizes the successor. While military or political collapse may bring down repressive leadership, unless the bad regime is also publicly discredited, its ideology often endures. An example is the trial of King Louis XVI, which served as a forum to deliberate over and to establish the evil of monarchic rule. Leading trials, whether of the major war criminals at Nuremberg, or the public trials of Argentina's military junta, are primarily remembered, not for their condemnation of individual wrongdoers, but, instead, for their roles in creating lasting historical records of state tyranny, and for representing a political shift.

Transitional criminal processes enable authoritative accounts of past evil legacies and collective history-making. There are many representations: the recreation and dramatization of the repressive past in the trial proceedings, and in the written transcript, the trial records, and the judgment. Radio and television reportage add to the many representational possibilities (consider The Hague today). One might add the Internet as well.

The contemporary post–Cold War period has given rise to even more complex and disaggregated understandings of responsibility, as well as to a problematizing of the public and the private realms. Consider the growing focus on the role of the multinationals in World War II, and other monetary settlements that attempt to legitimate the transforming global private regime.

The connections to law's role in the production of history that I discussed above advert to the broader role of law in constructing what I have termed the "narrative" of transition. The next part explores the distinct narrative structure of transitional rule of law.

*Narratives of Transition*

Narratives constructed in transitions—whether trials, administrative proceedings, or historical commissions of inquiry—make a normative claim about the relation of a state's past to its prospects for a more democratic future. As is explained further on, the transitional narrative structure propounds the claim that particular knowledge is relevant to the possibility of personal and societal change. Narratives of transition offer an account of the relation that construction of the political knowledge bears to the move away from dictatorship, as well as to the potential of a more liberal future.

Transitional narratives, I claim, follow a distinct rhetorical form: beginning in tragedy, they end in a comic or romantic mode. In the classical understanding, tragedy implicates the elements of catastrophic suffering by individuals, whose fate, due to their status, implicated entire collectives, and was followed by some discovery or other change from ignorance. In tragedy, knowledge seems only to confirm a fate foretold. Contemporary stories of transitional justice similarly *involve stories* of affliction on a grand scale. While such narratives begin in a tragic mode, in the transition they switch over to a non-tragic resolution; there is a turn to what might be characterized as a comic phase. Something happens in these accounts; the persons enmeshed in the story ultimately avert tragic fates, to somehow adjust and even thrive in a new reality. In the convention associated with transitional accounts, change necessitates a critical juncture, where, as opposed to tragic structure, knowledge's revelation actually makes a difference. The country's past suffering is somehow reversed, leading to a happy ending of peace and reconciliation.

The transitional narrative structure can be seen in fictional and nonfictional accounts of periods of political transformation. National "truth" reports read as tragic accounts that end on a redemptive note. Suffering is somehow transformed into something good for the country, into a greater societal self-knowledge that is thought to enhance prospects for an enduring democracy. Thus, after "Night and Fog" disappearance policies throughout much of Latin America, bureaucratic processes were deployed to set up investigatory commissions. Beginning with their title *Never Again,* the truth reports promise to deter future suffering. Thus, the prologue to the report of the Argentine National Commission on the Disappeared declares that the military dictatorship "brought about the greatest and most savage tragedy" in the country's history; but history provides lessons. "[G]reat catastrophes are always instructive." "The tragedy which began with the military dictatorship in March 1976, the most terrible our nation has ever suffered, will undoubtedly serve to help us understand that it is only democracy which can save a people from horror on this scale." Knowledge of past suffering plays a crucial role in the state's ability to make a liberating transition.

Confrontation with the past is considered necessary to liberalizing transformation. The report of the Chilean National Commission on Truth and Reconciliation asserts that knowledge and disclosure of past suffering is necessary to re-establishing the country's identity. The decree establishing Chile's National Commission declares "the truth had to be brought to light, for only on such a foundation . . . , would it be possible to . . . create the necessary conditions for achieving true national reconciliation." "Truth" is the necessary precondition for democracy. This is also the organizing thesis of the El Salvador Truth Commission. This storyline is seen in the report's title: *From Madness to Hope* tells a story of a violent civil war, followed by *"truth and reconciliation."* According to the report's introduction, the truth's "creative consequences" can "settle political and social differences by means of agreement instead of violent action." "Peace [is] to be built on [the] transparency of . . . knowledge." The truth is a "bright light" that "search[es] for lessons that would contribute to reconciliation and to abolishing such patterns of behavior in the new society."

Even where the reporting is unofficial, the claim is similar, that the revelation of knowledge—in and of itself—offers a means to political transformation. In the preface to the unofficial Uruguayan *Nunca Mas* or *Never Again* report writing, in and of itself, constitutes a triumph against repression. The claim is that the transitional truthtellings will deter the possibility of future repression. It is the lack of "critical understanding which created a risk of having the disaster repeated . . . to rescue that history is to learn a lesson . . . We should have the courage not to hide that experience in our collective subconscious but to recollect it. So that we do not fall again into the trap."

In transitional history-making, the story has to come out right. Yet this implies a number of poetic leaps. Was it the new truths that brought on liberalizing political change? Or was it the political change that enables the restoration of democratic government, and reconsideration of the past?

Despite ongoing processes of political change, without some form of clarification of the deception and ensuing self-understanding, the truth about the evil past is hidden, unavailable, external, foreign. In the post-communist transitions characterized by struggling with the accumulated past state archives, the region's transitional accounts begin with the story of invasion and popular resistance; the foe is represented as foreign outsider, progressing to the ever more troubling discovery of collaboration, closer to home and pervasive throughout the society. In the narratives of transition, whether out of a repressive totalitarian rule in the former Soviet bloc, or, out of authoritarian military rule; whether Latin America's truth reports, or post-communist "lustration," transitional stories all involve a "revealing" of supposedly secreted knowledge. What is pronounced is the tragic discovery.

What counts as liberalizing knowledge? These productions are not original, or foundational; but contingent on state legacies of repressive rule. Successor truth regimes' critical function is responsive to the repressive practices of the prior regime. For example, after military rule, where the truth was a casualty of disappearance policies, the critical response is the "official story." After communist rule, the search for the "truth" constituted a matter not of historical production as such, as previous uses of official history had been deployed as instruments of repressive control, but, instead, a matter of critical response to repressive state histories, to the securing of private access to state archives, to the privatization of official histories, and to the introduction of competing historical accounts.

Awareness of history means that the possibility of change is introduced through the potential of human action. The very notion of a knowledge that is objectified and exposed suggests somehow that there was "logic" to the madness, and intimates now that there is something to be done. The message propounded the notion that, had the newly acquired knowledge been known then, events would have been different. And, moreover, that now that the truth is known, the course of future events will indeed be different. Processes that illuminate the possibility of future choice distinguish the liberal transition. In the transitional accounts lie the kernels of a liberal future foretold. The revealed truth allows the switch from the tragic past to the promise of a hopeful future. A catastrophe is somehow turned around, an awful fate averted by the introduction of a magical switch. Transitional justice operates as such a device: Legal processes include persons vested with transformative powers, judges, lawyers, commissioners, experts, witnesses with special access to privileged knowledge. Reckoning with the past enables the perception of a liberalizing shift.

Narratives of transition suggest that, minimally, what is at stake in liberalizing transformation is a change of interpretation. In this process, political and truth regimes have a mutually constitutive role. Societies begin to change politically when citizens' understandings of the ambient situation change. As Václav Havel has written, the change is from "living within a lie to living within the truth." Consider that the Eastern European literature of the period such as Bernhard Schlink's *The Reader;* Ivan Klima's *The Ultimate Intimacy;* Pavel Kohout's *I Am Snowing* and *The Confessions of a Woman of Prague* are stories of precisely this move, from "living within a lie," to the revelation of newly gained knowledge and self-understanding, effecting a reconstitution of personal identity, and of relationships. These tales of deceit and betrayal, often stories of long-standing affairs, appear to be allegories of the citizen/state relation, shedding light on the structure and course of civic change.

What emerges clearly is that the pursuit of historical justice is not simply a response to, or representation of, political change, but itself helps to construct the political transformation. Change in the political and legal regimes shapes and structures the historical regime. New truth regimes go hand in hand with new political regimes; indeed, they support the change. Transitional accounts themselves construct a normative relation, as they connect the society's past with its future. Narratives of transition are stories of progress, beginning with the backward-looking reflection on the past, but always in light of the future. The constructive fiction is that, had the knowledge that has now been acquired been known then, the tragedy would have been avertable. New societies can be built upon this claim about knowledge. It is this change in political knowledge that allows the move from an evil past to a sense of national redemption.

Transitional narratives follow a distinct, structured form. Revelation of the knowledge of truth occurs through switching mechanisms, critical junctures of individual and societal self-knowledge. There is a ritual disowning of previously secreted knowledge, a purging of the past, as well as an appropriation of a newly revealed truth, enabling corrective return to the society's true course. A new course is charted.

The practices in such periods suggest that the new histories are hardly foundational, but rather explicitly transitional. To be sure, historical narrative is always present in the life of the state, but, in periods of political flux, the narrative's role is to construct perceptible transformation. Transitional histories are not "meta"-narratives, but discrete "mini"-narratives, always situated within the state's preexisting national story. Transitional truthtellings are not new beginnings, but rather, they build upon preexisting state political legacies. Indeed, the relevant truths are those that were implicated in a particular state's past political legacies. These are not universal, essential, or metatruths; a marginal truth is all that is needed to draw a line on the prior regime. Critical responses negotiate between historical conflict in contested accounts. As political regimes change, transitional histories accordingly offer a displacement of one interpretive account or truth regime for another, and in doing so, preserve the state's narrative thread.

Transitional law transcends the merely symbolic to become the leading ritual of modern political passage. The legal response epitomizes the liberal, secular, rationalist response to mass suffering and catastrophe, and expresses the notion that there is something to be done. Rather than accepting resignation to historical repetition, in the liberal society, hope is put in the air. Ritual acts enable the passage between the two orders, of predecessor and successor regimes. In contemporary transitions, characterized by their peaceful character within the law, legal processes perform the critical undoings of the predicate justifications of the prior regime, through public procedures that produce constitutive collective knowledge transformative of political identities. The paradigmatic feature of the transitional legal response is that it visibly advances the reconstruction of public knowledge comprehending operative features that enable the separation from the past, as well as integration processes. The importance of establishing a shared collective truth regarding the past repressive legacies has become something of a trope in the discourse of transitions. The meaning of "truth" is not universal, but rather is largely politically contingent to the transition. Accordingly, the paradigmatic transitional legal processes rely on discrete changes in salient public political knowledge for their operative transformative action. Legal processes construct changes in shared public justifications underlying political decision-making and behavior that simultaneously disavow aspects of the predecessor ideology and justify the ideological changes constituting liberalizing transformation. What is politically relevant to transformation is plainly constituted by the transitional context, as well as by the legacies of displacement and succession of the predecessor truth regimes.

Legal processes are ways of changing public reasoning in the political order, for these processes are predicated on authoritative representations of public knowledge. So it is that transitional legal processes contribute to the interpretive changes that create the perception of political social transformation. At the same time, transitional legal processes also vividly demonstrate the contingency in what knowledge will do the work of constructing the normative shift underpinning political regime change. The normative force of transitional constructions in public knowledge depends on critical challenges to the policy predicates and rationalizations of predecessor rule and ideology. Accordingly, what the relevant "truths" are in transition is discrete and yet of disproportionate significance. These reinterpretations displace the predicates legitimizing the prior regime, and offer newfound bases for the reinstatement of the rule of law.

Law offers a canonical language, and the symbols and rituals of contemporary political passage. Through trials and other public hearings and processes, legal rituals enable transitionally produced histories, social constructions of a democratic nature with a broad reach. These rituals of collective history-making publicly construct the transition; they divide political time into a "before" and an "after." Transitional responses perform the critical undoings that respond to the prior repression. The letting go of discrete facts that were justificatory of the predecessor regime is critical to political change. The practices of historical production that are associated with transition often publicly affirm only what is already impliedly known in the society, as transitional processes bring forward and enable a public letting go of the past.

Whether through trials or other practices, transitional narratives highlight the role of knowledge, agency, and choice. Though the received wisdom on historical responses to past wrongs is that these are popular in liberalizing states emphasizing structural causation, transitional histories are complex accounts, dense, layered narratives that weave together and mediate individual and collective responsibility. By introducing the potential of individual choice, the accounts perform a transitional liberalizing function. By revealing "truths" about the past, these accounts become distinctive narratives of progress, as they suggest that the course of events might have been different—had this knowledge been previously known, and advert to the potential of individual action. The message is of avertable tragedy. This expression of the hope for prospective individual freedom and human action goes to the core of liberalism and its rule-of-law discourse.

## Notes

1. Martin Krygier, "Transitional Questions about the Rule of Law: Why, What, and How?" *East Central Europe—L'Europe du Centre Est. Eine wissenachaftitche Zeitschrift* 28, no. 1 (2001): 1–34.

2. It is worth observing that, notwithstanding Martin Krygier's comments to the contrary, the context of the legal transformation is not only defined by the project or aims of the transition (see Krygier 2001: 25–26), but rather is also shaped by the mix of past and present variables that are almost definitional of transition.

*This essay was written at a time when the human rights community had increasing hopes pinned on the resuscitation of a centuries-old federal statute, permitting aliens to bring tort claims in U.S. courts for violations of "the law of nations." In several cases, victims of human rights abuses abroad succeeded in obtaining verdicts against their perpetrators whether in transition or ex ante. Yet these hopes would soon start to fade, as the majority of the U.S. Supreme Court would narrow the window for such actions to instances where the violation of the law of nations was at least of a general kind that could have been in the contemplation of the drafters of the statute. Now after a recent Supreme Court decision,* Kiobel[1], *where the Court insisted on a significant connection to the United States as a condition for bringing suit under the ATCA, many human rights activists have pronounced this avenue of accountability as essentially dead. Yet this estimate may be too narrow; lawsuits for violation of human rights abroad continue in state courts, and other national jurisdictions, such as Canada. And the Supreme Court emphasized that its judgment did not affect the operation of a much more recent companion statute, the Torture Victim Protection Act of 1991. Ultimately, this essay raises broader issues about interpreting transitional justice responses against a background of international law including the law of nations.*

# 10     The Alien Tort and the Global Rule of Law

THIS CHAPTER EXPLORES the significance of legal developments over the last decades whereby U.S. courts have become an avenue for civil litigation raising human rights claims on the basis of a form of "universal jurisdiction," under long-standing American law known as the Alien Tort Statute, or the Alien Tort Claims Act (ATCA), codified in U.S. law at 28 U.S.C. § 1350.

The chapter seeks to work on two levels.

First, it attempts to offer a historical account of the development of human-rights torts litigation. This account endeavors to show the nexus of legal developments to other political and social changes.

Second, the chapter traces the normative evolution of this line of litigation. With globalization, there is an apparent move to expanded jurisdiction, opening new sites for litigation of "alien torts." Here, the chapter makes a number of claims. First, it seeks to elucidate the important developments in this expansion of jurisdiction. It contends that the constructive work of human-rights litigation is inextricably bound up in the construction of the meaning of global rule of law. What is meant by this is that there is a move away from the traditional understanding of the association of the state with law and its protections. This is now understood on two levels, with respect to the creation of substantive and procedural jurisdiction, regarding the universality of the cause of action, but also in changes in legal personality and subjectivity in the international scene. These developments are currently animating substantial debate on a transnational level and they inform the sense of constitutive elements toward current transformation in the perception of rule of law in current globalizing politics.

## The Advent of the Transitory Tort: The ATCA in Historical Perspective

What is the course of reparatory justice when states fail to recognize rights? Where do the rights go? Is their vindication tied to the state and to the successor regime; or, where this fails, are they vindicable elsewhere?

A series of cases in the USA concerning the most serious wrongs, "gross abuses" of human rights, suggests that, in the most egregious cases of persecution, the vindication of victims' rights will not be restricted to the borders of the implicated country. Such transnational legal action is often seen in the early stages of transition, since during these times, above all, those implicated in prior wrongdoing commonly flee their countries in search of safe haven.

In a landmark case for victims of state abuses to vindicate their reparatory rights, relying on a two-hundred-year-old law, the Alien Tort Claims Act, jurisdiction was enabled in the U.S. courts for suits for violations of the "law of nations." Guided by the analogy to piracy, the appellate court held that "official torture" was a violation of the "law of nations" and, therefore, original jurisdiction lies in federal courts.[2] "For the purposes of civil liability, the torturer has become—like the pirate and slave trader before him—hostis humani generis, an enemy of all mankind."[3] Compensatory claims deriving from rights protected under the "law of nations" traditionally were considered transitory causes of action and, as such, could be brought in jurisdictions other than where the claim arose. Deliberate torture, like piracy, violated the law of nations; accordingly, reparatory rights arising out of official torture would be treated as transitory claims.

*Filartiga* gave rise to a long line of "alien tort" cases, generally involving either official torture or unlawful executions. *Forti* and *Siderman* involved Argentine torturers found in the USA. Acts of torture attributed to Argentina were held to constitute violations of "jus cogens" norms; peremptory norms of international law, with universal applicability and protection.[4] *In re Estate of Marcos* concerned a suit regarding torture in the Philippines that was brought against its former president, Ferdinand Marcos. In all of these cases of political persecution, victims or their families initiated suits against their perpetrators in the USA. The jurisdictional principle established that civil liability is transitory and follows the perpetrator.[5]

Guided by the piracy analogy, one could say that the Alien Tort Claims Act precedents relied on the fiction of an individual outlaw, and a classical idea of corrective justice where civil liability follows the lone wrongdoer. Perhaps, the extreme case is epitomized by a recent alien tort suit, in which Radovan Karadžić, the Bosnian Serbs' top political leader, was held civilly liable for atrocities committed under the policy of ethnic persecution he advanced in the Balkans. Going beyond prior litigation, the suit extended to the civil realm principles of command responsibility ordinarily associated with criminal justice.

The central idea is that of civil liability following the tortfeasor, extending beyond the borders of the state. This development may well seem paradoxical, in that we ordinarily tend to think of law and liability as linked up with sovereignty. Put another way, the question raised is where accountability for wrongdoing should fairly lie. Regarding torture that is generally committed under color of state law— commonly encouraged or condoned by the state—who should be held responsible? To what extent are reparatory claims arising out of modern state persecution fairly attributed to an individual wrongdoer? Moreover, what, ideally, is the right relationship between individual and collective responsibility?

One might conceive of the alien tortfeasor as a juridical construct characteristic of justice in non-ideal circumstances, following an idea more fully elaborated in *Transitional Justice*.[6] Such suits tend to arise in political conditions where a regime cannot be held accountable in the implicated country's courts. Furthermore, foreign governments are largely immune from suit in American courts for reasons of sovereign immunity. Therefore, the practical resolution is to resort to concepts of traditional private civil liability. Nevertheless, the paradox and complexity of the resort to the "alien tort" for redress of human rights violations is that, while the cause of action allows for individual liability, it explicitly recognizes that the wrongs at stake are committed against a background of state policy. Though the Alien Tort

Claims Act creates a cause of action against individual wrongdoers, jurisdiction has been largely based on "official" wrongs perpetrated under color of state law. One might expect only a small class of perpetrators to fit this bill: those who have acted in their official capacity, under color of state law, and whose actions have clearly violated the law of nations. At the same time, the claims must somehow also circumvent the defense of sovereign immunity, i.e., the general immunization of foreign states from jurisdiction, subject to a narrow exception. The violations on which there is the greatest consensus are torture, summary executions, and genocide, characterized as "jus cogens" norms with the highest status within international law, assuming a backdrop of state, or state-like, practices following a systematic policy.

Three decades since *Filartiga's* landmark holding, there is apparently a growing concern with accountability. During that time, there have been many declaratory judgments holding liable human-rights violators. Moreover, a form of the judicial remedy has been ratified into federal law: the Torture Victim Protection Act (TVPA—consolidated with the ATCA at 28 U.S.C § 1350) authorizes civil actions for monetary damages for abuses such as official torture and summary executions, where the perpetrator is within the jurisdiction.

Over the years, declaratory judgments have far exceeded payments. The ongoing nature of the suits suggests that the recognition of civil liability has an impact beyond monetary judgment. Even the simple ascription of civil liability often implies public sanction because of the media attention commonly associated with the public eye of litigation. The attribution of individual liability, notwithstanding its civil nature, often implies dimensions of the social censure associated with the criminal sanction. The incidence of reparatory justice-seeking measures across state borders reflects the dynamic role of these remedies in current globalizing politics. Although civil remedies ordinarily aim to vindicate victims' rights, like other transitional measures, the alien tort suit thus apparently serves purposes that are more commonly associated with the criminal sanction, such as the recognition and condemnation of wrongdoing. While the condemnation inheres in civil liability, it can also have broader effects, leading to the isolation of perpetrators from the community. Indeed, the transitory tort elucidates the linkage among vindication of victims' rights, recognition of individual wrongdoing, and state persecution. The emergence of the transitory tort, particularly in cases of persecution, reflects a conception of reparatory justice with affinities to other transitional legal responses.

By mediating the realms of the public and the private, the individual and the collective, the national and the international, the alien tort constitutes an alternative response to the offenses characteristic of modern repression. The transitory tort for human rights abuses illuminates a conception of a cause of action that transcends the ordinary confines of jurisdictions of time and space, which could be conceived as the "tort against humanity." This conception of tort emerges as a response to a distinctive form of contemporary governmental persecution, in a cause of action that brings together the implicated individuals in a broader persecutory policy. Furthermore, the tort against humanity challenges our ordinary intuitions, whereby civil causes of action are conceived as tied to particular jurisdictions, which only inadequately captures instances of grave wrongdoing that implicate the state itself in persecution. With the breakdown of ordinary jurisdictional parameters, the "foreign" is rendered "domestic," in turn redefining the understanding of what constitutes an international offense. By recognizing victims' rights, even though they may well be vindicated outside the national legal system, these actions nevertheless commence a process of normative transition. Wherever political transition may not yet have fully occurred, or the circumstances associated with vindication of justice remain largely absent, human-rights adjudication can, nevertheless, play a constructive role in fostering political change. These transitional legal responses reflect fluid, nuanced approaches to sovereignty and jurisdiction. These departures from conventional principles are rationalized in light of the nature of the state behavior, as well as the evolving principles relating to the extent to which it adheres to the international community's rule of law.

## The ATCA Jurisprudence: Contemporary Developments and the Shift to Corporate Accountability

This section explores what I characterize here as the second stage in the modern evolution of alien tort litigation. It discusses the meaning of these developments, and the role they appear to be playing in the construction of global rule of law. Hitherto, the phenomenon has been discussed as a pragmatic alternative to the uses of local legal systems, where these systems reflect an absence of full legitimacy, or political will, for human-rights protection. ATCA litigation appeared in this respect as part of an array of responses to persecution in the absence of full political or legal transition.

By contrast, I now discuss the next stage in the expansion of this area of human rights litigation, and explore how it came to transcend the response to past foreign wrongdoers. The analysis takes up the broader uses of this statute in responding to abuses associated with globalization. It explores the shift, beyond the site of litigation, to the full privatization of the suit through the institution of civil action against private parties, chiefly multinational corporations. This leads to consideration of the social meaning of this litigation by adumbrating the changes along several parameters, suggesting that the significance of these developments reflects the contemporary meaning of the threshold global rule of law.

The first move in *Filartiga*, as discussed above, was to situate the suit in national (federal) court rather than other local courts. The move to the U.S. courts has generally been pursued in situations when domestic institutions, for one reason or another, are unavailing. One might conceive of this latent principle of jurisdiction as "complementary," something that has now been ratified as a permanent feature of the global legal scene in article 1 of the new statute for the permanent International Criminal Court. Consider the link between the ATCA, taken historically, and its modern formulation. Initiated clearly as a "complementary" measure—an emergency or complementary form of jurisdiction—the idea was that U.S. federal court jurisdiction was necessary as a site for tort suits concerning diplomats, or piracy. To what extent do these historical uses help us conceptualize present-day corporate accountability?

The first stage of the ATCA in modern times, discussed above, appeared to posit a significant step in the privatization of human-rights protection. By taking matters into their own hands and initiating suits outside their countries, the litigants and assisting NGOs have become the motors of transitional justice.

In the next stage of litigation, there appears to be a further move in the privatization of justice in the area of human rights, whereby neither the plaintiff nor the defendant is any longer necessarily associated with the state. In the earlier years of modern alien tort litigation, there was a limit on those defendants who fit the very narrow requirements of having been officially connected enough to engage in state-sponsored crimes, but also, not so connected to the state as to run afoul of recognized categories of sovereign immunity, enshrined in the Foreign Sovereign Immunities Act (28 U.S.C §1330). For example, in the *Tel Oren* case, the D.C. circuit did not allow a suit to go forward against the PLO due to the lack of connection of a violation by state actors, saying any change would require an act of Congress. However, in the more recent landmark case against Radovan Karadžić, the Second Circuit held alleged war crimes, genocide, torture, and other atrocities actionable under the ATCA.[7] There have also been suits filed against a former El Salvadorian minister of defence for the murder of six U.S. nuns, against President Mugabe of Zimbabwe for intimidation and suppression of the country's opposition, against the Chilean military for actions taken in the country's 1973 coup, etc.[8]

For present purposes, however, the notable point is that, unlike in the more traditional alien tort suits, in more contemporary cases, the defendant is often a private company, commonly with transnational connections, i.e., a multinational corporation. Such was the case in *In re South African Apartheid Litigation*[9] and in *Doe v. Unocal*, a suit against a California multinational for assistance in human-rights violations in Burma.[10] Similarly, Coca Cola was sued regarding its alleged human rights violations in Columbia (including allegations of kidnapping and murder);[11] Chevron-Texaco for toxic waste in the rainforests of Ecuador;[12] Canadian oil producer Talisman for supporting the Sudan's military in the country's civil war.[13]

More and more private actors are being held to account for violations of what, so far, have been considered in the realm of state action and public law. Put another way, we are witnessing the privatization of human rights law. In this contemporary stage, the human rights lawsuit is structured as conducted by private citizens against private actors in a foreign court. This development has many implications. First, it forces the issue of the protection of human rights out of a narrow relation of the state and its victims, and into a more public debate. Even more significant is the direction of the debate: the line of litigation moves the focus from the periphery to the center, as the claim comes from abroad, but culminates in the U.S. federal courts.

Still, despite these significant changes, this version of the human-rights debate is still largely occurring in the judicial rather than the political sphere. Indeed, in the case of Humberto Alvarez-Machain, involving a Mexican kidnapping, the United States Supreme Court ruled on the ongoing vitality of this area of federal jurisdiction as a matter of constitutional law.[14] Claims brought under the ATCA must, the majority argued, "rest on a norm of an international character accepted by the civilized world and defined with a specificity comparable to the features of the eighteenth-century paradigms." Nevertheless, despite this exhortation, the Court failed to go further and to define the appropriate standards for universal civil jurisdiction.

## The ATCA and the "Law of Humanity" as a Global Rule of Law

This section elaborates further on the normative features of the line of litigation under consideration. Accountability is discussed in terms of the boundaries of criminal and civil; domestic and foreign; public and private; individual and collective; and, finally, international and universal jurisdiction.

### The Rise of Civil Accountability

First, and most important, the ATCA's expansion of civil liability, although limited to understandings of "universal jurisdiction," reflects the extent to which the sense of access to judicial redress lies at the core of the global rule of law. Access to the judiciary is a central theme in the norm of corporate accountability. And, relatedly, access to justice has become a critical element of the global rule of law. Indeed, the corporate sector has itself recognized the norm as generally helpful to globalization processes, and a significant indicator of the threshold rule of law.[15] While there is support for such litigation, it is generally understood as a matter of last resort.

At this point in the development of human-rights law, an increasingly common remedy for rights violations is monetary redress.[16] The remedy's dominance begins to emerge in the precedents in transitional justice, particularly with Velasquez-Rodriguez, the Honduras case in the Inter-American system, which gave rise to the "rights" of truth and compensation as the recommended form of human-rights protection.[17] The alien tort suits offer a remedy seemingly independent of the limits of national courts, and the struggle for domestic justice more generally. Instead, these suits focus upon the role and responsibility of private actors, and independent judiciaries, grounded on the basis of an obligation to minimal human-rights remedies.

The expansion in civil liability discussed here derives from a mix of developments in substantive jurisdiction, on both legislative and judicial fronts. Perhaps most significant is the previously mentioned TVPA, which ratifies a distinctive understanding of the substantive tort in the ATCA, which it defines as "extra-judicial killing" and "torture" when carried out under authority of law. Here, the U.S. Congress defined the relevant norms, and grounded them in state action. Another place where these norms appear through both national and international ratification of these developments is the American Convention on Human Rights, which provides for duties to investigate and redress that relate back to the landmark Velasquez Rodriguez decision, affirming the duty to "protect, investigate and compensate" under regional human-rights law.

In other instances, under regional human-rights law, the European Convention of Human Rights contemplates that, wherever there are violations of substantive rights, there ought to be the guarantee of a remedy: article 13 of the Convention promises an "effective remedy" and article 41 "adequate reparation." Other European projects focus on corporate liability: such as the Brussels Convention, article 2, providing for tort claims in third states.[18] To some extent, the rise of civil liability reflects a development apparently connected to globalization, and the attendant shift to individual responsibility and justice. Finally, there are the recently established International Criminal Court's expanded principles of individual sponsorship, such as "inducing" and "aiding," which contemplate proscription of human-rights abuses. Further, the new Court's charter also contemplates complex sanctions, such as reparations, in addition to the more traditional punitive penalties.

While civil liability may well be less coercive than criminal prosecution, it would nevertheless be difficult to interpret these adjudications as consensual. Indeed, opponents to the ATCA contrast such litigation, conceived as "hard law," with alternative "soft law" regulation involving voluntary codes of conduct. The question that arises is the extent to which such adjudicatory developments are a predicate to the moralization of capitalism.

## Shifting to Transnational Accountability

The ATCA litigation raises important normative issues about the location of vindication of human rights in a globalized economy. Where are questions of human-rights abuses best handled—in local or foreign courts? Debates in this area of human-rights litigation concern whether opening U.S. courts to foreign litigants represents a net gain to the rule of law, or, whether such access constitutes a form of judicial imperialism, to the detriment of the local judiciary and community.

Framing the debate this way may well be too neat, as there are, no doubt, conflicting rule-of-law values at stake: a view of the rule of law as neutral and dispassionate, which would, in turn, justify the turn to foreign judgment, versus other rule-of-law values which anchor the judiciary to local accountability. Where the injured community lies in Mexico or India, but the perpetrator is a company registered in the US, would the balance of rule-of-law values favor domestic, or foreign courts? And domestic or foreign, according to whom? To what extent should there be a requirement of exhaustion of local remedies? Further on, this is elaborated upon in exploring the tensions here between thinking of these developments as necessarily international, or universal norms. One way to reconciliation, I contend, is to conceive the guiding principle of global jurisdiction as viewing the options of foreign jurisdiction in "complementary" terms.

Historically, the eighteenth century enactment of the ATCA reflected the American constitutional founders' clear understanding of non-monist approaches to justice, and, in particular, the preference for national over local courts concerning the adjudication of the law of the nations. Similarly, the contemporary cases reflect the link between the turn to foreign courts and the related exercise of transnational jurisdiction. This change seems indubitably related to globalization, and to the increased presence and activities of multinationals abroad.

Consider the significance of the shift in litigation to U.S. courts, as opposed to its effect in the affected locale. Here, we have seen the extent to which the alien torts litigation illustrates a central dimension of globalization: the absence of periphery or center—or rather, the periphery coming to the center. Accordingly, there has been an outcry among multinationals regarding an anxiety that they will become vulnerable to the U.S. legal system as world courts of first instance. A growing principle of global jurisdiction that has arisen is that there should at the very least be "complementary" jurisdiction. Going abroad does not enable the corporate sector to avoid all norms. Still, this arguably constitutes a very limited check on normative development. For, after all, the ATCA jurisdiction is restricted to those norms considered "universal." As we shall see, this is limited to a very narrow set of claims that fall within the understanding of universality in the substantive jurisdiction.

## The Subject of the Human Rights Regime: From Public to Private

On the problem of personality, there has been substantial doctrinal evolution. At the beginning of this line of litigation, the subject of the law of nations appeared to be circumscribed, for example, as seen in the judgment in *Tel Oren*, which deals with terrorism and its relationship to state action.[19] However, in a series of cases, this notion has become more porous in the context of globalization; one can see the blurring of the realms of the public and the private. To what extent can private actors violate the "law of nations"? Through the Alien Tort Act, private actors are being held liable for complicity in the most grave of human-rights abuses, such as war crimes, slavery, and genocide: for example, in a previously cited case, Unocal for forced labor and slavery, regarding the building of a gas pipeline from Myanmar to Thailand;[20] and Royal Dutch Petroleum for confiscation and environmental damage in Nigeria.[21]

Similar developments are going on in the definitions of related violations, outside of tort, or, what might be considered criminal tort in the ICC statute, where private actors are being held accountable for genocide, war crimes, and crimes against humanity.

To what extent is it a departure to hold a private entity liable for violating the so-called "law of nations"? It may be helpful to consider this in a historical light. Historically, at common law, the subjects of the law of nations included not only states, but also persons. Whereas modern international law, the emphasis is upon states. With globalization one can see that there has been a revival of legal subjectivity in the person, often with transnational implications. Here, corporations, which are often conceived as persons, can be held responsible for the law of nations.

Nevertheless, the interpretation of the role of the law, here, is rather limited, and has generally been considered to be confined to instances where there are clear violations of community norms. What does this mean in light of the new corporate accountability? So far, the legal precedents in this area have converged on "jus cogens." Where corporations violate "jus cogens" what does it mean? Does it make sense to hold private actors responsible in national courts for such violations? Corporations are private actors that, in some ways, act like states, in that they engage in acts with systematicity. But, unlike states and like pirates, generally speaking, corporations act in an extraterritorial fashion, and, as such, lack other disincentives to their behavior. Further, unlike states, corporations do not have distinct national populations to which they must be accountable. These distinctions go some way toward explaining the alien tort's singular force and the behavior it delineates.

The ATCA litigation underscores what we know to be historically true: that, as a general matter, conflict and persecution is multi-causal, and commonly involves the close association and support of an economic elite. There is often profit making in undertakings such as dictatorships and war-like ventures. This was true of Germany's aggression in the Second World War, as well as more contemporary conflicts in Africa and the Middle East. Consider, in this regard, the likely first case for the International Criminal Court, involving atrocities in the Congo, which will expose the link among persecution, rights violations, and the flow of resources. One might conclude that these related geopolitical dimensions are present in the contemporary conflict in the Middle East.

## Individual and Corporate Accountability

To some extent, the above developments appear to be a move away from the post–Second World War responses, which emphasized a burgeoning interest in individual rights and responsibility. Indeed, the problem of who is the relevant subject of human rights might well be best understood in terms of cycles—after all, the post-war responses reacted to the punitive sanctions imposed after the First World War, and to concerns raised about punishing a country, interpreted as not allowing for a meaningful transition and implying an illiberal use of law. At present, one might understand the interest in corporate liability as, in some sense, a move away from individual responsibility. The conception of corporate responsibility, however, is distinguishable from historical sanctions punitive of the country as a whole.

While there is an emphasis in the ICC Rome Statute upon individual responsibility—for example, corporate actors cannot be prosecuted—nevertheless the ICC principles provide ways to go after those in leadership positions. For the court recognizes no immunity whatsoever: it does not waive the accountability of current political leaders, or others who aid or abet in any fashion. These principles (see articles 1 and 5) arguably transcend traditional understandings of criminal responsibility, though this may well be confined to the ICC context, and still not widely shared in the international community.[22]

Another significant normative development this area of litigation highlights is the tension between diverse principles of corporate civil liability. In particular, the extension of liability to private actors has implied the extension of principles of responsibility associated with humanitarian law, and, in particular, those associated with the law of war, to corporate actors. As these cases reflect, the principles of responsibility in the law of war are more stringent than in the area of corporate responsibility as a general matter.

## Developments in Jurisdiction: Internationalism Versus Universalism

To some extent, one can see with hindsight and in light of the latest developments that there is an overstatement in the meaning of "universality" of jurisdiction. This is so in at least two ways: to begin, most instances of procedural jurisdiction can be readily understood in more traditional terms. Indeed, "universality" in criminal prosecution in landmark cases, such as those of Adolf Eichmann (who was brought to trial in Jerusalem for Nazi crimes) or Augosto Pinochet (who was indicted in London, for Chilean crimes against humanity), reflects a narrower view of universality that overlaps, and, even coincides with, more traditional understandings of jurisdiction, whether of territoriality or passive personality.

Similar sorts of limits frequently apply in the civil context, where the ATCA litigation has confronted a variety of procedural doctrines such as "minimum contacts,"[23] and "forum non conveniens".[24]

At present, there are rather narrow grounds for the assertion of universal jurisdiction in ATCA human rights litigation. In *Filartiga*, the "law of nations" was understood to mean customary international law. Nevertheless while international customary law may well be understood to evolve over time, in subsequent decisions, this has been problematized. The law of nations is sometimes read not to refer to all customary law, but to "*jus cogens.*" This should be understood to comprehend a very narrow group of offenses, such as genocide, and certain crimes against humanity, while other cases suggest no limitation to the historical meaning of "law of nations."

Second, the substantive norms involved in these cases are highly limited, in deriving from notions of universality in civil litigation, rather than universal criminal litigation. Moreover, in recent years, universality in criminal litigation has also been limited. Consider, in this regard, the demise of the Belgium Genocide Act.[25] Consider, as well, the limits of the Pinochet litigation. There is a substantial scholarly debate, at present, over the meaning of universality in civil litigation. One might expect greater tolerance for extraterritoriality in civil jurisdiction. Where confronted with the question of how to interpret the "law of nations," the courts have ordinarily read this not to signify broad understandings of international law. Rather, over time, "the law of nations" has largely been read prudentially, limited to so-called violations of "jus cogens," the most serious peremptory norms.

## Conclusion

To conclude, the ATCA genealogy reflects dimensions of a form of transnational normative regulation associated with current global politics. The present debate over this judicial remedy may well shed important light on the treatment of a variety of extraterritorial behaviors. How these norms are defined, and adjudicated, can shed important light on other problems raising similar questions. So far, there appears to be significant consensus on such judicial access, from both the human rights and the corporate communities. Across the realms of the public and the private, there is some level of agreement on a modicum of judicial access as central to the global rule of law. Nevertheless, beyond this threshold, there is little consensus on the contribution of such human-rights litigation. Moreover, the judiciary is not a reliable source of the rule of law, as courts tend to be independent of political processes, and therefore not the most stable basis for building either procedural safeguards or deeper normative consensus.

## Notes

1. *See Kiobel v. Royal Dutch Petroleum Co.*, 456 F. Supp. 2d 457 (S.D.N.Y. 2006); *affirmed* in part, *reversed* in part, 621 F.3d 111 (2d Cir. 2010); rehearing *en banc* denied, 642 F.3d 379 (2d Cir. 2011); *cert.* granted, 132 S. Ct. 472 (2011); judgment *aff'd*, 133 S. Ct. 1659 (2013). On April 17, 2013, the Supreme Court unanimously affirmed the Second Circuit's decision. Despite its recognition of the presumption against the extraterritorial application of the ATCA, the majority opinion ruled that the presumption can be rebutted if the international law violation "touches and concerns" the United States with "sufficient force." Thus, in a post-*Kiobel* world, the issue of ATCA jurisdiction will require courts to consider the defendant's alleged misconduct and examine whether the conduct satisfies the standard of "substantially affecting an important American interest."

2. See *Filartiga v. Pena-Irala*, 630 F.2d 876 (2d Cir. 1980).

3. *Id.*

4. See *Forti v. Suarez Mason*, 672 F. Supp. 1531, 1540 (ND Cal.1987).

5. See *In re Estate of Marcos*, 103 F.3d 767 (9th Cir. 1996).

6. Ruti G. Teitel. *Transitional Justice*. Oxford: Oxford University Press (2000).

7. See *Kadic v. Karadžić*, 70 F.3d 232 (2d Cir.1995).

8. *Tachiona v. United States*, 386 F.3d 205 (2004) (suit brought against the President and Foreign Minister of Zimbabwe for intimidation and suppression of peaceful political opposition); *Ford ex rel, Estate of Ford v. Garcia*, 289 F.3d 1283 (S.D. Fla. 1999) (suit brought against a former El Salvadorian Minister of Defense and Director-General of the National Guard for the torture and murder of six U.S. nuns); *Estate of Cabello v. Fernandez-Larios*, 157 F. Supp. 2d 1345 (S.D. Fla. 2001) (suit brought against a member of the Chilean military for the murder of a Chilean governmental official in the immediate aftermath of that nation's 1973 coup). *Bao Ge v Li Peng*, 201 F. Supp 14 (D.D.C. 2000) (suit brought against former Chinese Premier Li Peng in respect of human rights abuses in the Chinese prison system); *Doe v. Islamic Salvation Front*, 257 F. Supp. 2d 115 (2003) (suit brought against an Islamic group in respect of crimes against humanity, war crimes, and other violations of international and domestic law).

9. *See Ntsebeza v. Daimler AG* (In re S. Afr. Apartheid Litig.), 617 F. Supp. 2d 228, 296 (S.D.N.Y. 2009) [Since the initial publication of this essay, the following developments have occurred. In November 2004, the district court granted the defendants' motion to dismiss. *See Ntsebeza v. Citigroup, Inc.* (In re S. Afr. Apartheid Litig.), 346 F. Supp. 2d 538, 543 (S.D.N.Y. 2004), aff'd in part, vacated in part, remanded sub nom. In 2007, on appeal, the Second Circuit reversed the district court and allowed the plaintiffs an opportunity to amend their original complaints. In 2008, the Supreme Court granted certiorari but affirmed by default for lack of a quorum. *See Am. Isuzu Motors, Inc. v. Ntsebeza*, 128 S. Ct. 2424 (2008). On remand, the district court narrowed the claims but allowed the case to continue against Daimler, Ford, General Motors, IBM, and Rheinmetall Group. The case is still pending at the time of the instant publication).

10. See *Doe v. Unocal*, 395 F.3d 932, 942 (9th Cir. 2002). The Ninth Circuit ultimately reversed the District Court's decision, allowing the lawsuit against Unocal to go forward. The Unocal case became the first instance wherein a federal court allowed a lawsuit against a corporation arising under the Alien Tort Act to proceed. The plaintiffs' claims of murder, rape, and forced labor were set for a jury trial in June 2005. However, in March 2005, the parties reached a confidential settlement thereby concluding the lawsuit.

11. *See Sinaltrainal v. Coca-Cola Co.*, 578 F.3d 1252, 74 Fed. R. Serv. 3d 410, 61 A.L.R. Fed. 2d 677 (11th Cir. 2009). The district court dismissed the claims against Coca-Cola USA and Coca-Cola Colombia in 2003 and the remaining claims in 2006. On appeal, the Eleventh Circuit upheld the dismissal for failure to satisfy the requisite pleading standards. The court explicitly stated that the circuit recognized such liability pursuant to the ATCA.

12. *See Aguinda v. Texaco, Inc.*, 945 F. Supp. 625 (S.D.N.Y. 1996), 157 F.3d 153 (2d Cir. 1998), 142 F. Supp. 2d 534 (S.D.N.Y. 2001), 303 F.3d 470 (2d Cir. 2002). In 1996, the district court dismissed the suit on the basis of forum non conveniens. In 1998, the Second Circuit reversed the district court for failing to require that Texaco was subject to jurisdiction in Ecuador. In 2001, the district court dismissed the case again after Texaco agreed to suit in Ecuador. In 2002 the Second Circuit finally dismissed the case.

13. *See Presbyterian Church of Sudan v. Talisman Energy, Inc.*, 244 F. Supp. 2d 289, 155 O.G.R. 409 (S.D. N.Y. 2003). The court rejected the defendant's motion to dismiss the plaintiffs' complaint under the Alien Tort Statute (28 U.S.C.A. § 1350) and held that where there is a violation of customary international law, a non-state actor would not be exempt from liability just because *jus cogens* had not been established.

14. See *Sosa v. Alvares-Machain*, 124 S. Ct. 2739 (2004).

15. E.G. Schrage, "Judging Corporate Accountability in the Global Economy," *Columbia Journal of Transnational Law*, 42, 153–76 (2003).

16. *See* Ruti G. Teitel, *Transitional Justice*. Oxford: Oxford University Press (2000); *see also* T. Van Boven, *Study Concerning the Right to Restitution, Compesantion and Rehabilitation for Victims of Gross Violations of Human Rights and Fundamental Freedoms*. Final Report. UN Doc. E/CN.4/Sub.2./1993/8 (1993).

17. *Velasquez-Rodriguez*, Inter-Am. C.H.R., 11 H.R.L.J. 127, P 25 (1989). The court here awarded the family of a "disappeared" person damages for loss of earnings and psychological injuries.

18. *See* Schrage, *supra* note 15.

19. *Tel Oren v. Libyan Arab Republic*, 726 F.2d 774 (D.C. Cir. 1984).

20. *See supra* at note 10.

21. *See Wiwa v. Royal Dutch Petroleum Co.*, 226 F.3d 88 (2d Cir. 2000), *cert. denied*, 532 U.S. 941 (2001).

22. *See Democratic Republic of Congo v. Belgium* (Int'l. Ct. of Justice 2002).

23. *See supra* at note 10.

24. *Sinaltrainal v. The Coca Cola Company*, 256 F. Supp. 2d 1345 (the court granted defendants' motion to dismiss with regard to lack of subject matter jurisdiction, under the TVPA, ATCA, and all RICO claims); *Villeda v. Fresh Del Monte Produce Inc.*, Case No. 01-CIV-3399 (S.D. Fla. 2001).

25. *See* Legality of the Use of Force (Serbia and Montegro v. Belgium), 2004 I.C.J. 279 (Dec. 15, 2004).

*We can see now that the judicialization of transitional justice, in engagement with constitutional and regional treaty norms, has become ever more common. This raises two sorts of questions: To what extent has the present conception of transitional justice been impacted by rights talk and constitutionalism? And, by the same token, how has transitional justice affected constitutional values and commitments? The evident trend toward the legalization and judicialization of transitional justice is a theme common to many of the essays in this book. Can we still really speak of an independent understanding of transitional justice particular to moments of radical political change, when mechanisms associated with traditional justice become institutionalized as general obligations of accountability for the past, required as a matter of constitutional and/or international law?*

# 11 Transitional Justice and the Transformation of Constitutionalism

THIS CHAPTER AIMS at exploring the mutual influence of transitional justice and constitutionalism. Constitutionalism herein is understood broadly, not just as the positive law of written constitutions but as the set of fundamental legal and political norms and practices that are constitutive of the polity, identified by Aristotle as the *politeia*. The chapter proceeds by tracing political and legal developments in various regions in relation to constitutional change, and by looking to relevant transitional justice developments.[1]

The predominant strands of constitutional theory in the twentieth century, particularly in the Anglo-American world, modeled constitutionalism as a form of pre-commitment and constraint on governmental or state action, usually in the name of individual rights. This form of constitutionalism is also reflected in a vision of separation of powers within the state and sometimes a federal division of powers, checks, and balances.[2] Here we can see the significant influence of the U.S. experience, given its contribution of a constitutional structure with restraints internal to the constitution and institutionalized in governmental structure, including judicial review, separation of powers, and federalism. This model was widely exported often notwithstanding context—political realities on the ground.[3]

The content of contemporary constitutionalism is also being shaped through developments in transitional justice, that is, systematic responses to the wrongs of the prior regime, or which occurred in the course of the political conflict that ultimately was resolved by or resulted in the new regime. Constitutions are created during periods of transition following political repression—indeed the post–World War II period has been characterized as the third wave of constitutionalism. Conversely, the new constitutionalism cannot help but shape our evolving assessment or evaluation of transitional justice itself.

Let us begin with the concept of "state action," which in the tradition of liberal constitutionalism has been central to defining the ambit of applicability of constitutional norms. As already suggested, twentieth-century constitutionalism at its core was shaped by the demand for limited government as is reflected internally by concepts of separation of powers and judicial review. Increasingly, however, we see in constitutionalism an important concern with *accountability* even for state *inaction*, reflecting an appreciation of the ability of the action of other actors and collectivities to affect underlying constitutional values and interests. Here, constitutionalism is evolving in a subtle relationship with conceptions of state responsibility in international law. Through the globalization of transitional justice, these conceptions have come to bear on understandings of constitutional obligation, further attenuating or nuancing the notion of constitutionalism in terms of the protection of the individual *against* the action of the state. Third, constitutionalism has no longer come to rest on the idea of defining the meaning for the individual of membership in the preexisting polity, with its claims regarding membership and identity. This is also reflected in the changing nature of rights protection, especially group conceptions of rights that may guide a way to deal meaningfully with the root causes of conflict and provide new parameters by which to identify and respond to political violence.

There is an ever-growing demand for *accountability*, captured by the core approaches to judicial guarantees and rights protection. Moreover, accountability appears not to be exhausted or fulfilled either by rights against the state or by democratic self-determination. In modern state constitutionalism, the subject of constitutional law is defined by the state and its aegis, seen in the basis of threshold of state action.[4] This is rooted in a distinct political history—the concern about abuses by the sovereign. It also reflects a distinctive view of the public sphere. Here, one might consider the ways that constitutions are informed by an obsession with a repressive past often associated with monarchical abuses and, later, with the legacies of fascism and mass totalitarian politics. To some degree, one can see elements of the essential features of the German Basic Law as responses to the experience of Nazism. Such laws do not merely set constraints on the state, but also reflect anxiety about mass politics and attempts to shape civil society, by putting limits on collective action at the social level.[5] Similarly, the European Convention on Human Rights explicitly prescribes limits on individual rights such as freedom of speech or conscience, wherever these may unduly impact upon other minority rights, or jeopardize democracy.[6] Thus, while Article 10 provides that "Everyone has the right to freedom of expression… (t)he exercise of these freedoms may be subject to such formalities, conditions, restrictions or penalties as are prescribed by law and are necessary in a democratic society."[7] This view of constitutionalism incorporates or embeds a dynamic understanding of civil society or social order as well as democracy as important values. One can see provisions which relate to historical, post-war experiences where expression rights instruments used to incite popular hatred of minorities and mobilize fanatical political prejudice. The more contemporary history in the Balkans and Rwanda has only reinforced a sense of these risks.[8]

Moreover, these historically derived approaches—arguably understood as transitional justice in its constitutional modality—appear to inform contemporary instances of "militant democracy" which are increasingly visible in Europe. Such instances are particularly apparent in regards to constraints upon exercises of political and religious expression: Burkha bans in several jurisdictions, the protest against the Danish cartoons, the Swiss plebiscite on public symbols of Islam, notably the minaret.[9] Indeed, one might perhaps best comprehend these developments in terms of a view of Europe itself in transition, that is, a Union in the midst of regional integration as well as processes of accession.[10]

Just what does the state owe its citizens as a constitutional matter? While twentieth-century constitutionalism had the state and its interests at its core, as reflected in the concern for abuse of state action, one can see that transitional constitutionalism in its twenty-first century has more primordial concerns. Here, we can see the vulnerabilities, for example in post-war Europe in the growing demand for a constitutionalism—beyond the state, notably in contexts involving conflict over religious expression where the state in a sense competes with peoples.[11] This is becoming even clearer with the increase in numbers of weak or failed states, giving rise to a twenty-first–century constitutionalism which addresses both state and nonstate actors—with evolving relevant understandings of responsibility beyond the state. This can be seen in the landmark prosecutions of international courts, such as the International Criminal Tribunal for the former Yugoslavia (ICTY) and International Criminal Court (ICC), which have often involved nonstate actors. Indeed, the landmark first cases in both tribunals fell into this category.

The evolving conception has in one way or another been informed by contemporary developments in transitional justice as well as international law. This is especially so where international human rights have been informed by precepts of international humanitarian law. Core questions of individual rights and state responsibility, as well as broader understandings of justice, are at issue. One can see the arc beginning earlier, with the post-war human rights covenants, such as the International Covenant on Civil and Political Rights, and the ways these conventions inform constitutional law and the normative commitment states owe their citizens, going to the changing view of individual responsibility in situations of conflict. One might also add the recently expanding jurisdiction of various ad hoc international criminal tribunals aimed at establishing individual responsibility. In *Prosecutor v Tadić*, the first international war crimes trial since World War II, jurisdiction was taken by the ad hoc tribunal although the relevant conflicts were largely internal, informing core obligations to humanity protection even where within the borders of the state, and hence not traditionally within international law understandings of principles of state responsibility. Another illustration is afforded by contemporary case law in the United States Supreme Court, for example, *Hamdan*, expounding upon the normative protections for detainees in U.S. custody under Geneva Common Article III. Indeed, there is an expanding understanding of individual responsibility evidenced by changes in the international conventions, such as the Convention on the Elimination of Discrimination against Women (CEDAW), whose scope reaches beyond the state to the private sphere where core discrimination is at stake.[12] What is now clear is that individual rights protection does not just follow from assertions of individual human rights concerns in the abstract, but rather, is connected to changing concepts of state responsibility. This can be seen in challenges surrounding changing principles of attribution, as in the landmark World Court decision in *Bosnia v. Serbia* and other case law at the cusp of individual and state responsibility.[13] Last, one can see evolution in the substantive norms of accountability in the changing parameters surrounding the protection of nonstate actors in inter-state affairs, and what duties are owed persons and peoples.

In the remainder of this chapter, drawing upon case law across regions, I aim to identify and discuss sites of contact between transitional and constitutional jurisprudence which I contend reflect normative transformation. From Africa to Eastern Europe to Latin America, developments in transitional justice are now having a significant influence on the evolving conception of constitutionalism, both in the way that judges apply constitutional norms, but also in the way others in the polity understand such norms. Transitional justice expounds a broader understanding of constitutionalism than the traditional account, one that implicates civil society as well as the state.

## The Changing Constitutional Self

In this section, I examine developments regarding the understanding of the self at the heart of two regimes and how these inform and mutually reinforce one another. I turn to the central example offered by the post-apartheid South African democracy. Here, one can see the evident link between a negotiated political transition and a distinctive perspective upon justice and constitution, in other words, the ways that the transitional legacy might well inform and prefigure constitutional injustice. The analysis might then be useful to understanding constitutionalism in other transitional contexts.

In South Africa, the interim 1993 constitution set out the basic political bargain informing the transition to democracy, including provision for amnesties. This provided the backdrop to the Promotion of National Unity and Reconciliation Act and the Truth and Reconciliation Commission (TRC) that it established.[14] As I argued in *Transitional Justice*, from the beginning, one can see the close association of the constitution-making and transitional justice processes, as the interim constitution is characterized as part of the 'bridge' out of apartheid.[15] Indeed, one can see that it is the parallel commitment to the constitution and its popular ratification processes that also lends the TRC much of its legitimacy. Without this commitment it would be hard to understand amnesties as a form of justice rather than the denial of justice. When the TRC's amnesty provisions were challenged under the permanent South African constitution by victims' groups, but sustained by its Constitutional Court, the decision thereby assimilated the norms governing the transition to constitutionalism as such: "If the constitution kept alive the prospect of continuous retaliation and revenge, the agreement of those threatened by its implementation might never have been forthcoming, and if it had the bridge itself would have remained wobbly and insecure, threatened by fear from some and anger from others. It was for this reason that those who negotiated the constitution made a deliberate choice, preferring understanding over vengeance, reparation over retaliation, *ubuntu* [Zulu for "humaneness: or generosity of spirit] over victimization."[16]

In the South African case, one can see the way the transitional commitment to transformation—and in particular, the central norm of *ubuntu*, the art of human-ity—operates as a constitutional value in setting out the parameters of compre-hension of perpetrators, victims, and the TRC and the constitution.[17] Indeed, the clearly asserted humanity value distinguishes the South African approach, even more meaningfully as the first of the new generation of constitutionalism—by its inclu-siveness and hence implied consociationalism that aims to cut across past political divisions, across state and nonstate actors. This explicit inclusiveness laid the basis that is key to the narrative of parallels put forth in the country's TRC report, which affirmed "gross violations of human rights were perpetrated or facilitated by all the major role-players in the conflicts of the mandate era."[18] And, moreover, this dual focus also informed the direction of the constitution, in that the inclusion of outside opposition provided the basis for unity constitutionalism, or consociationalism.[19] The distinctive transitional human rights–based framing, associated with *ubuntu*, has a clear appeal, as here is a norm at once aimed at addressing the wounds of the past, and yet also framed with a commitment to universalizability, as well as having a prospective, outward-looking direction.

Here are the dual optics of justice: the partially backward-looking aims of tran-sitional justice linked to the largely forward-looking constitutional process. From the one side, it seemed plain that the process underway of constitution drafting (going back to the first constitutional negotiations) helped legitimate the Truth and Reconciliation Commission processes. But, the converse also seems evidently true as the very inclusion of social and economic rights would be understood against the backdrop of the country's dire political and economic past and therefore in light of the evident problem of enforceability of such rights. It follows that their constitu-tionalization was inevitably predicated upon the transitional normativity (as seen in the draft ANC Bill of Rights), and therefore the ways that rights norms were constructed prefigure the constitution, and build upon the past legacy—namely of confiscation attendant upon state-affirmative duties to repair. One might consider in this regard the Constitution's socioeconomic rights, which on the one hand do not set out determinate positive remedies, and yet contemplate state action toward "progressive realization,"[20] rendering the norm in itself explicitly transitional.[21] This must be seen in light of the prior legacy of exploitation and land confiscation and in the commitment to the protection of groups. Consider also the Constitution's protection of language and culture rights both individual and in communal terms.[22] This brings front and center the idea of the constitutional self. More generally, a transitional context itself lends the constitutional project an implicit teleology.

To what extent can truth commission–type processes be exported elsewhere in the absence of a negotiated constitutional transition? On this point, we now have more evidence of the effects of the absence of such full constitutional legitimacy, especially in Latin America. This perspective helps to shed light on the question of just how and why, three decades later, these issues still garner the attention of civil society and have spurred demands for criminal and other justice processes despite the passage of time.

Accountability of actors beyond the state was incorporated expressly into the making of South Africa's transitional constitution. Moreover, going forward, these understandings have continued to shape the normative understanding of constitutional justice in the country. Consider the final South African constitution, which explicitly affirms a social and collective rights approach to these issues, contemplating an explicitly proactive state approach to the realization of these rights.[23] In referring to land rights, for example, the constitution expressly contemplates further legislative measures to redress past discrimination. "A person or community dispossessed of property after 19 June 1913 as a result of past racially discriminatory laws or practices is entitled,...either to restitution of that property or to equitable redress. No provision...may impede the state from taking legislative and other measures to achieve land, water and related reform, in order to redress the results of past racial discrimination."[24] And "(e)veryone has the right to have access to health care services...food and water...and social security...And [t]he state must take reasonable legislative and other measures, within its available resources, to achieve the progressive realization of each of these rights."[25]

Contemporary constitutionalism and, in particular, its more universalizable human rights–based group identity concept, where there is protection of affiliation on the basis of religion or ethnicity and any similar group affiliation, owes a debt to transitional justice developments over recent decades (particularly the South African case). This suggests a backward-looking direction, wherever the relevant categories were framed in terms of past violations and the related group claims for "restorative justice."

In *AZAPO*, the South African Constitutional Court upheld the constitutionality of a section of the Truth and Reconciliation Act granting amnesty to a perpetrator of an unlawful act associated with political objectives and committed prior to 6 December 1993.[26] Observing the "agonizing balancing act between the need for justice to victims of past abuse and the need for reconciliation and rapid transition to a new future."[27] the Court held that civil amnesty was supported by the epilogue to the Constitution. Moreover, as the *AZAPO* Court's decision suggests, a possible path to legitimacy may well be found in the commonality or overlapping process, the shared agreement at the time on the character of the relevant constitutional self, that is, who is in and who outside the constitution. These developments elucidate who is the constitutional self, as what became clear early on were the vulnerabilities in the country's transitional constitutionalism, especially regarding the victims, and the extent to which these citizens were largely left outside of the process—in light of the rationale of the transition for unity politics, as the constitutional case law of the time would reflect.[28] Here, one might compare the Brazilian constitutional court amnesty case, *Julia Gomes Lund et al. (Guerrilha do Araguaia)*, where the Supreme Federal Court, Brazil's highest court, upheld the country's 1979 law that provided full amnesty to members of the former military for crimes with a political basis committed during Brazil's military dictatorship of 1964–85,[29] which because of the country's popular process lay the basis for its ongoing legitimacy.[30]

It is therefore not surprising that there is now a widely proliferating phenomenon of transitional justice postponed—often decades after the fact, particularly in the African continent, as well as in parts of Latin America. In this transitional justice revisited, it is the victims, and their representatives, that are often the key civil society actors engaged in keeping the question on the table (South Africa's Khulumani support group is one example).[31] Victims' groups have benefited from the proliferation of tribunals and fora, including transnational litigation and tort suits under the U.S. Alien Tort Act (for example, *AZAPO*). In Chile, the demand for the extradition of Pinochet via universal jurisdiction from Spain had the effect of reopening transitional justice policy back home. This, of course, would ultimately raise questions for the status of the internal amnesty, as well as for their potential role in transnational lawmaking. Hence, one can see that the claim or stake of universal normativity is always applied in a particular context, and therefore drives a different negotiation even in the local context—via humanity the claim is reconfigured as connected to global society.

In any event, as one can see, wherever transitional justice has not been delivered, there is often a concomitant move away from the state, and its political monopoly, to claim for representation by and on behalf of its constituent peoples. Therefore, not surprisingly, when the *Khulumani* litigation began, the South African government initially raised, then dropped, its opposition—reflecting a changing strategy vis-à-vis transitional justice and state responsibility.[32] This precedent would ultimately guide responses to political violence, inserting itself in the debates about punitive versus restorative justice and individual versus collective responsibility. Yet, often these debates were waged eliding the fuller political context of a connection between Truth and Reconciliation commissions and constitutions, as they both deal with collectivities in such periods. Here, one might compare *Azapo* with *Barrios Altos*, a decision of the Inter-American

Court of Human Rights reopening amnesty policies in the Americas rationalized in terms of judicial protection—as it affords, in the context of amnesty, discussion and order of remedies establishing international rights to an investigation and reparation. In the African context, maintaining a dualist view is key to *Azapo*'s ruling of constitutionality, as the high court was called upon to address and distinguish the pertinent international law seen in terms of its relationship to constitutional adjudication, finding it "relevant only in the interpretation of the Constitution itself" insofar as it can meaningfully guide civil conflict of the sort here.[33] Regarding the amnesty laws, the Court explained, "[T]his incompatibility signifies that those laws are null and void, because they are at odds with the State's international commitments. Therefore, they cannot produce the legal effects inherent in laws promulgated normally and which are compatible with the international and constitutional provisions that engage the State of Peru. The incompatibility determines the invalidity of the act, which signifies that the said act cannot produce legal effects."[34]

The questions as to the impact on legitimacy of such contestations of domestic constitutionalism relate to a prior point regarding the extent to which prior transitional settlements have been legitimated via their constitutionalization. Hence the evolution of later jurisprudence is relevant to accountability. To what extent might regional rights precedents offer an alternative path to effect norm change within the rule of law—that is, change that might otherwise destabilize domestic constitutional doctrine?

## On the Evolution of State Responsibility in the Context of Tribunalization

The growing tribunalization of judgment concerning conflict-related political violence has constitutional implications, in particular, for changes in the principle of state responsibility. For the last decade has seen the establishment of a permanent criminal court with ongoing jurisdiction during conflict, with a new mandate to supervise the actions by both public and private actors at any echelon of power for grave violations of international humanitarian law, the most serious crimes of international society.[35] Once again, there is potential for significant impact in the generalization or normalization of transitional justice for the transformation of the constitutional subject. This judicialization at the regional level indubitably affects the developments in constitutionalism within the region. The tribunal creates a space for the adjudication of rights at a transnational level. Indeed, its decisions become constitutionalized in the broad sense through their influence on a range of actors, including domestic judiciaries.

To illustrate, consider the commitment to the International Criminal Court and its punitive reach for the contemporary understanding of the constitutional self on the African continent. From the start, since the Court's jurisdiction is premised on "complementarity," membership reflects a level of normative adherence; not merely mere compliance as a matter of simple cooperation with the tribunal, but rather including steps such as adoption of domestic legislation to facilitate substantive jurisdiction, such as to punish war crimes, analogous to those commitments to domestic measures guaranteed in the other conventions.[36] Beyond this, it would also imply a commitment to implementation at the level of the state. So understood, and scholarly writing to the contrary notwithstanding, the sense in which the ICC hardly comports to the zero-sum understanding of political competences and related changes anticipated by scholars regarding the current international/domestic allocation regarding jurisdiction over political violence.[37] Indeed, to the contrary, the significance of state cooperation here lies in assuming these added obligations reflexively and in light of other—potentially private— actors. This leads to situations where, so far, there are mostly private, not public, actors on the stand, reflecting the privatization of relevant action and accountability—pointing also to the role of this tribunal in the legitimation of the use of force. It was in the reaction to the convening of ad hoc criminal tribunals, especially the International Tribunal for Rwanda, that the exercise of "primacy," the assumed priority of international over local prosecution, would inspire opposition, and the critical challenge that any such permanent judicial institution should commence from the start by deferring to the jurisdiction of the state.[38] Yet, by the time the international tribunals become entrenched, it becomes clear that this is too statecentric a view, and that it fails to take in the role of other political actors here that have the potential to shape the constitutional structure, rivaling peoples and their representatives. While, in the mainstream view, the role of international justice tends to be evaluated in statecentric terms,[39] one might compare the effects of the ICTY to the 1990 Milošević prosecution and its political impact—a legal move credited with affecting an evident political disqualification, with obvious constitutional implications in the region.

Beyond this very prominent instance, one would see in the subsequent proliferation of tribunals that virtually all of the subjects of its supervision are private actors, shedding needed light on exactly where the courts might fit into global governance, important for understanding the judicial implications for maintaining democracy and constitutionalism. So, for example, the first case before the International Criminal Court involves Uganda's taking to court its murderous political opposition, with the rare exception to the ICC docket, via the traditional inter-state security framework, as in the Security Council's referral of

Bashir for his role in Sudan. The ICC's most recent indictments regarding Kenya and its post-election violence, again, demonstrate the potential of international justice in the attempt to strengthen constitutionalism and rule of law in the region. This is opening up a space for a new source of legitimation for the successor regime: cooperation with the Court. Here, we can see the court supervising the basic rule of law guiding democratic transition.

## Evolving Understandings of State Responsibility

Liberal rights depend essentially on the competent exercise of a certain kind of legitimate public power according to Stephen Holmes.[40] Yet, it is exactly the absence of such legitimate public power which frames the context for the phenomena discussed here. In particular, the shift in focus both within constitutionalism and transitional justice discourses toward dealing with what are seen as weak, failed, or divided states lies at the core of a new global transitional justice. This has clear implications for its relation to, and transformative effects on, contemporary constitutionalism.[41]

In earlier phases of modern constitutionalism, the focus on state action narrowly understood resulted from time to time in "tragic choices." One might recall in this regard a regrettable United States Supreme Court case, *Deshaney v Winnebago*, involving the failure of the state to intervene in a traditionally private area of family life. The case raised the question of what duty was owed children in foster care where, despite allegations of violence, the state did not act and was not held responsible for its omission in the absence of proof to make out state action.[42] Indeed, this norm had been a challenge for transitional justice in the past: how to obtain ruling as to state responsibility in cases of omission? Along with developments, discussed below, regarding the democratic expansion of action attributable to the state, one can see there is another related issue: what is the relation between the state, particularly weak or failed states, and the aim of protection of human beings or human security?

In the Southern Cone, the marked evolution of regional landmark individual rights case law draws in an ongoing way from periods of struggle to deal with the disappearances that pervaded the region for more than a decade. In *Velasquez-Rodriguez*,[43] the Inter-American Court of Human Rights addressed the question of accountability and impunity, directly engaging the nature of the state in the context of a lack of accountability or outright impunity with regard to past acts of political violence. A series of cases coming out of the Inter-American Court, as well as the high courts of states in the region, point to an interesting trend in the concept of state obligation, one that arguably gets beyond the state action limitation as well as the negative rights view, to posit that even where the state has failed to control past political violence, it ought to assume various affirmative obligations that go to the heart of the rule of law.

In *Velasquez-Rodriguez v Honduras*, the Inter-American Commission on Human Rights brought an action in the Inter-American Court of Human Rights regarding the 1981 disappearance of a Honduran student, Angel Manfredo Velasquez Rodriguez.[44] Holding Honduras had violated Articles 4, 5, and 7 of the American Convention on Human Rights, the Court held that "under international law a State is responsible for the acts of its agents undertaken in their official capacity and for their omissions, even when those agents act outside the sphere of their authority or violate internal law."[45] *Velasquez Rodriguez* was a landmark case in the Inter American Court, and would have effects far beyond the state and even the region in shaping the scope of state responsibility in transitions. Such regional precedents also elucidate the limits of constitutionalism in weak states undergoing transition.

In a context of lawlessness in the region, the question becomes, what is the meaning of state responsibility? Where thousands disappeared to their deaths, what is the state's duty to provide accountability? To what extent is the immediate successor regime responsible, and for what? In this landmark case, the problem at hand was what is the relevance and meaning of state action for purposes of accountability in the transition, in light of the disappearances that had occurred during the prior regime (and indeed as would later be revealed under Operation Condor throughout the region).[46] For purposes of state responsibility, the Court held that whether the abductors were state actors or not was of no consequence: the disappearance policy implied a presumption.[47] This move allowed the plaintiffs to link up the evidence of systemic harm, even where circumstantial, to establish a pattern of action. Hence, one can see a relaxing of the required nexus or criterion regarding attribution to the state: "An illegal act which violates human rights and which is initially not directly imputable to a State (for example, because it is the act of a private person)...can lead to international responsibility of the State, not because of the act itself, but because of the lack of due diligence to prevent the violation or to respond to it as required by the Convention."[48] What might this presumption tell us about the changing view of state responsibility in the context of political violence? For the court, "the State has a legal duty to take reasonable steps to prevent human rights violations and to use the means at its disposal to carry out a serious investigation of violations committed within its jurisdiction, to identify those responsible, impose the appropriate punishment and to ensure the victim adequate compensation."[49] Where there is violation of rights protected under the convention, the Court has referred to Article 63(1) of the American Convention, which provides that "the consequences of the breach of the rights be remedied and rule that just compensation be paid" "the injured party be ensured the enjoyment of his right or freedom."[50]

After this landmark opinion, the Inter-American Court's elaboration of state responsibility in the context of past human rights violations would influence the conception of state responsibility beyond international law, and would penetrate *within* states to impart their accountability to their own citizens. Accordingly, recent constitutional decisions out of Argentina—which reference the international human rights norms of the *Velasquez Rodriguez* line of cases—are often misread as being purely about setting limits to state power. They are apparently seen as limiting the political dealmaking of the past that had led to amnesties, for example in Chile and Uruguay. But, more important, these decisions appear to redraw and newly circumscribe the meaning of the state and its domestic competences, elaborating upon the duties of exercising its powers of judgment and establishing a set of fundamental obligations regarding the state and judicial protection.

In *Barrios Altos*,[51] involving a 1991 politically motivated massacre under the Fujimori regime,[52] the Inter-American Court of Human Rights invalidated the "self-amnesty," Law No. 26479, which had authorized amnesty to security forces and government officials for any alleged human rights violations. Instead, the Court found state responsibility for violations of core rights under the American Convention, including the right to life in Article 4, the right to a fair trial in Article 8, and rights to judicial guarantees and judicial protection in Article 25.[53] Moreover, the impact of the deprivation of such rights meant that other provisions were violated, such as the obligation to respect rights as well as the obligation in Article 2 to provide for domestic legal effect for the norms of the Convention.

This regional human rights case law is having a clear impact upon the evolution of both transitional justice and constitutionalism in the region and beyond. Of critical importance is the broader principle by which the regional court linked up the loss of the protection of personal integrity with the ongoing deprivation of meaningful judicial guarantees and protection: "This court considers that all amnesty provisions, provisions on prescription and the establishment of measures designed to eliminate responsibility are inadmissible, because they are intended to prevent the investigation and punishment of those responsible for serious human rights violations such as torture, extrajudicial, summary or arbitrary execution and forced disappearance, all of them prohibited because they violate non-derogable rights recognized by international human rights law." Beyond self-amnesty this is significant because the language of the opinion was not itself limited, referring specifically to "the manifest incompatibility of self-amnesty laws and the American Convention on Human Rights," but also to the measures at issue as inadmissible "provisions on prescription and the establishment of measures designed to eliminate responsibility" of "measures aimed at continuing to obstruct the investigation" and referring to "all amnesty provisions."

In the Americas, *Velasquez- Rodriguez'* influence would extend beyond its facts, where one can see its normative effects even without immediate state compliance. The norms drawn from this supranational court (albeit signed up to by member states in the region) have been picked up within the successor constitutions in the region, often explicitly or via judicial interpretation.[54] In particular, in Argentina, there has been an ongoing dynamic regarding the question of what relation transitional justice ought to have with the country's constitutionalism. Here, one might begin by first acknowledging the force of the line of decisions where the human rights provisions which at the time of the most recent transition have previously been incorporated in international human rights in the Argentine constitution.[55] Consider that the postauthoritarian Argentine constitution explicitly invokes international human rights law; yet, while the first post-successor Argentine constitution had incorporated human rights treaties in the immediate transition, at the time, mere textual inclusion would not turn out to be enough to guarantee meaningful enforcement.[56] Instead, one might best understand the initial policy on trials to have arrived at a rather hasty conclusion, one which now appears to enjoy rather diminished legality or legitimacy, since the demand for transitional justice clearly persists despite the passage of three decades since junta rule.[57] The question has become whether there is any possibility of accountability in this moment. Beyond the state, wherever these questions have been kept alive, it has been largely through civil society and private actors, especially victims' groups and their representatives.

How have these questions, which were associated with the first generation debates on transitional justice, shaped the more contemporary reconceptualization of constitutionalism in the region? One can see the pursuit of transitional justice is underway in the courts now, which is calling the judiciary to a more activist review of transitional precedents, decisions which now are being reconceived in light of human rights developments, regional precedents, and rights conventions. These decisions are having a broad effect in the region, as they have shaped both the course of transitional justice as well as of constitutional review. Hence, in the case of *Simon, Julio Hector y otros*, involving illegal detention, torture, and disappearances, Argentina's high court wrestled with the critical question of the extent to which the country's amnesty policy was reconcilable with its constitution and binding international law. In the most recent set of precedents,[58] the Court appeared to reverse prior transitional justice policy, in that this Supreme Court decision struck down amnesties, even those that had been politically arrived at and validated within the existing constitutional system.[59] Amnesties had apparently been accepted within the Argentine constitutional system, despite the legally prevailing context of incorporating human rights treaties into its domestic law.[60] These parallel developments inevitably had an effect on the legitimacy of domestic constitutionalism, particularly given the perceptions of the strength of the country's commitment to international human rights. Indeed, one might see this latter wave of transitional justice as reflexive and responsive to predecessor judicial review and its shortcomings, with consequences for human rights protection in the prior period of repressive rule.

Now, let us turn to the constitutional developments occasioned as a result of the changes in doctrine and normativity discussed above. With the passage of time, non-state actors turned to alternative fora, whether international or regional, or domestic courts via "universal jurisdiction," as well as new transitional justice institutions. The ad hoc international criminal tribunals have given new meaning to these treaties. They have been applied and interpreted to vitiate standing amnesties, with implications over the long run for our constitutional balance of powers. Indeed, as we will see, where punishment involves offenses such as the "crime against humanity," this norm is broad enough to become a placeholder, to evolve over the years with both internal and inter-state ramifications, as well as, more broadly, for the course of current foreign affairs discourse.

These developments reflect the evolution of the relevant freedoms at stake—in the direction of the reconceptualization of relevant state power, where the meaning of state action for purposes of transitional justice and constitutionalism is no longer seen as limited or "negative" as in earlier phases, but, rather, implies the protection of a range of other rights as well. Moreover, these rights weren't conceived purely as limits on state power, but instead, as establishing a basis for action, indeed, presenting obligations for the state and nonstate actors. In *Simon*, 2005, the Argentine Supreme Court ruled the Ley de Punto Final and the Ley de Obediencia Debida unconstitutional. Because these crimes fell within the law of the time, that is, Ley de Obediencia Debida, the Court found the legislation "unconstitutional" largely in terms of international human rights norms, violating the American Convention on Human Rights, the ICCPR, and the Convention against Torture.[61] With this case, although close to two decades after the repressive period, the Argentine Supreme Court struck down the laws that had limited prosecutions. In doing so, it drew upon the regional American norms that had evolved in the meantime and were seen as incorporated within the country's constitutionalism.[62]

How should we evaluate this change? One might say that the first transitional and constitutional response in the region was to limit the state. This can be seen in post-authoritarian constitutionalism, with its notion of strong states *with* strong constitutions. For this purpose a form of restoration of the constitutionalism that had preceded the authoritarian rule was enough; but, with the passage of time, it is clear that this is no longer deemed sufficient to establish and convey the rule of law.

To what extent could the change in constitutionalism be effected without a loss of legitimacy? There is a return to a prior normative dimension of transitional justice in constitutional law, as it would be the post-Alfonsin administration that would give human rights treaties constitutional standing when the first successor regime had moved to amend the constitution in 1993.

*Simon* appears to present a complete overturning of the prior consensus on transitional justice, reflecting an apparent rebalancing of the values of justice of transition, with effects for domestic constitutionalism as well. It reflected a division in the criminal justice power, which would seem to go to the core of enforcement of laws, at least where certain core crimes are no longer completely within domestic jurisdiction. The Argentine Supreme Court held that where crimes against humanity are at stake, there is no temporal limitation on prosecution, despite the three decades and substantial passage of time since the event.[63] The continuity of state responsibility becomes a constitutional principle.

## Reconstituting Europe: Transitional Justice for Its Peoples

Last, I turn to the ways post–Cold War transitional justice is informing understandings of the state and inter-state relations, and the conceptualization of the public and the private, of internal and international conflict in the European space. In particular, how does the evolution of current instances of militancy fit into the category? They clearly, for example, share the historical concerns of constitutionalism, which is confirmed by past political pathologies. Here we can see the context for modern European instances as linked to actual contemporary constitutional transitions in the makeup of European constitutional states.

Once again, we will see the effect of judicialization on the direction of development of conceptions of state responsibility, as well as of the view of its state's relation to other actors as well. Let us begin with the International Tribunal for the former Yugoslavia which, in response to the post–Cold War Balkans conflict, reaffirmed Nuremberg's central principle of the subjectivization of responsibility for crimes against humanity and underscored the message of accountability for ethnic persecution, that is, for crimes against peoples. This was a principle of jurisprudence with constitutive dimensions with regard to states and the role of peoples on the continent.

Even more significant for understanding the normativity of constitutionalism, beyond its role in conflict, *strictu sensu*, is where we can see the institutions of punishment offering a basis for the renunciation of military and/or other collective sanctions. Cooperation with judicial processes is seen as evidence of reconciliatory aims and tantamount to a promise to cooperate with other European purposes and institutions. Thus, European Commission President José Manuel Barroso speaking of the arrest of Radovan Karadžić, the war architect of ethnic cleansing: "This...very positive development...will contribute to bringing justice and lasting reconciliation in the Western Balkans." Here we can see the EU accession process being made conditional on signs of adoption of transitional justice of a conciliatory nature. And, in so doing, taking what might amount to a stance on just war and demilitarization, plausibly of relevance going forward to integration in the region.

The complexity of the regional transitional justice project would commence with a private actor—a radical transformation in the understanding of state action and responsibility. *Tadić* was the first case before the ICTY and one in which it was confronted with a defendant who was a private, not a state, actor, but where the connection to the state remained an important question. As the tribunal opined, "It is nevertheless imperative to *specify* what *degree of authority or control* must be wielded by a foreign State over armed forces fighting on its behalf in order to render international an armed conflict which is *prima facie* internal. Indeed, the legal consequences of the characterization of the conflict as either internal or international are extremely important. Should the conflict eventually be classified as international, it would *inter alia* follow that a foreign State may in certain circumstances be held responsible for violations of international law perpetrated by the armed groups acting on its behalf."[64]

The EU accession process required Serbia to cooperate with the ICTY in a number of ways, including making efforts to apprehend suspects and turning them over to international justice.[65] Whether in regard to constitutionalism within states in the region, or to the European Union as a transnational constitutional order, we can see now the ways that transitional justice appears to operate as a precondition for the EU constitutional project. European Commission President José Manuel Barroso said of the Milošević trial, "It proves the determination of the new Serbian government to achieve full cooperation with the ICTY. Observers agree that the EU strategy of conditioning the progress of ex-Yugoslav countries towards joining the union on their cooperation with the International Criminal Tribunal for the former Yugoslavia, ICTY, 'has been a key tool in ensuring that perpetrators of war crimes committed during the Nineties Balkans wars face trial and victims see justice.' It is also very important for Serbia's European aspirations." Then EU foreign policy chief Javier Solana has said, "it shows the commitment of the new Serbian government to cooperate with international organizations." Here, the ICTY—as an institution both transitional and international—operating to reconstitute the relevant community of judgment—offers a rule of law that gestures toward an alternative normative future. Moreover, the Tribunal's purposes reflect the role of politics in rationalizing the broader humanity (human security) bases of these trials.

One can see the ways in which this dimension of transitional justice promotes constitutionalism in Serbia in the broader sense. It shows some willingness to move forward with respect to issues of states' responsibility, breaking with the previous regime and also addressing the role of nonstate actors as to accountability. This approach has now taken off with the RECOM.[66] This would reinforce local justice processes and point in a new direction as to the commitment to protect minorities.

Likewise, we can see in the consideration of other countries, for example, Turkey, respecting EU membership, there has been a need to address a number of unresolved long delayed conflicts. After decades of silence, it is only in the context of EU accession aspirations that Turkey has indicated willingness to engage regarding its past conflicts, involving Armenians and Kurdish peoples. With respect to the Armenians, Turkey has said it has been prepared to acknowledge the past and to address repair, referring the matter to a historical commission.[67] For Prime Minister Erdogan, "Today is the beginning of a new timeline and a fresh start," saying with regard to its Kurdish population, that it would recognize them and pay compensation: "fresh start: overhaul would expand use of minority language in a number of settings including national media and politics."[68] As at the start of the Balkans conflict, the protection of such rights is seen as key to the state's legitimacy in the new union.[69]

The assumption regarding these attempts at accountability seems to be that dealing with a state's past grievances reflects on its democratic potential for the future—although dealing with the past may well be easier than showing such capacities exist to deal with conflicts in the here and now. But, more fundamentally, it is predicated on the view that justice is the path to transformation in the treatment of transitional peoples in the region.

## Constitutionalism as the Law of Peoples

Now let us turn to the meaning of self-determination and political equality within the polity. The European Court of Human Rights, in a recent case, *Sejdic and Finci v Bosnia and Herzegovina*, conceded the transitional value of ethnically based representation following the Balkans conflict, but held nevertheless that such arrangements must respect individual democratic rights.

> When the impugned constitutional provisions were put in place a very fragile cease-fire was in effect on the ground. The provisions were designed to end a

brutal conflict marked by genocide and "ethnic cleansing." The nature of the conflict was such that the approval of the "constituent peoples" (namely, the Bosniacs, Croats and Serbs) was necessary to ensure peace…a challenge to the existing power sharing arrangements in Bosnia-Herzogovina on an ethnic "constituent peoples" basis excluding out representatives other than Bosnian Croats and Serbs, where the Court ruled that such structures were racially and ethnically discriminatory. "Racial discrimination is a particularly egregious kind of discrimination…requires from the authorities special vigilance…the authorities must use all available means to combat racism, thereby reinforcing democracy's vision of a society in which diversity is not perceived as a threat but as a source of enrichment."[70]

Indeed, by ratifying a Stabilization and Association Agreement with the European Union in 2008, the European Court of Human Rights found that the respondent State had committed itself to "amend[ing] electoral legislation regarding members of the Bosnia and Herzegovina Presidency and House of Peoples delegates to ensure full compliance with the European Convention on Human Rights and the Council of Europe post-accession commitments" within one to two years.[71]

Here, one can see a growing connection between transitional justice and what Joseph Weiler and others have described as the federal trajectory of Europe.[72] Reconciliation processes undertaken in the midst of the accession process, more generally, have resulted in evolution toward protection of indigenous peoples, reflecting newfound capacities for an array of effective judicial and other responses beyond the recognition and protection of individual rights. The state's responsibility in relation to the collective rights of indigenous peoples, a transitional response to "ethnic cleansing," had already become part of the canon of transitional justice (for example, *Velasquez-Rodriguez*), where affirming these rights implies attendant rights to judicial guarantees such as identification, prosecution, and reparations, or other past persecution–oriented rights. In the words of the Court, "The State has a legal duty to take reasonable steps to prevent human rights violations and to use the means at its disposal to carry out a serious investigation of violations committed within its jurisdiction, to identify those responsible, to impose the appropriate punishment and to ensure the victim adequate compensation."[73]

Beneath the surface lurks the perennial question about Europe's old divisions, and where exactly the peoples might fit within the modern state, as well as within the new entity of Europe. The element of a persecutory motive[74] uniquely mediates protection of individual and group identities so long as there are systematic mechanisms of state or state-like policy.[75] Indeed, to adjudicate the responsibility for humanity also means reaching the public and the private—whether in its perpetration, going beyond state sponsorship, but also, concern as to the protected person, and the sense of victimhood that goes beyond its relation to the state to the protection of various dimensions of civil society. It also entails protecting and accounting for individuals—as they are—with their affiliations,[76] and related political identities, delineating clear limits on what is, and what is not, legitimate state and parastate action in the twentieth century, and informing a standard of global accountability and governance.

Here, there are at least two lessons, one regarding the impact of transitional justice at the level of the state and the other informing the principles guiding interstate relations. First, and foremost, one can see that such discriminatory tactics can no longer be used to rationalize the state—that a state's constitutional identity can no longer be rationalized or entrenched around the *ethnos*—with implications internally for the conception of the constitution itself. And so for the interstate realm as well: the line of insistence on compliance reflects the clear limits to ethnonationalism being established in suits for corrective justice, such as that brought by Bosnia against Serbia, in the World Court. Laying down strict principles as to the permissibility of "ethnic cleansing" also offers guidance as to the parameters of legitimate political identity.

This could explain, without necessarily justifying, the absence of representatives of the other communities (such as local Roma and Jewish communities) at the peace negotiations and the participants' preoccupation with effective equality between the "constituent peoples" in the "post-conflict society." However, in this landmark case, the Court went on to set constitutional limits to such exercises of justice, ruling that, even if at an earlier point in the transitions, such political structures might well have a legitimate aim such as peace, at present such measures had to be said to be evaluated in terms of their proportionality:

> … the maintenance of the system in any event does not satisfy the requirement of proportionality…while the Court agrees with the Government that there is no requirement under the Convention to abandon totally the power-sharing mechanisms peculiar to Bosnia and Herzegovina and that the time may still not be ripe for a political system which would be a simple reflection of majority rule, the Opinions of the Venice Commission…clearly demonstrate that there exist mechanisms of powersharing which do not automatically lead to the total exclusion of representatives of the other communities…it is recalled that the possibility of alternative means achieving the same end is an important factor in this sphere (see Glor v. Switzerland, no. 13444/04, § 94, 30 April 2009).[77]

Given that the *ethnos* is no longer an unquestionable basis for state formation, to what extent can its preservation afford a basis for intervention, and if so, in what way? On the question of the direction of state external sovereignty, to some extent one can see that current developments in the conceptualization of state action and state responsibility (for example in the *Bosnia v Serbia* case) are explicitly broadening the nexus to the state. This naturally impacts accountability and the view of the state for constitutional purposes. As the World Court held, "The Court is however of the view that the particular characteristics of genocide do not justify the Court in departing from the criterion elaborated in the Judgment in the case concerning Military and Paramilitary Activities in and against Nicaragua (Nicaragua v. United States of America). The rules for attributing alleged internationally wrongful conduct to a State do not vary with the nature of the wrongful act in question in the absence of a clearly expressed *lex specialis*. Genocide will be considered as attributable to a State if and to the extent that the physical acts constitutive of genocide that have been committed by organs or persons other than the State's own agents were carried out, wholly or in part, on the instructions or directions of the State, or under its effective control."[78]

Here, it is interesting to think about the ways the Bosnia case has been influenced and informed both by the ICTY's transitional justice following the World Court decision, and to consider other ECHR decisions recognizing the clear limits of ethnonationalism. In the landmark case of *Sejdic and Finci v Bosnia and Herzegovina*, discussed above, the European Court of Human Rights, in supervising the transitional agreement in the region, sharply circumscribed the potential of legislating along ethnic lines, explaining that "no difference in treatment which is based exclusively or to a decisive extent on a person's ethnic origin is capable of being objectively justified in a contemporary democratic society built on the principles of pluralism and respect for different cultures."[79]

From the perspective of this justice-oriented case law, we can better understand the site of some of these recurring issues of religion, gender, and ethnicity as involving the balancing and reconciliation of the relevant preservation rights of persons and peoples, where group claims can be grounded on part of their traditions. These varying claims help to clarify the reconciliation/accommodation needed at the level of the state.

## Conclusion: Transitional Justice as Twenty-First Century Constitutionalism

This discussion yields observations as to the relation today of transitional justice and constitutionalism, namely that what we are seeing indubitably amounts to a new constitutionalism—one with distinct subjectivity and rule of law. The evolving normativity is enmeshed with contemporary politics and can tell us something about the conundra that lie at the heart of state politics today.

Principles of state responsibility that cut across the public and the private are being recognized via transitional justice, with implications for the reconceptualization of constitutionalism. There are some interpretations that assert the emergence of a global constitutionalism, representing in Habermas' words "the unity of the global legal system."[80] By contrast, the perspective that informs this chapter emphasizes neither systemic unity nor normative hierarchy but the dialogic character of interpretation and the mutual influence of diverse legal orders.

The very problem of justice is being reconceptualized, and it no longer centers on the state. If the classic understanding of the role of the state is to protect its citizens, via its central control of use of force, then these contemporary instances point to instances where there has been a loss of such control.

Rather than the centrality of the state, and the related aim to constitutionalize delimitation of state power, transitional constitutionalism poses a challenge that directly engages nonstate actors and their behavior at all levels and entails changing social norms. One can see dimensions of the above paradigm shift reflected in phenomena that address globalizing politics of a transitional nature. In the move away from the immediate post–Cold War conflicts that span international to internal conflict, such as in Milošević's Balkans or Saddam's Iraq, we start out by emphasizing state action, missing relevant transitional justice. We then move to evident weak and failed states, such as Afghanistan or Lebanon, to the paramilitaries in Sudan, where the relevant problem has changed: accounting for the varieties of transitional justice, in light of the growing pursuit of forms of accountability beyond the state. Appreciating fully this shift in perspective helps to explain the rise of international criminal justice, illuminating the role of the institutions of judgment.

The shift will have consequences for the evaluation of transitional justice and its relation to other political questions of conflict and resolution.[81] This chapter's normative take is that better understanding of this recent stage of aims, actors, and interests, and associated important changes, will have a significant impact upon the relevant measure for assessment of transitional justice and its relation to constitutionalism in the new century.

As seen above, transitional situations have set the stage for the evolution of constitutionalism such that, in many such situations, it targets rights abuses not committed by official state actors. One can see also the ways group claims have driven the aspiration of transition to a new polity, and, moreover, the reclamation of individual freedom. The task is creation of a legitimate polity in the first place, with transitional justice and constitution-building both being about construction/reconstruction of identity building, informing a transformed relationship among collectivities—one which is not simply reflective of the preexisting structure and identity of society.

# Notes

1. Ruti Teitel, *Transitional Justice* (Oxford: Oxford University Press, 2000).

2. Norman Dorsen, et. al., *Comparative Constitutionalism: Cases and Materials* (St. Paul, MN: Thomson West, 2010).

3. Mark Tushnet, *Taking the Constitution Away from the Courts* (Princeton, NJ: Princeton University Press, 1999).

4. Larry H. Tribe, *Constitutional Choices* (Cambridge, MA: Harvard University Press, 1986).

5. See German Constitution, art. 19; see also Ruti Teitel, 'Militating Democracy: Comparative Constitutional Perspectives', *Michigan Journal of International Law* 29 (2008):49.

6. Article 19 of the European Convention on Human Rights provides: 'To ensure the observance of the engagements undertaken by the High Contracting Parties in the present Convention, there shall be set up: 1. A European Commission of Human Rights hereinafter referred to as "the Commission"; 2. A European Court of Human Rights, hereinafter referred to as "the Court".'

7. Convention for the Protection of Human Rights and Fundamental Freedoms, 4 November 1950, 213 UNTS 221: Art. 10.

8. See *Prosecutor v Ruggui*, Case No. ICTR-97-32-I, Judgment and Sentence (1 June 2000); *Nahimana, Barayagwiza and Ngeze v Prosecutor*, Case No. ICTR-99-52-A, Appeals Chamber (28 November 2007); *Prosecutor v Kambanda*, Case No. ICTR 97-23-S, Judgment and Sentence (3 September 1998).

9. Ruti Teitel, "Militating Democracy: Comparative Constitutional Perspectives," *Michigan Journal of International Law* 29 (2008): 49.

10. Joseph Weiler, *The Constitution of Europe: 'Do the New Clothes Have an Emperor?' and Other Essays on European Integration* (Cambridge: Cambridge University Press, 1999).

11. Treaty of Lisbon Amending the Treaty on European Union and the Treaty Establishing the European Community, *Lisbon*, 13 December 2007, OJ [2007] C306/1; Bundesvervassungsgericht, Lisbon decision of 30 June 2009, http://www.bundesverfassungsgericht.de/entscheidungen/es20090630zbve000208en.htm.

12. Convention on the Elimination of All Forms of Discrimination Against Women ('CEDAW'), adopted 18 December 1979, GA Res. 34/180, UN GAOR 34th Sess., Supp. No. 46, UN Doc. A/34/36 (1980) (entered into force 3 September 1981).

13. See Application of the Convention on the Prevention and Punishment of the Crime of Genocide (Bosn. & Herz. v. Serb. & Mont.) (Judgment of Feb. 26, 2007), http://www.icj-cij.org/docket/index.php?p1=3&k=8d&p3=4&case=91 [hereinafter Bosnia v. Serbia case]; see also James Crawford, *The International Law Commission's Articles on State Responsibility: Introduction, Text and Commentaries* (Cambridge: Cambridge University Press, 2002).

14. See Promotion of National Unity and Reconciliation Act of South Africa, 1995.

15. Ruti Teitel, *Transitional Justice* (Oxford: Oxford University Press, 2000); see also *People's Organization (AZAPO) v The President of the Republic of South Africa*, 1996 (4) SALR 671, para. 19 (South African Constitutional Court) [Hereinafter *AZAPO* case].

16. *AZAPO* case, para. 19.

17. Drucilla Cornell, "Exploring Ubuntu: Tentative Reflections" *African Human Rights Law Journal* 5 (2005): 195.

18. See 'Truth and Reconciliation Commission of South Africa Report', Vol. 5, *Truth and Reconciliation Commission* (29 October 1998), para. 66.

19. For discussion of this form of political arrangement, See Ian Shapiro, *Democratic Justice* (New Haven: Yale University Press, 1999).

20. See Constitution of the Republic of South Africa (1996), arts. XXV–XXVII.

21. See ibid. (in relation to property, housing, health care, food, water, 'the state must take reasonable legislative and other measures, within its available resources, to achieve the progressive realization of these rights.').

22. See Constitution of the Republic of South Africa (1996), arts. XXX, XXXI.

23. Marion Smiley, "Democratic Jusice in Transition," *Michigan Law Review* 99 (2001): 1332; see also Ian Shapiro, *Democratic Justice* (New Haven, CT: Yale University Press, 1999).

24. See Craig M. Scott and Philip Alston, "Adjudicating Constitutional Priorities in a Transnational Context: A Comment on Soobramoney's Legacy and Grootboom's Promise," *South African Journal of Human Rights* 16 (2000): 206. See also *Government of the Republic of South Africa and Others v Grootboom and Others* (CCT11/00) [2000] ZACC 19; 2001 (1) SA 46; 2000 (11) BCLR 1169; (4 October 2000) (holding there is a right to housing); *Minister of Health and Others v Treatment Action Campaign and Others (No 1)* (CCT9/02) [2002] ZACC 16; 2002 (5) SA 703; 2002 (10) BCLR 1075 (5 July 2002) (finding a right to health care and access to HIV/AIDS treatment).

25. Constitution of the Republic of South Africa (1996), art. XXVI.

26. *AZAPO* case, para. 4.

27. *AZAPO* case, para. 22.

28. Indeed, the court's conceptualization opposes victimhood. See *AZAPO* case, para. 19 (referring to choice of 'ubuntu…humaneness over victimization').

29. "Brazil Court Upholds Law that Protects Torturers," *Amnesty International*, 30 April 2010, http://www.amnesty.org/en/news-and-updates/brazil-court-upholds-law-protects-torturers-2010-04-30; see also "Brazil: No Change to Amnesty Law," *New York Times*, 1 May 2010, http://www.nytimes.com/2010/05/01/world/americas/01briefs-Brazil.html.

30. On 20–21 May 2010, the case was heard at the Inter-American Court of Human Rights. See *Caso Gomes Lund y otros v Brasil*, Communicado de Prensa, CIDH_CP-08/10, http://www.corteidh.or.cr/.

31. See Khulumani v Barclay National Bank Ltd., 504 F.3d 254, 258 (2d Cir. 2007), see also America Isuzu Motors, Inc., et al. v Ntsebeza, 128 S. Ct. 2424 (2008).

32. See ibid.

33. See *AZAPO* case, paras. 26, 27, 30, 31.

34. *Case of Barrios Altos v Peru*, Series C No. 75 [2001] IACHR 5 (14 March 2001), para. 15 (concurring opinion of Judge Ramirez). [Hereinafter Barrios Altos Case].

35. See *Rome Statute of the International Criminal Court*, Article 28, UN doc. A/Conf. 183/9, (17 July 1998).

36. See American Convention on Human Rights, arts. 1(1) and 2, whereby states parties are 'obliged to take all measures to ensure no deprivation of judicial protection'. See also Robert Howse & Ruti Teitel, "Beyond Compliance: Rethinking Why International Law Really Matters," *New York University Journal of International Law* 19 (2010): 769.

37. Jean L. Cohen "Rethinking Sovereignty," Special Issue, *Constellations* 12 (2005): 2.

38. Jośe Alvarez, "Crimes of State, Crimes of Hate, Lessons from Rwanda," *Yale Journal of International Law* 24 (1999): 365.

39. *Prosecutor v Milošević*, Case No. IT-02-54 (International Criminal Tribunal for the former Yugoslavia 1999).

40. See Stephen Holmes, "What Russia Teaches Us Now: How Weak States Threaten Freedom," *The American Prospect*, 30 June 1997.

41. Ruti Teitel, "Militating Democracy: Comparative Constitutional Perspectives," *Michigan Journal of International Law* 29 (2008): 49.

42. *Deshaney v Winnebago*, 489 U.S. Sup. Ct. 189 (1989) ('our cases have recognized that the Due Process Clauses generally confer no affirmative right to governmental aid, even where such aid may be necessary to secure life, liberty, or property interests of which the government itself may not deprive the individual. . . . a State's failure to protect an individual against private violence simply does not constitute a violation of the Due Process Clause.').

43. See *Velásquez Rodríguez v Honduras*, Case 7920, Ser. C., No. 4, IACHR 35, OEA/ser. L/V/III.19 doc. 13 (1988), reprinted in *International Legal Materials* 28 (1989): 291.

44. Ibid.

45. See ibid., para. 170.

46. See ibid., para. 172.

47. See ibid., para. 124 (allowing circumstantial evidence to make out particular disappearance claim).

48. Ibid.

49. See ibid., para. 174.

50. *See Barrios Altos v Peru*, IACHR Ser. C. No. 75 (14 March 2001), para. 189.

51. See ibid., paras. 41, 44.

52. Ibid., para. 2(j).

53. Ibid., para. 39.

54. Eyal Benvenisti, "Judicial Misgivings Regarding the Application of International Law: An Analysis of Attitudes of National Courts," *European Journal of International Law* 159 (1993); see also Yuval Shany, "How Supreme is the Supreme Law of the Land? A Comparative Analysis of the Influence of International Human Rights Conventions upon the Interpretation of Constitutional Tests by Domestic Courts," *Brooklyn Journal of International Law* 31 (2006): 341.

55. See National Constitution of the Argentine Republic (1994), § 75(22)–(24) (stating that international treaties are part of the hierarchy of law in Argentina and authorizing Congress to enact laws giving force to international human rights treaties); see also Janet Koven Levit, "The Constitutionalization of Human Rights in Argentina: Problem or Promise?," *Columbia Journal Transnational Law* 37 (1999): 281.

56. Martin Bohmer, "Hybrid Legal Cultures, Borrowings and Impositions: The Use of Foreign Law as a Strategy to Build Constitution and Democratic Authority," *University of Puerto Rico Law Review* 77 (2008): 411.

57. On the course of the transition and prosecution policy, see Carlos S. Nino, "The Duty to Punish Past Abuses of Human Rights Put into Context: The Case of Argentina," *Yale Law Journal* 100 (1991): 2619. On the limits of textual incorporation, see Janet Koven Levit, "The Constitutionalization of Human Rights in Argentina: Problem or Promise?," *Columbia Journal Transnational Law* 37 (1999): 281.

58. *Simon, Julio Hector y otros*, 328 Fallos 2056 (2005) (striking unconstitutional Argentine amnesty laws).

59. Jose Sebastian Elias, "Constitutional Changes, Transitional Justice and Legitimacy, The Life and Death of Argentina's Amnesty Laws," *Hastings International and Comparative Law Review* 31 (2008): 587.

60. Janet Koven Levit, "The Constitutionalization of Human Rights in Argentina: Problem or Promise?," *Columbia Journal of Transnational Law* 37 (1999): 281.

61. Christine A.E. Bakker, "A Full Stop to Amnesty in Argentina: The Simon Case," *Journal of International Criminal Justice* 3 (2005): 1106.

62. Corte Suprema de Justicia [CSJN], 22/06/1987, 'Camps, Ramon Juan Alberto y otros Causa incoada en virtud del decreto 280/84 del Poder Ejecutivo Nacional', Coleccion Oficial de Fallos de la Corte Suprema de Justicia de la Nacion [Fallos] (1987-310-1162) (Arg.).

63. See *Arancibia Clavel, Enrique Lautaro y Otros*, Corte Suprema de Justicia (CSJN), 24/8/2004.

64. *Prosecutor v Tadić*, Case No. IT-94-1, Judgment (International Criminal Tribunal for the Former Yugoslavia, 15 July 1999): para. 97.

65. The relations between Serbia and the European Union deteriorated in spring 2006 due to the negative assessment of Serbia's cooperation with the International Criminal Tribunal for the former Yugoslavia in The Hague that had insisted on the extradition of Serbian suspected war criminals to the ICTY. Failure of Serbian authorities to locate and arrest remaining fugitives led the European Commission to call off negotiations on the Stabilization and Association Agreement with Serbia and Montenegro on 3 May 2006. See Simon Jennings, "EU Urged to Boost Balkan Reconciliation Efforts," *Institute for War and Peace Reporting*, May 2009), http://www.iwpr.net; see also Simon Jennings, "Calls for Bigger EU Role in Balkan Stability Efforts," *Institute for War and Peace Reporting*, 26 May 2009, http://www.iwpr.net/report-news/call s-bigger-eurole-balkan-stability-efforts ('A total of 161 individuals suspected of war crimes have been charged and 60 convicted—is not being followed up with sufficient backing for regional war crimes trials and efforts to counter ethnic divisions still prevalent across the region.').

66. The new civil society project regarding transitional justice in the region; see Humanitarian Law Center, http://www.hlc-rdc.org/.

67. Although regrettably not accepted by Armenia, see "Turkey in Europe: Breaking the Vicious Circle," Second Report of the Independent Commission on Turkey (September 2009): 30–31.

68. See Sebnem Arsu, "Turkey Unveils Plan for Kurdish Rights," *New York Times*, 10 November 2009, A3 (seeking a 'fresh start: overhaul would expand use of minority language in a number of settings including national media and politics').

69. See *Conference on Peace in Yugoslavia, Arbitration Commission*, Opinion No. 1, 11 January 1991, reprinted in *International Legal Materials* 31 (1991): 1494.

70. Case of Sejdic and Finci v Bosnia and Herzegovina, Judgment, Application Nos. 27996/06 and 34836/06 (European Court of Human Rights, 22 December 2009): para. 49. [Hereinafter Case of Sejdic].

71. *Case of Sejdic*, para. 49. The applicants, Mr. Dervo Sejdić and Mr. Jakob, brought their complaints relating to their ineligibility to stand for election to the House of Peoples and the Presidency of Bosnia and Herzegovina on the ground of their Roma and Jewish origin.

72. Joseph Weiler, *The Constitution of Europe 'Do the New Clothes Have an Emperor?' and Other Essays on European Integration* (Cambridge: Cambridge University Press, 1999).

73. Velasquez Rodriguez Case, Judgment, (Ser. C) No. 4 (Inter-American Court of Human Rights 1988).

74. See *Convention on the Prevention and Punishment of the Crime of Genocide* (1948) entered into Force, 12 January 1951, 78 UNTS 277 (defining 'genocide' in terms of acts committed 'with intent to destroy, in whole or in part, a national, ethnical, racial or religious group, as such'). Regarding the recognition of crimes against humanity, see Agreement for the Prosecution and Punishment of the Major War Criminals of the European Axis, and Charter of the International Military Tribunal, 82 UNTS 279 (1945): Article 6(c).

75. See *Prosecutor v Kupreskic*, Case No. IT-95-16, Judgment (Trial Chamber, International Criminal Tribunal for the former Yugoslavia, 14 January 2000): para. 543. In the 1987 prosecution of Klaus Barbie, a Nazi chief in occupied Lyon, France's High Court defined persecution as committed in a systematic manner in the name of '[s]tate practicing a policy of ideological supremacy,' *Federation Nationale des Deportes et Internes Resistants et Patriotes and Others v Barbie*, 78 ILR 125, 128 (Criminal Chamber, French Court of Cassation, 1985).

76. See Jurgen Habermas, *The Postnational Constellation: Political Essays* (Cambridge: Polity Press, 2001) (discussing the significance to preservation of identity of such affiliations for persons).

77. *Case of Sejdic*, paras. 46–50.

78. *Case Concerning the Application of the Convention on the Prevention and Punishment of the Crime of Genocide* (Bosnia and Herzegovina v Serbia and Montenegro) 2007 ICJ 91 (2007): para. 401.

79. *Case of Sejdic*, para. 44.

80. See Jurgen Habermas, *The Divided West* (Cambrdige: Polity Press, 2006) (laying out Habermas's view of constitutionalism beyond the state and grounded in international law.). For a discussion of Habermas's view of non-state-based constitutionalization of international law, see Jurgen Habermas, "The Constitutionalization of International Law and the Legitimation Problems of a Constitution for World Society," *Constellations* 15 (2008): 444-45. For an analysis of other pockets of international law characterized as involving the constitutionalization of international law, see Jeffrey Dunoff and Joel Trachtman, *Ruling the World: Constitutionalism, International Law and Global Governance* (Cambridge: Cambridge University Press, 2009). See also Robert Howse, "Human Rights, International Economic Law and Constitutional Justice: A Reply," *European Journal of International Law* 19 (2008): 945; see Ernst-Ulrich Petersmann, "Human Rights, International Economic Law and Constitutional Justice," *European Journal of International Law* 19 (2008): 769.

81. *The Rule of Law and Transitional Justice in Conflict and Post-Conflict Societies: Report of the Secretary General*, UN Doc. S/2004/616 (2004).

# Epilogue: The Return of the Political

The global paradigm of transitional justice raises difficult questions. We can see a need to reckon with the tension between the normativity evoked by justice-seeking, with the political considerations associated with transition. These tensions are recognized in a number of essays in this volume, such as the "law and politics of contemporary transitional justice" raising the critical question of what is the potential for punishment in case of ongoing conflict? In addressing that question, to what extent should explicitly transitional goals be part of the consideration? Indeed, in a context of more persistent conflict of a non-interstate nature, we saw that transitional justice offers a more capacious forward-looking framework than that of international criminal justice, which may explain the discourse's appeal and its normalization.

Nevertheless, the tensions show no sign of abatement but rather continue to multiply as can be seen now that the normalization of international law has become a permanent feature of the global paradigm. Indeed, one can see that this is giving rise to raised expectations, and in some cases, backlash.

Consider, for example, just how the 2013 confrontation of the ICC in Kenya reflects the possible tension between political transition and international criminal justice. Following Kenya's President Uhuru Kenyatta's indictment and election, in a summit in fall 2013, the African Union had demanded a postponement of proceedings, and threatened as a bloc to pull out of the Court.[1] Consider also following the Libya referral and after regime change, the fraught questions regarding admissibility in the ICC and the possibility of complementarity in the Libyan context.[2] Despite these confrontations, nevertheless, the ICC maintains that it cannot take into account considerations of a political nature. Yet, might this view of international justice threaten rather than advance the asserted goals of democratization and peacemaking during transitions? Ultimately, the ICC has exercised the option to postpone.[3] Similiar issues are being confronted today, for example, in Latin America, where regional human rights tribunals constituting a supranational judiciary decades after postmilitary transitions are insisting on formal obligations of the law. These have sparked controversy over how to measure the rule of law. Has transitional justice become a default measure?[4]

Other recent interventions reflect the ongoing bureaucratization of transitional justice at the UN and other NGOs, where a set of transitional practices is being reframed or packaged in terms of human rights obligations, and has become de rigeur policy for new states in transition. In Tunisia, for example, it is the UN transitional justice unit that appear to be the driver of transitional justice duties, along with other international NGOs that appears to be neutral and disinterested, yet such exercises can foment divisiveness and serve to carve up political interests along perpetrator/victim lines at a time of a fragile path toward democratization.[5]

Several conclusions emerge from the experiences of the recent period: First, it is clear that there is no going back to before the global paradigm; henceforth transitional justice is no longer solely the purview of domestic policy and decision-making, but rather engages global interests. But the new modalities associated with the global paradigm, whether "legal/formalist" or "praxis/bureaucratic," each in their own way reflect disembodied approaches to transitional justice, and, therefore, lack the normative principles to guide global transitional justice.

The questions that lie at the heart of the global paradigm, such as of what the relationship ought to be of the local to the international, as the experiences of the last decade reflect, defy categorical answers. In this regard, we currently lack and urgently need to have a meaningful understanding of "complementarity": the idea that stands for a preference for domestic over international accountability mechanisms, such that there should only be international criminal accountability where domestic institutions fail or are unavailable.[6] The spirit of complementarity has broader implications for the division of labor between domestic and transnational institutions. This is a principle that is apt for the global paradigm, as it addresses the tensions in the domestic and the international regimes and can give guidance regarding how to reconcile multiple levels of decision-making. In referencing political will and capacity, the global paradigm recognizes the discretion both domestically and at the international level, particularly where the exercise of criminal justice would imperil important goals of transition, such as peace and democratization. Complementarity at the international level needs to be exercised in keeping with the rule of law, that is, transparency and reason-giving, as well as in keeping with relevant international human rights.

Next, even where because of domestic state failure or absence of political will, there is a threshold or colorable basis for international intervention, what this will mean in any given case in part will depend upon international law principles of interpretation. International law norms are absolutes; rather traditional principles of legal interpretation contemplate considering the object and purposes of these treaties, such as the Rome Statute, in accordance with other international law (i.e., the Vienna Convention on Treaties). In international criminal jurisprudence, this has taken the form of teleological interpretation.

The turn to international law and judicialization is often seen as somehow anti-political, when the international criminal tribunals' constitutive instruments are themselves often justified in broader terms of political goals such as peace and security, especially so of tribunals convened during conflict with particular aims in mind. As such, the legitimacy of the international judiciary will be implicitly relativized by political goals and considerations. The touchstone is global transitional justice and its often competing goals and values. Its judicialization implies a greater role for international law principles of interpretation, and brings to the forefront the importance of interpretation in bringing to bear the relevant considerations to advance justice in a given case. The resolution of these questions may reveal defining choices and involve a resetting of the terms of political engagement.

## Notes

1. http://www.theguardian.com/world/2014/jan/23/uhuru-kenyatta-trial-postponed-internation-criminal-court. *See generally* Security in Transition. *See* Nicholas Kulish & Benno Muchler, *African Union Urges International Court to Delay Kenyan President's Trial*, N.Y. TIMES, Oct. 13, 2014, at A11.

2. See In the Case of *The Prosecutor v. Saifal-Islam Gaddafi and Abdullah Al-Senussi*, ICC-01/11-01/11, 11 Oct. 2013.

3. *See* Ruti Teitel, Transitional Justice and Judicial Activism: A Right to Accountability? 48 Cornell Int'l Law Journal, 2015.

4. http://www.theguardian.com/world/2014/jan/23/uhuru-kenyatta-trial-postponed-internation-criminal-court. See generally SecurityinTransition, http://www.securityintransition.org/commentaries/judging-and-judgment-in-the-21st-century-the-iccs-confrontation-with-africas-leaders/

5. *See As Tunisia Finalizes Transitional Justice Law, ICTJ Advocates for Victims' Rights and Participation*, INT'L CENTER FOR TRANSITIONAL JUSTICE, Jul. 8, 2013, http://ictj.org/news/tunisia-finalizes-transitional-justice-law.

6. *See* Rome Statute, Preamble and Article 17.

# Index

CPSIA information can be obtained at www.ICGtesting.com
Printed in the USA
BVOW08s1614181015

422779BV00002B/4/P